T0163101

Rethinking Kennedy

Rethinking Kennedy

AN INTERPRETIVE BIOGRAPHY

Michael O'Brien

Ivan R. Dee
CHICAGO

www.ivanrdee.com

First paperback edition 2010

Library of Congress Cataloging-in-Publication Data:

The hardback edition of this book was previously cataloged by the
Library of Congress as follows:
O'Brien, Michael, 1923–
   Rethinking Kennedy : an interpretive biography / Michael O'Brien.
      p. cm.
   Includes bibliographical references and index.
   1. Kennedy, John F. (John Fitzgerald), 1917–1963. 2. Presidents—
United States—Biography. 3. United States—Politics and
government—1961–1963. I. Title.
E842.O24 2008
973.922092—dc22
   [B]   2008024895

ISBN: 978-1-56663-790-9 (cloth : alk. paper)
ISBN: 978-1-56663-871-5 (pbk. : alk. paper)

To Kathy Skubal,

without whom I would not have been

able to publish this and other books

Contents

Preface

RATHER THAN a full-scale biography of John F. Kennedy or a comprehensive history of his era, this book is designed to be a concise analytical portrait of the man.

Kennedy had a special magnetism—flair, aspirations to great deeds, and contagious confidence. He was a president with superior intelligence, imagination, and curiosity, and he wielded power with grace and verve. His brief tenure in the White House occurred in the midst of dramatic events and personalities—the civil rights movement and Martin Luther King, the cold war and the Berlin Wall, the Cuban Missile Crisis, Khrushchev, de Gaulle, Castro, and the Peace Corps. Revisionist writers disdain the usual glamorous portrayal of Kennedy, and their views deserve a hearing. Their work, plus important new information that has come to light and must be incorporated into our judgment of the man, have moved me to write this book in the wake of my much more detailed earlier biography of Kennedy.

Rethinking Kennedy

1

The Kennedy System

AS A YOUNGSTER John Kennedy was shaped by a full measure of wealth and luxury, inherited physical good looks, zealous parents, Irish Democratic politics, and a dash of Catholicism and morality. There followed, in his young adulthood, late-blooming intellectual interests—particularly for history, biography, and current events—the searing effects of a world war, and his pathological pursuit of sex.

In the 1840s John Kennedy's great-grandparents came from Ireland, in the mid-nineteenth century probably the poorest and most backward country in Europe. Two centuries earlier England had brutally conquered Ireland, redistributed Irish property, and persecuted its people. Wars, plague, and famine of the time killed one-third of Ireland's population. Penal codes deprived the Irish of civil and political rights, and England hounded Ireland's Catholic church.

Although battered and impoverished, the stubborn Irish held on to their families, their memories, and their speech patterns. Since most of the Irish couldn't read or write, they came to prize oratory, many dreaming of winning fame as orators. Despite persecution, the Irish Catholic church survived, providing a common bond and comforting the wretched.

In the 1840s calamity again devastated Ireland. Their staple crop, the potato, became infested with a fungus, and the blight brought famine. Morale was shattered, and scurvy, typhoid, and cholera killed 800,000 people. During and shortly after the catastrophe, a million and a half Irish immigrants fled to the United States. Many of the new arrivals ended up in Boston, where they settled in America's first large urban slums.

Critics stereotyped them as corrupt, drunken, illiterate, and priest-ridden. "Protestants only" and "No Irish need apply" were frequent captions in newspaper want ads. Hatred of the Irish was unusually intense partly because they bitterly resisted denigration and took to politics as an avenue to express their grievances.

The Boston Irish formed their own Catholic bloc of voters in opposition to the Brahmins, the Protestant Yankee oligarchs. Block by block they organized politically until they captured control of precincts, wards, and finally the city government. Fascinated with politics, the Irish viewed an election as a contest that had to be won; a moral victory was no victory at all. Irish politicians were gregarious, and they became skilled conciliators and compromisers. Historian Dennis Ryan notes that Irish-American politicians entertained people with their "penchant for flamboyant rhetoric, vivid metaphors, witty anecdotes, and personal invective." Boston's Irish taverns were the setting for ward-boss politics as proprietors circulated nomination papers and corralled votes from their customers on election day.

John Kennedy's maternal great-grandfather, Thomas Fitzgerald, and his wife, Rose Mary Murray, both came from Wexford, Ireland. They had eleven children. Their third child, John (Honey Fitz) Fitzgerald, was born February 11, 1863. Most Irish youths completed only grammar school, but young John continued his education at the elite Boston Latin School.

Energetic, full of blarney and cunning, Honey Fitz won a city council post in 1892 and moved up to the Massachusetts state senate the following year. As a state senator he advocated progressive social measures: maximum hours for workers, workmen's compensation insurance, and old-age pensions. From 1895 to 1901 he served as U.S. congressman from Boston's Eleventh District. Four years later he won election as Boston's mayor, and served until 1914.

Although he campaigned against rascality and corruption, his own administration was shamelessly tainted with unscrupulous practices. Graft was blatant. On the other hand, Honey Fitz's accomplishments were equally large. His administration built the City Hall Annex, the aquarium in South Boston, and the Franklin Park Zoo. Vocational schools, libraries, gymnasiums and playgrounds in poorer areas, a measles hospital and a child hygiene system to protect the health of the city's children were all part of his legacy.

Honey Fitz and his wife Josie had six children, of whom Rose, born July 22, 1890, was the oldest. Rose loved her parents and always thanked them for shaping her character. "My mother and father instilled in me the same enthusiasm for life and thirst for knowledge that I am proud to see in my own children. . . . My father's love of public life could not help but be contagious, the way he made history and headlines come alive."

A month before her sixteenth birthday, Rose graduated from Dorchester High School, one of the youngest graduates in the school's history—and she ranked in the top three academically in a class of 285. To crown her success, she was voted Boston's prettiest high school senior.

As a young lady Rose Fitzgerald was in the spotlight. Since Mrs. Fitzgerald hated public appearances, Honey Fitz brought along his beautiful and articulate daughter to act as his official hostess. Rose assumed a full round of political and social duties, smiling through banquets and rallies, appearing at the mayor's side for wakes and funerals, dedicating public buildings, and hosting prominent visitors at city hall.

Young Rose seemed blessed. Historian Doris Kearns Goodwin describes her as having "an open, ardent nature filled with wonder and belief; a radiant complexion and eyes full of laughter; a fine, slim figure and plenty of new clothes, a strong active mind and abundant opportunity to engage it in stimulating conversation."

John Kennedy's ancestors on his father's side did better financially than most Irish Americans. His widowed great-grandmother, Bridget Kennedy, purchased a small notions shop in East Boston. Crafty and acquisitive, she made the store successful. Her son Patrick Joseph (P.J.) attended the neighborhood parochial school and helped his mother at the store.

Later, with financial assistance from his mother, P.J. purchased a dilapidated saloon and made it prosper. Like many tavern owners, he moved into politics, becoming a shrewd and powerful ward boss in Boston. He offered discreet counsel, free drinks, a small loan before payday, and coal in the winter, and he smoothed over people's problems with the police.

P.J. was elected to the Massachusetts legislature, but he didn't like campaigning and was not a good public speaker. With little interest in officeholding, his forte was working quietly behind the scenes. He was so unassuming, generous, and kind that old-timers, who often found fault with Boston's political leaders, seldom said a bad word about Pat Kennedy. In the mid-1880s he entered the wholesale liquor business, eventually owning two dealerships. He also bought a coal company and helped establish a bank, became its president, and accumulated a substantial estate.

When Patrick's son Joe Kennedy was ten, Patrick was a banker, one of Boston's most powerful politicians, and the family lived in a stately mansion. His father's example taught Joe that with perseverance and determination a man could take the world as he found it, improve himself, and be successful. Ambitious and energetic, young Joe particularly enjoyed making money. Whenever he met a childhood friend on the street, young Kennedy would always broach the question, "How can we make some money?"

At Boston Latin, Joe was such an indifferent student that school officials forced him to repeat one year to make up his deficiencies. But he excelled at sports and extracurricular activities. Classmates elected him president of his senior class, and he captained the baseball team for two years. Somehow he finagled his way into Harvard, but he remained an indifferent student, and his perception of anti-Irish prejudice often made his college experience unpleasant.

Joe Kennedy and Rose Fitzgerald met as children while Rose accompanied her father on his visits to East Boston, and on October 7, 1914, they married.

Rose delivered their first child, Joseph Patrick Kennedy, Jr., in 1915, and on May 29, 1917, she delivered her second. Since the first child had been named after a Kennedy, Joe and Rose decided their second son should be named after her beloved father. So they named him John Fitzgerald Kennedy.

More children followed—Rosemary in 1918, Kathleen in 1920, Eunice in 1921, Patricia in 1924, Robert in 1925, Jean in 1928, and Edward in 1932.

As his family grew, Joe Kennedy was making millions. In the 1920s he mastered the intricacies of the unregulated stock market, including the predatory practices of insider trading and stock pools. He made five million dollars in the motion picture industry. In the early 1930s, as Prohibition was ending, he earned a fortune after he convinced British distillers to appoint him as their U.S. agent. But many people who conducted business with Joe complained of treachery, deceit, and brutal tactics. P.J. had been respected and well liked, but Joe's feverish ambition overwhelmed any moral standards he may have had, resulting in a slew of enemies.

Fiercely independent, Joe had a flair for organization and management. The telephone was his Stradivarius. Cultivating a talent for soliciting expert advice, he asked questions and listened carefully. "What do you hear?" "What do you know?" "What do you think?" From associates and advisers he culled what he needed and applied it.

Joe entered politics in 1932, forming a partnership with presidential candidate Franklin D. Roosevelt. When Roosevelt won the presidency, he appointed Joe to chair the new Securities and Exchange Commission, and Joe handled the chairmanship admirably, earning accolades for his administrative ability, public relations, political acumen, and conflict mediation.

Because of their wealth, the Kennedys could have become dilettantes, but Joe and Rose had a unique vision for their family, plus the drive and the determination to achieve it. They spent countless hours together discussing the children, going over each youngster's activities, and planning each child's future. They tried to inculcate in their children that the Kennedys were an extraordinary family. Away from his work, the children preoccupied Joe. In most respects he was an excellent child psychologist, insightfully appraising the strengths and weaknesses of each child and relentlessly encouraging the fulfillment of the child's potential.

It is critical to understand that the brutal, unethical businessman that outsiders saw was not the Joe Kennedy that his children knew. They saw a warm and gentle father who was never too rushed to ask them about their progress in school or their plans for the day. He played games and sports with them, jaunted to the water's edge to watch a beginner swim, and stood on the pier awaiting the start of a sailboat race. His children had to have the finest athletic equipment, schools, hospitals, and travel experiences.

"Mr. Kennedy was somehow able to do it right," observed Lem Billings, Jack's friend, "not to spoil his children and yet not to make them resentful with his strictness. He was able to follow a very fine line . . . make them want to improve themselves and please him, and he did this without undue force. He did it with love, and yet with strictness."

Mealtime was a focal point in the Kennedy family—it was important that the whole family gather to eat. A strict schedule was followed: lunch was served at 1:00 and dinner at 7:15, except for the young children who ate an hour earlier. Meals were a time for the family to share information and express themselves. The children must read the newspapers, with special attention to the "News of the Week in Review" in the Sunday *New York Times*. Then the children would discuss news items at Sunday's lunch. Rose also hung a bulletin board and tacked up news items.

When Joe presided during the evening meals, sparks flew. "It was something!" said Billings, a frequent dinner guest. Joe kept the conversation on a high level, concentrating on world affairs, making the discussions exhilarating and fun. He wanted his children to argue and debate, and didn't force his views on them, yet he purposely played the devil's advocate. "He never wanted them to agree with him," said Billings. "All this talk about [John Kennedy] being influenced by his father is crazy because he was raised *not* to be."

Both parents, but especially Joe, inspired an intense competitive spirit. In every competitive activity their children should strive to be first. For Joe, second best was not good enough. He was passionate—sometimes obsessed—about excellence, winning, and the virtues of competition. Seldom introspective, he spoke in the simple imperatives of the pep talk, giving powerful emphasis to platitudes and clichés ("When the going gets tough, the tough get going") and influencing his children with the force of his personality.

Intense competition does improve self-discipline, initiative, perseverance, and determination. Unfortunately, competition often causes collateral damage leading to a host of destructive consequences, including the moral evils of deceit, lying, and hypocrisy—vices that characterized Joe's business career. Although serious problems can follow in its wake, competition provides a means for assigning position along with power and excellence. Without competition's powerful stimulant, potentialities may fail to develop.

Joe Kennedy stressed winning and excellence, but he taught little about ethics and morals. He regularly attended Sunday Mass and usually received Communion. Overall, though, he was not a religious or moral person. While Rose believed that religion was the finest molder of character, Joe put his faith in experience.

Generous and outgoing, Rose could also be stingy, selfish, and withdrawn. She studied theology and philosophy, Catholic church history, and current events. She assembled scrapbooks and loose-leaf notebooks filled with inspirational thoughts, a hobby she maintained all her life. An intrepid world traveler, including a dangerous tour of the Soviet Union in 1936, she reported back to her family about all the fascinating people she met. "Tea at [American] Embassy today. Lunch with Winston Churchill tomorrow."

Most people admired Rose, but she had a few private unattractive traits, and several of the children's friends chuckled at her eccentricities. Sometimes she caked "pasties" on her face all day to avoid wrinkles. Because she developed the habit of pinning her "to-do lists" to her blouse or dress, in the morning she looked like a walking bulletin board. "As she finished with one reminder," said a member of the household staff, "she would tear it off and go on to the next." At the end of the day, her paper corsage plucked clean, she was proud of systematically accomplishing all her tasks. These peculiar habits led some visitors to judge her as dull-witted.

In her autobiography, *Times to Remember*, Rose made her feelings clear. For her, being a good mother was a more noble goal than anything else. "What greater aspiration and challenge for a mother than the hope of raising a great son or daughter? . . . A mother knows that hers is the influence which can make that little precious being to be a leader of men, an inspiration, a shining light in the world." Excellent values, traditions, and habits, she believed, would sustain her children for their entire life. They must use their mind to the fullest; discover the world through reading, study, and travel; and welcome new adventures. Life was exciting.

To raise her children properly, Rose looked to experts. One book she consulted was pediatrician L. Emmett Holt's *The Care and Feeding of Children*, first published in 1894 and still being read fifty years later. Enormously influential, Holt was the Dr. Spock of his age, followed by millions of mothers.

"Babies under six months old should never be played with," Holt declared, because "they are made more nervous and irritable, sleep badly, and suffer from indigestion and cease to gain weight." Don't express affection, either. "Tuberculosis, diphtheria, syphilis, and many other grave diseases may be communicated in this way," he warned. "The kissing of infants upon the mouth by other children, by nurses, or by people generally, should under no circumstances be permitted." Rose hewed to Holt's advice and did not normally express affection with her children. She cared deeply about them, but she remained reserved and emotionally distant.

A daily communicant, Rose made the Catholic church the center of her life, its tenets the foundation for her children's moral training. When the children were toddlers, Rose read them bedtime stories; when they were ill and bedridden, she read to them several hours at a time. She carefully selected books from the library and other places—books with educational and inspirational value, not just entertainment. She took the children on historic tours of the Bunker Hill Monument, the *USS Constitution*, Old North Church, and the Boston Common.

*

One enormous burden disrupted Joe and Rose's idealistic family goals and caused incessant concern. Rosemary, their third child, was retarded. Slower to walk and to talk than her brothers, during her early school years she couldn't perform simple assignments. The parents consulted experts and hired special tutors, and Rose spent an inordinate amount of time seeking to overcome Rosemary's disability. The other Kennedy children were protective and tried to help.

Joe Jr. had been a healthy child and grew strong and robust, but Jack suffered numerous illnesses. The most serious, diagnosed on February 20, 1920, when he was two years old, was scarlet fever, a dreaded disease, sometimes fatal and often crippling in its aftereffects.

Partly because he was so often convalescing, reading became Jack's major entertainment. He loved stories of adventure and chivalry, biographies of famous and fascinating people, subjects having to do with history, "so long as they had flair, action, and color," said Rose. A romantic and idealistic streak inclined Jack to daydreaming. "I often had a feeling his mind was only half occupied with the subject at hand, such as doing his arithmetic homework or picking his clothes up off the floor, and the rest of his thoughts were far away weaving daydreams."

Discrimination against the Kennedys as Irish Catholics infuriated Joe. "I was born here," he exclaimed in an interview. "My children were born here. What the hell do I have to do to be an American?" Boston was no place to bring up Catholic children, Joe said in disgust. With that, in September 1927 he relocated his family to Riverdale, New York. Two years later he again moved the family to the exclusive Westchester County community of Bronxville, New York.

In the fall of 1928 the Kennedys bought a large cottage in Hyannis Port, Massachusetts. The sprawling white-clapboard, green-shuttered house sat on a bluff overlooking Nantucket Sound and included two and a half acres of lawn sloping to a wide stretch of beach.

When Jack was sixteen the Kennedys added a third dwelling, a Palm Beach, Florida, vacation home on North Ocean Boulevard, known locally as "Millionaire's Row." After 1933 the Kennedy family moved three times a year—to Palm Beach for Christmas and Easter holidays, to Hyannis Port for the summer, to Bronxville during school sessions.

Jack had noteworthy relations with two of his siblings. Joe Jr. was the "golden child" but often tormented young Jack. Disciplined, hard working, and mature for his age, young Joe was, in Doris Goodwin's words, "reverent the way the mother wanted, ambitious the way the father wanted. He was clearly the favorite child of both his parents."

Kind and patient with his younger brothers and sisters—aside from Jack—Joe Jr. willingly accepted his role as family exemplar, spending many hours with the young ones teaching them to ride a bicycle, throw a football, play tennis, and sail. Jack was like a pal to the little Kennedys; Joe Jr. acted like a father. "While Joe was an orderly child at home and a serious student at school, even tackling things he did not like," writes Goodwin, "Jack was unpardonably sloppy at home and lazy at school, interested only in the things that pleased him."

With Jack—the rival for his throne, a challenge to his status in the family—Joe Jr. was often sarcastic, overbearing, disapproving, a taunting bully. Young Joe would lob a football to Rosemary or Eunice but would smash the ball into Jack and laugh when he dropped it or had the wind knocked out of him. Having an older brother was a convenience for Jack, though, because it relieved him of his father's pressure to excel. In high school and college Jack would tell close friends, "Thank God Joe Kennedy's there so that my father's not on my back."

Jack had a close relationship with his sister Kathleen. They shared the same self-deprecating humor, free-spiritedness, and unharnessed energy. They showed up together at all the activities on the Cape—the barn dances as well as the Saturday matinees at the Idle Hours movie theater in Hyannis Port.

*

In some ways Joe and Rose had a satisfactory marriage. Each was considerate and respectful with the other. Their correspondence radiated affection. "Joe dearest," Rose wrote her husband around 1936, "Just a short note, my darling, to tell you again that I love you very, very much—more all the time and more than I can ever write." But one critical feature of their marriage was dysfunctional, and that feature strongly influenced John F. Kennedy.

Rose was so chaste that she almost denigrated sex, even within marriage. Joe, on the other hand, became a notorious philanderer. While working in Hollywood he rented a large house on Rodeo Drive in Beverly Hills, where he often beguiled dazzling young women. Because Joe flaunted his women in front of townspeople in Bronxville and Hyannis Port, many residents detested him. Later he even tried to date and bed his sons' girlfriends. Alone in the darkened theater in the Hyannis Port home, he pinched his daughters' girlfriends. Many were bewildered by Joe's lechery. "One night I was visiting Eunice at the Cape," recalled Mary Pitcairn, "and he came into my bedroom to kiss me goodnight! I was in my nightgown, ready for bed. Eunice was in her bedroom. We had an adjoining bath. The doors were open. He said, 'I've come to say goodnight,' and kissed me. Really kissed me. It was so silly. I remember thinking, 'How embarrassing for Eunice!'"

"I think all this confused Jack," Pitcairn speculated. "He was a sensitive man and I think it confused him. What kind of object is a woman? To be treated as his father treated them? . . . When he did get involved with someone, what kind of a woman was she? Like his mother or like his father's girls?"

Rose repressed the unpleasant reality of her husband's lechery. She acted as if the other women didn't exist, willing the unpleasant knowledge of her husband's affairs out of her mind. "After all, Rose seemed to have what she wanted in her marriage: children, wealth and privilege," Goodwin observes. "At the same time, the marriage satisfied what may have been her own desire for sexual distance." Better to suffer privately in silence than risk public disgrace or a divorce that would shatter the Kennedy family.

For many years Joe and Rose earned praise as model parents. *Reader's Digest* described the Kennedys as "one of the most interesting family groups in the world." Recently, though, a new critical perspective has emerged. Several authors, most notably Nigel Hamilton in his best-selling and influential book *JFK: Reckless Youth,* judge both Kennedys as far less than admirable. According to Hamilton, Joe Kennedy was a "Boston-Irish braggart," "a foul-mouthed, controlling, frightening, evil-eye his children could not escape." He was "bigoted, almost psychotic . . . ignoble," a "despot" whose life Hamilton summarizes as "odious."

At times Joe displayed most of those traits, particularly in his business career, and his philandering had a profoundly detrimental impact on his second son. Nonetheless Hamilton's assessment ignores Joe's deep love for his family and his admirable fatherly traits.

Joe Kennedy inspired in Jack and his other children some of his own qualities—his doggedness, perseverance, ambition, interest in public affairs, love of the limelight, and a flaming competitive spirit. He meddled in his children's social life and was too controlling, but he encouraged his children to think for themselves and provided superb opportunities for them to grow and succeed.

Hamilton thinks Joe Kennedy's tyrannical approach to winning damaged his children. "To win, for the Kennedy children," Hamilton writes, "meant to gain their father's love; to lose, conversely, was to forfeit it—hardly a recipe for relaxed and self-confident children." The young Kennedys did feel pressured and did worry about temporarily losing their father's respect, but Hamilton exaggerates the resulting damage. The children certainly didn't think they forfeited their father's love by losing a swimming race or a football game. Besides, they learned important lessons in self-discipline, initiative, perseverance, and determination.

Recent biographers and historians have disparaged Rose as well. "A theme in the recent literature on the Kennedys," writes one historian, "is that Rose was not the model mother depicted in earlier writings." Nigel Hamilton savages Rose Kennedy. He sees her as a pathetic figure, a maternal monster—"cold," "unmotherly," "severe," "distant," "sanctimonious," and guilty of a "vengeful piety" toward her children.

Hamilton's most telling point concerns Rose's global travel, particularly while Jack attended high school at Choate and was often ill. "If Rose Kennedy was anxious in Palm Beach, she had a strange way of showing it. She had ventured abroad seventeen times in four years, but could not manage the journey to Connecticut, where Jack lay in the hospital a further month."

According to Hamilton, Rose caused one of Jack's major character flaws. "Jack's lifelong need not simply to flirt with women but compulsively to lie with them—obsessively, maniacally, to the point of sexual addiction—would owe much to his twin obsessions: sexual revenge against his mother and, quite simply, the need for a quality of physical touching denied him from infancy."

In truth Jack occasionally praised his mother, but his comments masked his deep bitter feelings. "She's not as forceful as my father, but she was the glue," he said. "I thought she was a very model mother for a big family." He specifically credited her with stimulating and encouraging his reading, and appreciated that she spent many hours reading to him as a boy. "She was great on self-improvement," he added.

In general, though, there is no doubt that Jack loved and respected his father far more than his mother. In private he expressed resentment that his mother was "either at some Paris fashion house or else on her knees in some church. She was never there when we really needed her. . . . My mother never really held me and hugged me. Never! Never!" Angry over this maternal frostiness, he allegedly told a friend: "My mother is a nothing." When historian Arthur Schlesinger noted that the Kennedy children turned out better than the Roosevelt children, Jack observed, "Well, no one can say that it was due to my mother. It was due to my father," who always made Jack feel important and loved when he was around.

Both the critics and Jack Kennedy were unfair to Rose, underestimating her strengths and her contributions to the family. She supervised a variety of family matters—from visiting the orthodontist to arranging picnics, from meals to swimming lessons. She taught, inspired, and disciplined her nine children, a daunting task. Considering the burden of raising her brood—and providing time-consuming special care for Rosemary—she needed a leisure outlet, and her favorite was travel.

Rose was pregnant with her ninth child during part of the time Jack was at Choate. Joe visited Choate several times. In any case, as one observer noted, Joe and Rose both "rained down upon the headmaster at Choate a constant barrage of letters, telegrams, and notes, a correspondence unprecedented in the history of the school." Harold Tinker, an English teacher at Choate, praised Rose's concern for Joe Jr. and Jack. "She was marvelous all the time they were there," said Tinker. "She kept track of everything about all of her children."

Columnist Arthur Krock of the *New York Times,* a family friend, described Rose as "a marvelous mother, calm, serene, reserved, extremely well educated." The Kennedy children may have been hobbled by too much prescribed behavior and regulated activity, but as Goodwin contends, "Living in the shadow of the disintegrating twenties—the dizzying decade of flappers and bootleggers, of sensuous music, scandals and fads—Rose believed that adherence to daily ritual offered the best hope for the family's survival."

If John Kennedy's later obsessive sexual philandering stemmed from Rose's lack of affection, why didn't the same pathological behavior emerge from the sons of millions of other conscientious mothers? They raised their children like Rose, read the same advice from parenting experts, and yet didn't produce sexually addicted sons. Joe Kennedy's obsessive behavior provided the roadmap for Jack's sex life.

Although subsequent critics and Jack mocked Rose, Dr. L. Emmett Holt might have selected her as an exemplar of his approach to modern progressive child care.

2

Education

IN 1930 thirteen-year-old Jack entered eighth grade at Canterbury, a Catholic boys' boarding school in New Milford, Connecticut, the only Catholic school he ever attended. Although lackadaisical and absentminded, Jack enjoyed reading. "We are reading *Ivanhoe* in English," he wrote to his father, "and though I may not be able to remember material things such as tickets, gloves and so on I can remember things like *Ivanhoe*, and the last time we had an exam on it, I got ninety-eight."

Joe Jr. was attending the prep school Choate, and his growing maturity and accomplishments impressed his father, who decided to send Jack there as well, hoping for similar results. For the next four years Jack would attend Choate.

In his teenage years Jack was impulsive and undisciplined yet witty and charming; although an indifferent student, he displayed intellectual promise. His disdain for rules and disrespect for authority figures almost resulted in his expulsion from Choate. Near the end of his prep-school experience, an insightful psychologist helped him gain perspective on his attitude and his relations with his older brother.

Founded in 1896 as a boys' boarding school, Choate was located in Wallingford, Connecticut, a few miles north of New Haven. The longtime director, or "head," was Reverend George St. John, a stern, no-nonsense fellow.

At the close of his freshman year Jack had failed both French and Latin and barely passed algebra. Mr. Davis, his French teacher, was fond of Jack but couldn't inspire him to learn the language. There was little "except physical violence that I haven't tried!" Davis reported. Jack's papers were "chaotic, and he invariably forgets books, pencil or paper."

In 1933 Jack first met LeMoyne Billings while serving on the business board of *The Brief*, the Choate yearbook, where Billings was the advertising manager. They roomed together during their final two years at Choate and became close friends until Kennedy's death.

Billings came from Pittsburgh, where his father, a physician, had lost heavily in the 1929 crash and died early in 1933. With his high forehead, grizzly-bearish appearance, and awkward manner, Lem was physically unattractive. He shared a major burden with Jack: both were second sons who for years had submitted to bullying, patronizing older brothers who were highly successful and admired.

Not long after they met, Lem's feelings for Jack went beyond friendship. He fell in love with Jack and gently solicited sex. "I'm not that kind of boy," Jack replied. Lem wisely backed off. "But unlike most straight men confronted with this situation, certainly at that time, Jack didn't break off the friendship with Lem," observes David Pitts, who studied their relationship. "Jack liked Lem, enjoyed good times with him, and was determined that the friendship would continue, despite Lem's apparent sexual desires."

Homosexuality was a huge taboo at the time and for decades afterwards. Most gays remained isolated in the closet, fearing rejection and discrimination. "That John Kennedy maintained a deep friendship with a man whom he knew to be gay and did so in an age of homophobia—at great potential risk to his political career and reputation—is an extraordinary demonstration of loyalty and commitment," suggests Pitts.

At Choate, Jack was noted for practical jokes rather than academic achievement. He intensely disliked math and physics and refused to apply himself in those courses. In English he enjoyed poems and short essays, and had a flair for phrasemaking and style. Still, his teachers complained of the gap between his high potential and his daily performance. Brown graduate Harold Tinker, a specialist on the English poet and novelist Thomas Hardy, was one of Jack's English teachers. He liked Jack and saw potential in him. Tinker judged Jack's spelling and punctuation erratic but his vocabulary exceptionally good. When Tinker explained something, Jack was often gazing out the window, apparently daydreaming. But after class Jack asked probing questions showing a depth of understanding. "He learned not what you wanted him to learn," Tinker recalled, "but what he wanted to learn."

In one fascinating essay, written in April 1934 for advanced English composition, Kennedy addressed the problem of justice. How can a Christian God allow evil in the world? Specifically, how can God be just when people are born into widely different circumstances?

Justice is always linked with God, he began. "But should this be so?" Webster's dictionary said justice meant "The rendering to everyone his just due." Does "God render to everyone his just due?"

He alluded to his own luxurious upbringing when he continued:

A boy is born in a rich family, brought up in [a] clean environment with an excellent education and good companions, inherits a fool-proof business from his father, is married and then eventually dies a just and honest man. Take the other extreme. A boy is born in the slums, of a poor family, has evil companions, no education, becomes a loafer, as that is all there is to do, turns into a drunken bum, and dies, worthless. Was it because of the [rich] boys abylity [sic] that he landed in the lap of luxery [sic], or was it the poor boys fault that he was born in squalor? The answer will often come back "The poor boy will get his reward in the life hereafter if he is good." While that is a dubious prospect to many of us, yet [there is] something in it. But how much better chance has [the] boy born with a silver spoon in his mouth of being good than the boy who from birth is surrounded by rottenness and filth. This even to the most religious of us can hardly seem a "square deal." Thus we see that justice is not always received from "The Most Just" so how can we poor mortals ever hope to attain it.

Jack doubted that the unfortunate, living in poverty and squalor, would benefit much from the traditional Christian notion that things would even out in heaven, where they would gain their reward. Heaven was supposed to reward those who lived an exemplary life on earth. Yet the disparities of environment and upbringing made living a morally good life much more daunting for those born into poverty and squalor. So the problem of injustice remained. Given the problem, if people on earth didn't strive to overcome injustice, no one else would.

More than just the guilt of a young rich boy who sympathized with the downtrodden, Jack's perspective showed a spark of social conscience, his awareness of the metaphysical injustice in life for which Christianity had no answer.

He enjoyed reading about current events. "In those days, it wasn't the ordinary boy who subscribed to the *New York Times* in prep school," said a classmate. "But Jack did, and as far as I know, he was the only one who did." At sixteen, said Tinker, Jack knew more about world affairs than most men much older. He read the editorial pages of newspapers rather than just the sports pages.

Jack probably missed more classes due to illness than any other boy at Choate. Repeatedly in the infirmary, he suffered from chronic colds, pinkeye, flu, swollen glands, boils, scraped legs, an injured knee, and fallen arches. Throughout his bouts with illness he remained stoic, like his mother, and never complained except jokingly.

But there was no joking about the mysterious and scary disease Jack developed in January 1934. No one at Choate could diagnose it, and he was losing weight. Doctors initially feared he had leukemia and regularly checked his blood count. They never diagnosed the illness conclusively, but one doctor in Boston settled on agranulocytosis, a rare disease that impaired the production of granulated white blood cells by bone marrow.

Jack spent most of June 1934 at the Mayo Clinic in Rochester, Minnesota, undergoing a battery of tests. Tests of his colon were normal. Paul O'Leary, his primary physician at Mayo's, concluded that Jack had a blood infection, a decline in the number of white cells, and was allergic to dogs, cats, horses, and house dust. O'Leary recommended that Jack be treated with injections of bone marrow, get plenty of rest, and avoid strenuous exercise.

Considering how much worry their underachieving son caused them, Rose thought that Joe's response was a model of reasonableness, which indeed it was. In reply to one of Jack's letters, in which he was contrite about his underachieving, Joe expressed "great satisfaction" over the "forthrightness and directness that you are usually lacking." He didn't want to nag, but after "long experience in sizing up people I definitely know you have the goods and you can go a long way. Now aren't you foolish not to get all there is out of what God has given you?"

Unfortunately Jack didn't have the self-discipline to follow through on his good intentions, and was nearly kicked out of Choate for his shenanigans. The school gave three troubled boys the chance to visit the psychologist Prescott Lecky at Columbia University. Apparently feeling he could benefit from the counseling, Jack took advantage of the opportunity. Lecky subsequently described Jack's psychological predicament. He was very able, "but definitely in a trap, psychologically speaking. . . . He has established a reputation in the family for thoughtlessness, sloppiness, and inefficiency, and he feels entirely at home in the role."

Lecky asked him how he could amount to anything if he had to be thoughtless and sloppy. This stumped Jack. When Lecky pointed out the great handicap he would be under in the business world, Jack responded, "Yes, that is true enough."

Lecky continued his report: "He thinks of himself as a self-reliant, intelligent, and courageous boy, but he has never recognized the difficulty he will have in maintaining those definitions unless he sacrifices the defense devices that he has built up through the years."

In probing Jack's sibling rivalry with Joe Jr., Lecky struck a nerve. Much of Jack's trouble was due to comparison with his older brother, Lecky found. Jack remarked, "My brother is the efficient one in the family, and I am the boy that doesn't get things done. If my brother were not so efficient, it would be easier for me to be efficient. He does it so much better than I do." Lecky concluded that "Jack is apparently avoiding comparison and withdraws from the race, so to speak, in order to convince himself that he is not trying."

Twenty-five years after graduating from Choate, John Kennedy soberly reflected on his high school years. "I didn't know what I wanted to do and I didn't do much of anything. I was just a drifter. I didn't really settle down seriously to study until the last couple years at Harvard. Why? I don't know."

*

In the fall of 1935 Jack went to London to study under Harold Laski, the brilliant political scientist, and a socialist, who was considered one of the world's greatest teachers. Earlier Joe Jr. had spent a year under Laski's tutelage. Joe Sr. had arranged the educational adventures. After he arrived in London, though, Jack became ill, apparently with hepatitis, and studied under Laski only briefly. Joe and Rose decided that he should return home to be closer to his doctors. Meanwhile Jack had convinced his father to let him enroll at Princeton instead of Harvard because Billings and Ralph Horton, a

Choate classmate, were both there. It was a happy reunion for the three roommates at Princeton, but after only two months Jack's illness forced him to withdraw from school during the Christmas holiday.

The following fall, his health restored, Jack transferred from Princeton to Harvard, the college his father preferred he attend. For the next two years he remained lackadaisical about most of his studies. He listed government as his primary field of concentration, followed by a combination of history and literature. His freshman adviser reported that "he is planning to work in government." Jack's early academic record at Harvard reflected his attitude and resulted in the "gentleman's C." As a freshman he received a B in Economics, Cs in English, French, and History. No better his sophomore year, he managed one B, four Cs, and a D.

During that second year one professor saw potential in Jack. In addition to its usual classes, Harvard had a tutorial system in which the student met with a professor to discuss research and readings. In the fall of 1937 Payson Wild, assistant professor of government and acting master of Jack's dorm, Winthrop House, tutored both Jack and Joe Jr. once a week. He remembered vividly his first contact with Jack. The young sophomore came to Wild's office, sat down on the sofa, and said candidly, "Dr. Wild, I want you to know I'm not bright like my brother Joe." Wild thought that Jack obviously had an inferiority complex in relation to his older brother. Gradually, though, Wild became more impressed with Jack than with his brother, because Jack's work was more substantial.

He had several girlfriends in college, but he casually dated many others. Jack was highly successful in squiring women. He romped with coeds, models, stewardesses, nurses, showgirls, and prostitutes—a seemingly endless supply. "Every time he went to New York for a weekend he returned with ten new names," said his friend Jim Rousmanière.

During Jack's Harvard years he made three trips to Europe: a two-month sight-seeing excursion with Billings in the summer of 1937, a brief vacation in the summer of 1938, and a major seven-month tour in 1939. The first trip provided Jack with an opportunity to study fascism. Always inquisitive, he insisted on picking up hitchhikers, many of whom were students who spoke English. Then he would grill the new traveling companion about European politics and current events, especially about fascism in Franco's Spain, Mussolini's Italy, and Hitler's Germany. He compared these comments with those of the book he read during the journey, John Gunther's *Inside Europe*. While he pondered the often conflicting judgments, he mused about them in his diary and in letters to his father.

As he and Billings approached the Spanish border with France, Jack briefed himself on the Spanish Civil War, which had been raging for a year. Since the establishment of its republic in 1931, Spain's situation had been tense and unstable. The efforts of the republic's first government to enact reforms—freedom of action for trade unions, separation of church and state—had led conservatives to believe the country faced imminent social revolution. In July 1936 Gen. Francisco Franco led a military revolt against the government, plunging Spain into civil war. (In 1939 Franco's victory would end the gruesome fighting.)

At first Jack found the arguments of pro-Franco supporters convincing, but after reading Gunther's critical assessment of the Spanish fascist leader and his supporters, he changed his mind. "Not quite as positive now about Franco victory," he wrote. "Shows that you can be easily influenced by people around you if you know nothing and how easy it is for you to believe what you want to believe."

He wrote his father, "While I felt that perhaps it would be far better for Spain if Franco should win—as he would strengthen and unite Spain—yet at the beginning the [elected] government was in the right morally speaking as its program was similar to the New Deal."

*

On January 5, 1938, President Roosevelt appointed Joe Kennedy as ambassador to Great Britain. Delighted and proud, the Kennedys packed for London in time for Joe to assume his official duties on March 8.

As war clouds darkened Europe, the thought of armed conflict horrified Joe Kennedy, partly because of his deep sense of foreboding for the safety of his children. War would reduce Europe to rubble, he thought, and would destroy capitalism and probably accelerate the triumph of communism. Considering these dreadful possible consequences, Nazism, despite its obnoxious features, seemed clearly preferable. Joe steadfastly opposed American intervention in Europe and had no faith that the British could survive a war with the Nazis. Throughout the years of Hitler's dictatorship, neither John Kennedy nor his father expressed any empathy for the terrible plight of Jews in Germany. Joe in fact was anti-Semitic, and when his attitude became public, his reputation suffered.

When Joe Kennedy suggested that Jack take a semester's leave of absence from Harvard to work in the London embassy and travel throughout Europe, Jack jumped at the chance. Harvard granted him permission to withdraw during the spring semester of 1939, and he remained in Europe for seven months, until the following September.

During the spring and summer of 1939 he traveled throughout Europe, the Soviet Union, the Balkans, and the Middle East. From each capital he wrote letters to his father about the political and economic situation. It was a unique opportunity to get behind the scenes of the coming war.

The European situation was so "damn complicated," Jack wrote to Billings in late March. And, in a remark he was to make often in 1939, he concluded, "The whole thing is 'damn interesting.'"

While in Poland he predicted accurately that the Germans would maneuver to make Poland appear the aggressor in any conflict, "and then go to work." "Poland has an army of 4,000,000 who are damn good—but poorly equipped." He predicted inaccurately that Poland's poor roads would "nullify Germany's mechanical advantage." Since neither France nor Great Britain could help, Poland would have to fight alone. "But they are tough," he concluded, "and whether they get help or not they will fight."

After Poland, Jack traveled through the Soviet Union— Leningrad, Moscow, Kiev, and the Crimea. Then it was on to Hungary, Lithuania, Latvia, Estonia, Romania, Turkey, Egypt, and Palestine.

In the last ten days of August he had a front-row seat in the riveting drama as he shuttled between Prague and the German cities of Munich, Berlin, and Hamburg. The pervasive, incredibly powerful propaganda of Hitler's totalitarian regime shocked him.

> The anti-Polish campaign is beyond description. Every edition of the newspapers has a more gruesome tale to tell of Polish outrages against the Germans, of planes being attacked and of German soldiers tortured. In the newsreel about two minutes was given over to showing the real German background of the city of Danzig. The Nazi banners, the fascist salute, and the goose-stepping soldiers were all featured. After this they showed the women and children who had been turned out of their homes by the Poles. With tears streaming down their cheeks they bawled into the microphone their tale of grief. Even children told theirs.

War broke out on September 1, 1939, when Germany invaded Poland. A lull in the war followed the easy German victory, but the calm ended in May 1940. In England Neville Chamberlain's inadequate handling of the war crisis aroused intense opposition, leading to a loss of parliamentary and public confidence. On May 10, 1940, he resigned, and Winston Churchill formed a national coalition government.

On the same day Churchill assumed power, the Germans struck in the West. German forces invaded the Netherlands, knocking out the Dutch army, brushing aside the Belgians, and continuing their assault into France. The German spearheads crushed the resistance and forced France to capitulate on June 22. Suddenly Hitler was triumphant and the British were left to resist alone. In August 1940 the German Luftwaffe began sustained night bombardment of English cities; the Battle of Britain lasted until mid-May 1941. Like many Americans, the shocking German success and the dire threat to England forced Jack to reevaluate his thoughts about the war and America's role in it.

Meanwhile, in his junior and senior years at Harvard Jack had taken his courses far more seriously. Because he intended to join his father in Europe during the spring semester, in the fall of 1938 he selected six courses instead of the usual four, and did remarkably well—five Bs and one C, earning him a spot on the Dean's List.

As Jack completed his college career, the quality of his intellect increasingly impressed his friends and other observers. He liked to probe a person's mind. When history professor William G. Carleton of the University of Florida spent an evening of conversation with the Kennedys at Palm Beach, Jack impressed him most. "It was clear to me," Carleton recalled, "that John had a far better historical and political mind than his father or his elder brother." He could see current events in historical perspective and project historical trends into the future.

For his senior thesis Jack proposed to write about Great Britain's controversial appeasement policy up to the Munich Conference of September 1938, a conference that shamelessly dismembered Czechoslovakia. Created in 1918 following World War I, democratic Czechoslovakia comprised seven million Czechs, two million Slovaks, plus three and a quarter million Germans living in the Sudetenland, a mountainous region between Bohemia and Silesia, bordering Germany. Hitler exploited nationalist sentiment in Germany by demanding the return of the Sudetenland to the Reich. In 1938, aided by his agents in the Sudetenland, Hitler manipulated complaints by Sudeten Germans over high unemployment and repressive security measures to manufacture a crisis.

To solve the crisis, Mussolini suggested a conference of major powers, which took place in Munich in September. England, France, Italy, and Germany attended; neither the Czechs nor the Russians were invited. To "appease" Hitler, Czechoslovakia's democratic friends abandoned her and forced the country to surrender the Sudetenland to Germany, mortally wounding the new Czech state.

After he returned to England, Chamberlain boasted that the Munich agreement meant "peace in our time." Hitler had promised him, Chamberlain said, that the Sudetenland was his final demand and that all future problems would be settled by peaceful talks. Chamberlain naively believed Hitler's promises. At the time, though, the Munich settlement was wildly popular in Great Britain.

At the beginning of 1939 Hitler and his agents created disorder in the rest of Czechoslovakia, until finally, demoralized and browbeaten, the president of Czechoslovakia, Emil Hacha, capitulated. On the morning of March 15, 1939, German troops marched into Prague. Independent, democratic Czechoslovakia had been destroyed. Hitler's takeover of Czechoslovakia went far beyond simply bringing Germans into the Reich and rectifying the Treaty of Versailles. Evidently Hitler's promises made at Munich were worthless, souring public opinion toward him in France, Great Britain, and the United States.

Jack's thesis rejected the prevailing attitude, both in Britain and the United States, that British unpreparedness had been primarily the fault of a group of appeasers led by Stanley Baldwin, Britain's Conservative prime minister from 1935 to 1937, and his successor Chamberlain. Jack contended that the critics of Munich had been aiming their barbs at the wrong target. The Munich Pact itself should not be the object of criticism; rather the "underlying factors" made "surrender inevitable."

He insightfully traced British appeasement policy and the country's delay in rearmament to varying moods and interests in England in the 1930s: blind faith in the weak League of Nations, petty and self-indulgent political partisanship, foolish pacifism, obsession with a balanced budget, the feeling that specific German claims were legitimate, self-seeking business, trade-union opposition to industrial conscription, and the fear that social services would be trimmed to provide money for rearmament. Thus Jack blamed the failure on almost everything—except British political leaders. Explaining this omission, he argued ineffectively that "leaders are responsible for their failures only in the governing sector and cannot be held responsible for the failure of a nation as a whole."

What Jack learned about Britain up to Munich would influence his views for more than two decades. A dictator like Adolf Hitler had superior power to control his country's foreign policy, Jack argued. Hitler could change its direction overnight and bring the power of a unified nation into any issue, whether his followers liked it or not. In the long run, under a democratic system, the people unite in support of policy once a war begins. But before that, a democracy may suffer strategic defeats that jeopardize its ultimate hope of victory. This was the price to be paid for living in a democracy. "In the end it is felt the democratic way is the best way," Jack wrote. Unlike a dictatorship, he observed, a democracy does not take the long-range view. In the final two pages of his thesis, Jack pointedly used the word "sacrifice" three times: a democracy must sacrifice when confronted by aggressive dictatorial regimes. Munich, he concluded, was the price England had to pay for enjoying the luxury of democracy during the preceding six years.

Many historians subsequently agreed with Jack's argument. Neville Chamberlain had no other realistic choice at Munich; the pact was the best he could have negotiated under the circumstances, considering that in 1938 Britain was unprepared for war. Following the seizure of all of Czechoslovakia, the British became more united, determined, and prepared than they had been at the time of Munich. The Commonwealth was now behind them, and Hitler had exposed for the first time his determination to dominate all Europe, whether German or non-German.

Yet the Munich Pact was nonetheless dishonorable, a point Jack did not address. The commitment to peace on which Chamberlain's appeasement rested displayed a moral blindness to the evils and dangers of fascism in Europe.

"Finished my thesis," Jack wrote exultantly to his father in early spring. Titled "Appeasement at Munich: The Inevitable Result of the Slowness of the British Democracy to Change from a Disarmament Policy," it "represents more work than I've ever done in my life," Jack said.

In the Harvard system, a senior thesis could receive a grade of summa cum laude, magna cum laude, cum laude, or simply nondistinction. Jack earned magna cum laude, bettering the thesis grade of cum laude that Joe Jr. had received for his thesis.

Despite Jack's mediocre academic record in his first two years, he did well enough in his junior and senior years to graduate cum laude, placing him better than 70 percent of his classmates.

Until the fall of France in the spring of 1940, Jack believed, with his father, that the United States should not become entangled in another European war. But he never shared the ambassador's tolerant view of Hitler's Germany. "He was very much disturbed by Nazism," observed Payson Wild. "He was somewhat embarrassed by his father's position, but he didn't get on any stands or pulpits to declare his difference of opinion. He was a very loyal son."

Before Jack graduated he had already begun revising his thesis for publication. Normally a college senior thesis isn't sufficiently polished to lure a publisher, but his father's friend Arthur Krock liked the thesis and encouraged Jack to publish it. It was Krock who came up with the arresting title, *Why England Slept*, which deliberately paraphrased the title of an earlier Churchill book, *While England Slept*.

On May 20, 1940, Joe offered his son astute criticism. Jack had let "[Stanley] Baldwin off too easily." Joe focused on the responsibilities of leadership:

> The basis of your case—that the blame must be placed on the people as a whole—is sound. Nevertheless, I think that you had better go over the material to make sure that, in pinning it on the electorate, you don't give the appearance of trying to do a complete whitewash of the leaders. I know that in a democracy a politician is supposed to keep his ear to the ground; he is also supposed to look after the national welfare, and to attempt to educate the people when, in his opinion, they are off base. It may not be good politics but it is something that is vastly more important—good patriotism. . . . Why not say that British national policy was the result of British national sentiment and that everyone, leaders and people alike, must assume some share of the responsibility for what happened. . . . For some reason, Britain slept. That means pretty much all Britain, leaders and people alike.

Jack immediately agreed: "Will stop whitewashing Baldwin." He incorporated portions of his father's letter almost verbatim into the book's concluding pages.

Krock and several others helped revise Jack's manuscript. "He brought the stuff to me and we worked over it," said Krock. "I may have supplied some of the material as far as prose is concerned, but it was his book." Krock contacted a literary agent, who found a publisher, and the book appeared in 1940.

Written with becoming modesty, the book had an appealing quality of freshness and understanding. Most reviewers found it dispassionate, clear, scrupulously objective, and, above all, timely. *Time*'s review called it "startlingly timely, strenuously objective," and added, "To Americans who believe that democracy always triumphs because of its moral superiority over fascism, *Why England Slept* is a warning and challenge." The book sold eighty thousand copies in the United States and England. Jack earned modest fame and forty thousand dollars in royalties.

Meanwhile Ambassador Kennedy remained perplexed about the war and continued to underestimate the diabolical nature of Hitler's system and its dire threat to England and the United States. His speeches continued to compare Western democracies with totalitarianism, always lamely concluding that the Western system was preferable. Certainly Germany was no paradise, he admitted, but was the Reich really as bad as the interventionists made her out to be? "Democracy is finished in England," he declared in an interview. "It may be here."

When the United States had pledged every possible assistance to England short of war, and when popular opinion overwhelmingly sympathized with Britain's heroic fight, Ambassador Kennedy's statement met withering criticism. The interventionist *New York Herald-Tribune* accused him of encouraging the enemies of democracy and discouraging democracy's defenders. It was realistic to recognize "unpleasant facts [about England's predicament] and fight to overcome them," but emotional despair "concedes a fight before it is put to the test. . . . Despair can stab democracy in the back quite as fatally as treason."

On December 5, 1940, Jack gingerly, lovingly advised his father on how to extract himself from his public relations nightmare. To counter the popular view that his father was a defeatist and an appeaser, Jack urged him to write an article that emphasized the courage and sacrifice of the British. At the same time Jack clarified his own evolving thoughts about the war. He urged his father to support U.S. rearmament and aid to Great Britain. As Munich awakened England, so the defeat of France "awakened us," he wanted his father to say. "But like England we are rearming in much the same leisurely fashion." In advising America to stay out of the war, the ambassador should not make the plea at the expense of minimizing aid to Britain. Despite his son's advice, throughout most of World War II Joe Kennedy remained gloomy and defeatist.

Between 1938 and 1940 Jack was often hospitalized—in February 1938 at the Mayo Clinic, two weeks in June at New England Baptist Hospital, and another trip to Mayo's in February 1939. During the last hospitalization Dr. Walter Alvarez hinted that Jack's stomach pain might stem from hypochondria, a view that Joe Kennedy also suspected. When all the major tests of Jack's stomach were negative, Dr. Alvarez suggested that Jack's stomach problems might be caused by "an inherited nervousness or sensitiveness of the nervous system. We see this sort of thing commonly in college students who get over it as they grow older and as responsibilities come upon them."

In 1938 Jack also began experiencing back pain. Gradually his back became stiffer and more bothersome. After getting out of bed in the morning, his left sacroiliac region would hurt, forcing him to walk stiff-legged. Occasionally the soreness would cross over to the region of the right sacroiliac. For the moment Jack decided not to have surgery.

After his graduation from Harvard, Jack thought about attending Yale Law School, but he was undecided and worried about his health. Why not head west and audit some graduate classes at Stanford? It would be an adventure—meeting new people, especially attractive coeds. He told friends that he planned to study business law, first taking courses at Stanford's business school and later entering Yale Law School.

"Have become very fond of Stanford," Jack wrote Billings on November 14, 1940—"everyone is very friendly—the gals are quite attractive—and it's a very good life." A month earlier he had registered for the draft, and the prospect of being drafted concerned him. "They will never take me into the army—and yet if I don't [get into military service] it will look quite bad—I may be able to work out some sort of thing." He probably worried about being viewed as the son of a millionaire who was dodging the draft.

Because his interest in politics remained acute, Jack audited courses from two of Stanford's most eminent professors of political science, Thomas S. Barclay and Graham H. Stuart. Barclay taught a graduate seminar in politics where eight students discussed the presidential campaign of 1940 and other political issues. Barclay thought Jack was well informed and intelligent in the field of politics and international relations.

The news from Europe and the Battle of Britain captivated Jack. He listened to every radio broadcast. "I turned it off once when we were driving around San Francisco, and he was furious," said one of his girlfriends. "He was really angry."

On May 7, 1941, Jack Kennedy set sail aboard the *Argentina* for a tour of South America. By then U.S. military preparedness for war was almost in full swing; it was time for him to enlist.

3

World War II and Aftermath

DESPITE his medical problems, Kennedy was determined to enter military service. Initially he failed the physical exams for both the army's and the navy's officer candidate schools. In desperation he allowed his father to use his connections, leading the navy to change its mind. After a perfunctory exam, the navy's medical examiners declared him "physically qualified for appointment" as an officer in the naval reserve.

Kennedy officially joined the navy in October 1941 and was immediately assigned to the Foreign Intelligence Branch of the Office of Naval Intelligence (ONI) in Washington, where he began tedious duty collating reports and rewriting them clearly. He rented a small apartment in Washington only a few blocks away from his sister Kathleen, who had recently moved to the city.

While in Washington in early 1942, he engaged in a torrid love affair with Inga Arvad, a friend of Kathleen's. Born in Denmark, multilingual, well traveled, sophisticated, perfumed, and sexually experienced, Inga was also stunningly beautiful. "Luscious, luscious is the word," remarked Kathleen Kennedy's friend John White. "Like a lot of icing on a cake."

The events of December 7, 1941, altered the nature of this affair. Following the Japanese attack on Pearl Harbor, the United States declared war on Germany, Italy, and Japan. With rumor and paranoia permeating the atmosphere in Washington, Inga's past soon attracted suspicion. As a reporter in Denmark she had interviewed Nazi leaders and had been photographed with Hitler. Judging her a possible spy, observes Nigel Hamilton, the FBI "resorted to surveillance, interception of mails, phone tapping, burglary, and information from janitors and postmen to piece together its own picture of Inga's past and present, guaranteeing a comic mishmash of distortion, paranoid speculation, and plain ignorance." When Kennedy's relations with Inga were publicly exposed by gossip columnist Walter Winchell, his worried navy boss immediately transferred him to a desk job in Charleston, South Carolina.

Kennedy had presidential ambitions as early as 1941 and confided his hopes to Inga. He told her that he was torn between his postwar dreams of relaxing by moving to a ranch out West, or pursuing an extraordinary political ambition, as she rephrased it, "to be a White-House-Man." She took his White House ambition seriously. "Put a match to the smoldering ambition, and you will go like wild fire," she advised him. "It is all against the ranch out West, but it is the unequalled highway to the White House." By late February 1942 their relationship had ended, except for a few brief encounters.

On reflection Kennedy considered World War II to have been a defining moment in his life. "I firmly believe," he wrote, "that as much as I was shaped by anything, so was I shaped by the hand of fate moving in World War II." He thought the same was true for others: "The memory of the war is a key to our characters. It serves as a breakwall between the indolence of our youths and earnestness of our manhoods. . . . No other experience could have brought forth in us the same fortitude and resilience."

The war also "savaged" his family. "It turned my father and my brothers and sisters and I upside down and sucked all the oxygen out of our smug and comfortable assumptions." It took a while to get the oxygen back.

In late July 1942 Kennedy received a long-awaited telegram transferring him to midshipmen's school at Northwestern

University. After a stint there, the navy accepted him for PT-boat training in Melville, Rhode Island. He was going to torpedo boat school, he wrote Billings, adding, "The requirements are very strict physically—you have to be young, healthy and unmarried—and as I am young and unmarried, I'm trying to get in."

Low, squat, and eighty feet long, the high-speed PT boats (patrol torpedo) carried four twenty-one-inch torpedoes and mounted four .50 caliber machine guns in two twin turrets. A boat's normal complement was three officers and nine men.

Kennedy's ardor to fight the enemy was now deep and sincere. "His whole attitude about the war has changed," Rose chronicled in her family newsletter. "And he is quite ready to die for the U.S.A. in order to keep the Japanese and the Germans from becoming the dominant people on their respective continents, believing that sooner or later they would encroach upon ours."

Kennedy was assigned to the Solomon Islands in the Pacific. For two decades before the war, the Solomon Islands, stretching for six hundred miles just east of New Guinea and Australia, slumbered as a remote portion of the British Empire. After the U.S. victory at Guadalcanal in the Solomons, however, Adm. William Halsey's amphibious forces leapfrogged up the islands, bypassing and isolating Japanese strongholds, and constructing new airfields and bases to prepare for the next landing. By the end of July 1943 the Americans had more than fifty PT boats operating from two bases in the Solomons.

At Tulagi on April 24, 1943, Kennedy was assigned to PT-109, a filthy, battle-scarred veteran of the Guadalcanal campaign. Together with his mostly unseasoned crew, he cleaned the dirt and grime, eliminated the rats and cockroaches, and began repairs and training.

"For Jack it was the beginning of the most dramatic episode of his life," notes Hamilton. "Indeed it would be no exaggeration to say that the next few months in the Southwest Pacific would be the making of Jack Kennedy."

As the commander of PT-109, Kennedy had his first real taste of leadership, and by all accounts his peers and his crew respected him. His squadron commander gave him an excellent performance rating in May: a perfect 4.0 for shiphandling and a 3.9 for his ability to command. "I thought he was a real good officer," recalled Ens. Johnny Iles. "His boat was shipshape and his crew was well organized."

In mid-July Kennedy received orders to move PT-109 to Rendova, where the navy had established a new forward base in the middle of the current battle zone, bringing Jack the closest he would come to engaging the enemy. His new boss was Lt. Cdr. Thomas Warfield.

From their powerful base at Rabaul, the Japanese moved soldiers and supplies at night down the New Georgia Sound, renowned since Guadalcanal days as "the Slot." Usually they transported by motorized barges, but when the Japanese needed a major reinforcement they organized an "Express," consisting of several destroyers, and rammed it down the Slot. The primary responsibility of the PT boats was to intercept nightly Japanese shipments.

At anchor the PT boat smelled of engines, damp life jackets, stale coffee, and sweat. Kennedy lived on the boat, ate canned army rations (beans and fried spam), and went out nearly every night. By midday the crew's quarters were hot and airless, making sleeping below deck unbearable. Despite the burning sun, the crew preferred to sleep on deck. Sleeping in the heat produced torpor; no one could sleep for very long.

Kennedy's letters gave his impressions of conditions in the Solomons and his views on the Pacific war. The war confirmed his strong belief in military preparedness, a view he held for the rest of his life; but he also related stories of military inefficiency and poor military leadership.

He criticized the military leadership for logistical bottle-necks:

> A great hold-up seems to me to be the lackadaisical way they handle the unloading of ships. They sit in ports out here weeks at a time while they try to get enough Higgins boats to unload them. . . . Don't let any one sell the idea that everyone out here is hustling with the old American energy. They may be ready to give their blood but not their sweat. . . . They have brought back a lot of old Captains and Commanders from retirement and stuck them in as the heads of these ports and they give the impression of their brains being in their tails as Honey Fitz would say.

The navy screwed up everything it touched, Kennedy reported. "Even the simple delivery of a letter frequently over-burdens this heaving puffing war machine of ours. God save this country of ours from those patriots whose war cry is 'what this country needs is to be run with military efficiency.'"

Many of his letters were unusually thoughtful and often hilarious. "Admiral Halsey inspected us yesterday," Jack wrote the family in June 1943, "and I tried to look broken-down so he would send me home—but he said we were a 'fine looking crowd'—which was obviously a lie—and said it was a 'privilege for us to be where we are' which made me edge away from him in case God hit him with lightning."

In Rabaul in July the Japanese decided to ferry nine hundred men and supplies to Kolombangara on three destroyers with a fourth, the *Amagiri*, as an escort. On the afternoon of August 1, 1943, after Commander Warfield received a message warning him to expect an Express that night, he called an emergency meeting of the PT skippers. To meet the Express he organized fifteen boats into four divisions, each to operate independently. He assigned PT-109 to a group of four boats under the command of Lt. Henry Brantingham, twenty-six, a career officer and Annapolis graduate.

As PT-109 set out that evening, the crew consisted of Torpedoman Raymond Starkey, Motor Machinist Mate Gerard Zinser, Seaman Raymond Albert, Gunner Harold Marney, Gunner's Mate Charles Harris, Seaman Edgar Mauer, Radioman John Maguire, Motor Machinist Mate William Johnston, and, at thirty-seven the oldest crew member, the stoic, uncomplaining Motor Machinist Mate Patrick McMahon.

Another crew member, Torpedoman Andrew Kirksey, initially had seemed as brave, bold, and steady as any of the others. But since the last week of July he had become convinced he was going to die, and no one could dispel his premonition.

Kennedy relied most on his second in command, Ens. Leonard Thom of Sandusky, Ohio. A blond-haired giant weighing 210 pounds, Thom had played left tackle at Ohio State in 1939 and 1940. "He had no fear," Charles Harris said of Thom. "[He] could rule anybody. You'd just look at him and do what he told you; he was that big. He was an awful nice man."

During the afternoon of August 1 Kennedy had run into an acquaintance from Melville days, Ens. George "Barney" Ross, whose PT boat had been sunk twelve days earlier. Ross wanted to ride on PT-109 that evening, and Jack readily agreed.

All the boats were ordered to maintain radio silence. "When the leading boat saw something and attacked, the other boats were to follow right along without further ado and no further conversation," Lieutenant Brantingham later said. He conceded, though, that it may not have been the practice in other squadrons. Unfortunately for Kennedy, this was the first time he had ever patrolled with Brantingham, and the Annapolis graduate never informed Kennedy of his procedures.

Of the four boats in Kennedy's division, only Brantingham's had radar. Ross recalled that "it was extremely difficult to keep station on the other boats for it was so dark—an extremely black night."

Shortly after midnight, when Brantingham saw blips on his radar screen, he thought they were Japanese barges and tore off after them. A second boat, PT-157 under the command of Lt. William Liebenow, followed him. Confused and left behind were PT-109 and PT-162, commanded by Lt. John Lowrey. Shocked to be greeted by salvos from the Japanese destroyers, Brantingham and Liebenow fired their torpedoes, which all missed their targets, and then fled the scene, never rejoining the two boats they had left behind. Some of Kennedy's crew were angry at Brantingham. Charles Harris recalled:

> We had no idea there were ships out there that night. We didn't know the Express had gone down to Vila. We thought it was shore batteries firing. Our lead boat, the radar boat, picked something up but they didn't tell us anything about it. They took off after it and left us sitting there. . . . When we got back we were really going to look up that skipper and give him the business for leaving us high and dry like that.

Since Kennedy and Lowrey had no radar and heard only garbled, panicked radio transmissions, they were left in a quandary. Kennedy resumed his patrolling, paired with Lowrey in PT-162. While they eased their way up Blackett Strait, a third boat, PT-169, under the command of Lt. Phil Potter, emerged out of the darkness and joined them. Potter had lost contact with his division leader the same way as Lowrey and Kennedy.

At about 2:30 a.m. on August 2, a ship suddenly appeared on PT-109's starboard bow, about 250 yards away. While standing at the helm of 109, Kennedy glanced at the object at the same moment Ross was pointing to a shape suddenly coming out of the darkness. As the shape became clearer they both realized that it wasn't a PT boat. It was the *Amagiri*, a new 2,000-ton Japanese destroyer carrying 13 officers and 245 men under the command of Lt. Cdr. Kohei Hanami.

The *Amagiri* slashed through PT-109. Harold Marney was immediately crushed to death. Kirksey, the quiet Georgian with the premonition of death, also perished. The engine portion of the boat sank immediately; the bow stuck out of the water at a steep angle.

The collision threw Kennedy into the cockpit, where he landed on his sore back. "So this is how it feels to die!" was his first thought. Once he realized he was still alive, he developed an implacable desire to survive. His indomitable spirit over the next six days sustained him and bolstered his crew.

"Mr. Kennedy! Mr. Kennedy!" Harris shouted in the darkness. "McMahon is badly hurt." On the floating bow, Kennedy removed his shoes, his shirt, and his sidearm, dove in, and swam toward Harris's voice. McMahon and Harris were a hundred yards away. When Kennedy reached them, he found McMahon in serious condition with terrible burns over 70 percent of his body. Kennedy took McMahon in tow and brought him back to the wreck. Having successfully towed in McMahon and prodded Harris, Kennedy swam from one man to another, checking their condition. All of those who had survived the crash were still afloat, thanks to their life jackets. Finally, eleven men were accounted for.

As they huddled at the floating bow and waited, fortunately the Japanese never returned. Unfortunately neither did the Americans. "Those sons of bitches ran away from us," Maguire recalled bitterly. "We were left."

Shortly after 1 p.m., still on August 2, Kennedy ordered the men to abandon ship. They must try to reach land before dark. He directed them toward a group of islands east of Gizo, his best guess of land not occupied by the Japanese.

"I'll take McMahon with me," he said. Under Thom's direction, the others tied their shoes and a battle lantern to a two-by-eight-foot plank to which they would cling.

As the men gathered about the plank, Kennedy put the straps of McMahon's life jacket between his teeth and began swimming. He and McMahon were back to back with

Kennedy low in the water beneath McMahon. It was an epic swim.

Jack did the breast stroke for ten to fifteen minutes, rested briefly, then resumed swimming.

Near sundown Kennedy and McMahon arrived on the shore of Plum Pudding Island. It had taken nearly four hours for Jack to make the three-and-a-half-mile swim across Blackett Strait. As he and McMahon stumbled onto the island, coral spikes and spurs lacerated their feet and shins and bruised their thighs. Kennedy lay panting, his feet in the water, his face on the sand. The others, clinging to the plank, arrived shortly after.

From his hideaway on Kolombangara several hundred feet above Blackett Strait, the Australian coastwatcher, Lt. Arthur Reginald Evans, overlooked the Japanese base at Vila. One of a network of courageous coastwatchers engaged in intelligence work in the Solomon Islands, Evans used his binoculars and a telescope to report by radio to his superiors on Guadalcanal all the Japanese movements he detected or were reported by the native scouts assisting him.

At 9:30 a.m. on August 2, the base notified Evans that PT-109 had been lost in action—"Request any information." Late in the afternoon Evans told his native scouts to watch for survivors of the PT wreck.

Kennedy decided he would swim alone into Ferguson Passage that evening, hoping to signal a patrolling PT boat. None of the crew attempted to stop their determined skipper. "It was Jack's refusal to be defeated, even when they could see no sign of help or rescue coming, that would earn the admiration and devotion of his crew," notes Nigel Hamilton.

He stripped down to his skivvies. Carrying the battle lantern, wearing a rubber life belt around his waist and shoes to protect his feet on the reefs, his .38 revolver hanging from a lanyard around his neck, he entered the water at dusk. His trek in the dark over the coral reefs, a distance of about two and a half miles, was eerie. Strange creatures flitted through the water; he worried about mutilation by sharks or barracuda. In the Ferguson Passage he treaded water looking for PT boats, ready to signal them with his lantern. He didn't know that instead of patrolling in Ferguson Passage that night, the boats were operating farther north.

Hoping to secure coconuts for his hungry crew, and wanting to be closer to Ferguson Passage and possible rescue, on Wednesday, August 4, Kennedy moved his group to Olasana Island, just one island removed from Ferguson Passage. At midday the men dragged the plank into the water, and Kennedy again towed McMahon, this time for a distance of a mile and three-quarters. Several hours later, as the eleven men gathered in the trees behind the curved beach of Olasana, Kennedy could see another island, Naru, a half-mile away. The far side of Naru Island faced Ferguson Passage. From there it might be easier to flag down friendly boats.

Shortly after noon on Thursday, Kennedy and Ross crawled up on Naru, a narrow, four-hundred-yard-long island. They quickly crossed to the side facing Ferguson Passage. On the reef, about a mile away, they spotted the wreckage of a small Japanese ship. Exploring the vessel, they found nearby a crate containing hard candy and a dugout canoe with a large tin of precious rainwater.

While Kennedy and Ross quenched their thirst, two of Evans's native scouts, Biuku Gasa and Eroni Kumana, happened to stop at Naru to explore the Japanese wreck. Both pairs of men spotted each other at the same time from a mile away. Afraid that Kennedy and Ross were Japanese from the wreckage, the two scouts paddled furiously away in their canoe.

Instead of returning immediately to their base, Biuku and Eroni made a fateful decision. They would stop at Olasana. "I was thirsty, so I told [Eroni] to leave me at the island so I could get a coconut," recalled Biuku. "[While] I was going ashore, I saw a white man crawling out from the bushes near the shore. I said '[Eroni], a Japanese here.'" They pushed their canoe out to get away. Neither scout spoke English, only pidgin. The white man tried to communicate with them but failed.

Then Lenny Thom emerged from the bushes.

Eroni and Biuku were far enough away to stop and listen. "Me no Jap," said Thom, rolling up his sleeve to show his white skin. Biuku and Eroni were still dubious. Thom tried several other approaches. "Me know Johnny Kari," he blurted out. John Kari was a prominent native scout known to the PT men.

"At this point I began to believe the soldiers and to understand what had happened," said Biuku. The natives waded ashore.

Using his newfound canoe, Kennedy returned to Olasana before dusk with the candy and water, leaving Ross to sleep on Naru. When Kennedy arrived, crewmen yelled to him, "We're saved! Two locals have found us!" Kennedy put down the water and candy and ran over and embraced the two natives.

On Friday, August 6, new excitement animated the stranded Americans. With two canoes, and the natives assisting them, perhaps they could now help themselves.

Without a definite plan, Kennedy persuaded Biuku to paddle him back to Naru for another look at Ferguson Passage. There he had Biuku quarter a coconut. Using his sheath knife, Kennedy scrawled a message on the coconut. Thom, still on Olasana with the men, had a similar plan. Using the stub of a pencil and a blank invoice that Maguire found in his pocket, Thom also wrote a message. When Kennedy returned to Olasana, he entrusted Biuku and Eroni with both messages and sent them by canoe to Rendova Harbor, thirty-eight miles away.

The two natives set off but wisely made a stop at a nearby island to tell Benjamin Kevu, an English-speaking scout, about the survivors. In turn, Kevu sent another scout to inform Evans of the news. With Evans's resources—a radio and the native scouts—the rescue effort accelerated. The coastwatcher immediately dispatched seven of his scouts in a large war canoe to Naru with a message inviting Kennedy to his hideout. Seven scouts, led by Kevu, made their way to Olasana, followed footprints into the underbrush, and found the survivors.

The arrival of Evans's scouts on Olasana seemed like a miracle to the crew. The canoe itself was a cornucopia of food, water, and kerosene. After finishing their feast, Kennedy and the natives began the journey to meet Evans. Over tea at Evans's hideout they discussed the rescue plan. Two PT boats would meet Kennedy at 10 p.m. near Patparan Island. Kennedy insisted that he accompany the rescue boats to Olasana. Well after 10 p.m., the PT boats arrived and hauled Jack aboard. Cdr. Alvin Cluster, Biuku, and Eroni were there to share the jubilation. Then the party made their way to Olasana, arriving shortly after midnight to rescue the survivors.

The rescue party and the eleven survivors reached Rendova at dawn on Sunday, August 8. Several war correspondents had heard the news about the rescue and rushed to interview the son of the prominent former ambassador. After debriefing by Rendova intelligence officers, Kennedy talked with the correspondents in a tent.

After the interview he strode outside and walked to a broken-down army cot under a tree, where Commander Cluster squatted next to him. The accumulated strain of Kennedy's weeklong ordeal exploded. Clenching his fists, tears running down his cheeks, he bitterly told Cluster that the two lost crewmen might have been saved if the other boats had tried to rescue the crew of PT-109. Trying to calm Kennedy's emotions, Cluster explained that the other boats had seen the crash but assumed that all the crewmen had been killed.

Although Jack's PT-109 exploits made him famous, some historians later minimized and criticized his actions. The primary source for the revised version of the PT-109 story is Joan and Clay Blair's *The Search for JFK*. PT-109 was the only PT boat ever hit by a Japanese destroyer during the Pacific war, they note. Kennedy was told to expect Japanese destroyers, so why wasn't he more vigilant?

Before the crash, the Blairs contend, Kennedy ignored "prescribed procedure" by not following his section leader, Lieutenant Brantingham, when he attacked. Kennedy should have known that Japanese destroyers were in the area. When the Express came down Blackett Strait, there was pandemonium for about thirty or forty minutes. Didn't Kennedy hear any of this?

The Blairs doubt that Kennedy had his crew properly alert. He should have had everyone at general quarters. "It seemed incomprehensible that at a tense moment like this, two of the thirteen men who could have served as lookouts were asleep and that Thom and Kirksey were lying down."

Earlier writers had praised Kennedy's heroism for swimming into Ferguson Passage to try to flag down a friendly boat. But the Blairs disagreed. It was impulsive, reckless, a failure, and Kennedy could have been killed.

Finally, the Blairs point out that contrary to most published reports of the six-day survival episode, Kennedy did not "save" his crew. The PT base alerted coastwatcher Evans, who with his native rescue group ultimately rescued the survivors. Kennedy's famous coconut message was useless.

In short, Kennedy "was not a war hero."

On one point the Blairs are probably correct. Kennedy admitted that just before the crash his engines were idling with the mufflers closed. When he saw the destroyer he pushed the throttle forward, and the engines stalled. He had neglected to open his flaps first.

Nonetheless all the witnesses agree that on the night of the crash it was as dark as the inside of a well—no moon, no stars. Lieutenant Brantingham had failed to explain his procedures and tactics to Kennedy, who was riding with him for the first time. Jack didn't follow when Brantingham attacked because he had no idea what the division leader saw or intended. And he was too far away from the "pandemonium" caused by the enemy destroyers coming down Blackett Strait. The only clear message Radioman John Maguire heard that evening was "Let's get the hell out of here." "There were no instructions at all," Maguire recalled. "Once we got out there we never heard from anybody . . . about the destroyers."

Did Kennedy have his crew sufficiently alert? Two of the men were asleep; two others were lying down. That left nine other crewmen, at least five of whom were serving as lookouts at the time of the crash. "The lookouts were out," said Ross. "I was up on the bow, I was a lookout. . . . We weren't all laying around sleeping."

Kennedy's swim into Ferguson Passage was dangerous and didn't accomplish its goal, but it wasn't reckless or impulsive. Risk was involved, but in his judgment there was a good possibility of success. If a boat appeared, he would be astute enough to assess the situation and judge whether it was friend or foe. That the PT boats didn't patrol that night in Ferguson Passage was simply bad luck.

The Blairs correctly set the record straight on the rescue of the eleven survivors. Contrary to the view of countless reporters, historians, and biographers, Kennedy did not "save" his crew with his coconut message. Coastwatcher Evans and his native scouts, assisted by PT-boat headquarters, rescued the crew. But Jack Kennedy agreed and consistently praised his rescuers.

The crew of PT-109 were unanimous in their judgment of their skipper. Long after the ordeal, Gerard Zinser insisted that Kennedy was a genuine hero:

> None of us felt the base did enough to save us but Kennedy had done everything he possibly could to save us. . . . He had extraordinary energy, he just wouldn't give up. . . . That's what made him go out and try to flag down a PT boat. He was exhausted each morning when he got back in.

Charles Harris agreed:

> He saved our lives. I owed him my life. I tell everybody that. If it wasn't for him I wouldn't be here. I really feel that. I

venture to say there are very few men who would swim out in that ocean alone without knowing what was underneath you. That took a lot of guts. I thought he was great. Everybody on the crew thought he was top-notch.

The day after his rescue, on August 9, Kennedy was treated at the thatched hospital in Tulagi for fatigue and for many deep abrasions and lacerations of his entire body, especially his feet. Seven days later, on August 16, he left the hospital, apparently much improved.

Back home in Hyannis Port, Joseph Kennedy knew that Jack was missing, but, not wanting to worry the family, he hadn't told anyone. Rose, hearing a radio report, rushed toward Joe, crying: "I just turned on a news broadcast. They say Jack's been saved. Saved from what?"

News of the PT-109 rescue made the front pages of America's major newspapers. The stories focused on Lieutenant Kennedy because he was the officer in charge and his name was the best known. "Kennedy's Son Is Hero in Pacific as Destroyer Splits His PT Boat," read the headline in the *New York Times*. In the *Boston Globe,* James Morgan praised Kennedy's resourcefulness and described the incident as "one of the great stories of heroism in this war." The PT-109 story later became one of Kennedy's greatest political assets and a major theme in his early campaign literature.

After his adventure, Jack promptly wrote his parents. "On the bright side of an otherwise completely black time was the way that everyone stood up to it. Previous to that I had become somewhat cynical about the American as a fighting man. I had seen too much bellyaching and laying off. But with the chips down, that all faded away. It was a terrible thing, though, losing those two men."

Kennedy emerged from the war wiser, mentally tougher, and with self-respect for having done his patriotic duty. Unlike many officers whose men hated their cowardice or insensitivity, even arrogance, Kennedy's crews respected their skipper for his modesty, initiative, fortitude, and bravery, and for accepting the responsibility for the safety of his men.

Kennedy never naively believed that World War II was the war to end all wars. Having witnessed war's horror, its death and destruction, he emerged with an intense interest in maintaining peace in the postwar era. In a world of tyrants, he believed, peace could be maintained only by vigilance and continued military preparedness.

*

Following Kennedy's return from the Pacific, he tried to relieve the anxiety of the relatives of his comrades still in the war zone. He wrote Barney Ross's father and visited Pat McMahon's wife, giving her an account of the collision and assuring her that Pat was recuperating from his burns. (McMahon eventually did recover.) Afterward Mrs. McMahon, with tears in her eyes and a shaky voice, commented that "my husband wrote home to me that Lt. Kennedy was wonderful, that he saved the lives of all the men."

Jack's immediate goal was to regain his health. He spent a large portion of 1944 in hospitals and clinics. On January 12 that year, before heading home to Palm Beach from the Pacific, he again entered the Mayo Clinic. The orthopedic physician who examined him at the clinic found some "sagging" of the left gluteal muscles and "mild" atrophy and weakness of the back muscles, but the evidence was "not sufficient" to warrant an "operation at the present time." Dr. Paul O'Leary concluded that Jack had no specific illness or injury but that his overall condition was poor:

> In other words, it would seem that with the duodenitis, the weight loss, the backache, and the anemia, Lieutenant Kennedy at the present time is in a state of fatigue and nervous exhaustion which I believe would require more than a month for him to recuperate. He seemed anxious to return to the South Pacific at the completion of his leave of one month,

but it was the impression of all the men who saw him here that a month's time would not be sufficiently long for him to recuperate from his present difficulty.

Meanwhile Kennedy also had his back examined by orthopedists at the Lahey Clinic, who concluded that he probably had a protruded disk and needed an operation. They pushed for back surgery, but orthopedists at Mayo's dissented and urged conservative, nonsurgical treatment. Tragically, Jack and his father made the wrong decision: they opted for surgery.

On June 23, 1944, Dr. James L. Poppen of the Lahey Clinic operated on Kennedy's back to explore herniation of his fifth lumbar intervertebral disk. But the operation proved to be a failure. Poppen removed "degenerative . . . cartilage," but the surgeon did not find a protruded disk. "Upon having the patient get up and about, . . . severe muscle spasms in the low back took place," the mortified Dr. Poppen explained in his medical report. These required large doses of narcotics to keep Kennedy comfortable. "I have had nine other patients in a series of over five hundred ruptured intervertebral discs with a similar experience. They have all subsided in a few days or few weeks. I am indeed sorry that this had to happen with Lieutenant Kennedy."

On August 17, 1944, Kennedy underwent rectal surgery by a Dr. Hensen at the Chelsea Naval Hospital. Once more the operation failed. While the "back pain and leg pain is less," and the patient could "walk with less discomfort," Hensen reported, abdominal symptoms remained. Shortly after the doctor's report, Kennedy's back pain returned as well.

While he struggled with his health and two failed operations, the story of his gallantry in the South Pacific was trumpeted to the entire nation after a chance encounter with John Hersey, one of America's prominent writers. Acclaimed for his direct style and eye for detail, Hersey was a journalist, novelist, and eventually the author of two dozen books.

When Hersey became interested in Kennedy's story, at Jack's request he traveled to the Motor Torpedo Boat training center at Melville, Rhode Island, to interview William Johnston, Patrick McMahon, and John Maguire. He then interviewed Kennedy at the New England Baptist Hospital in Boston where Jack was having his back examined. "He asked if the crew had given a decent account of him and I assured him they had," recalled Hersey. "His insistence that I see the crew first struck me very favorably. It didn't seem to me to be self-serving. . . . They were wildly devoted to him, all of them."

When Hersey submitted his story to *Life*, the magazine surprised him by turning it down. After the *New Yorker* accepted it, it appeared under the title "Survival" in the magazine's issue of June 17, 1944. To gain wider readership, Joe Kennedy—and probably Jack—lobbied editors at the *Reader's Digest* to reprint the article in condensed form. Following extensive negotiations, the *New Yorker* granted rights to the *Reader's Digest*, and the condensed article, appearing in August 1944, made Kennedy a national hero.

*

During World War II the Kennedy family suffered three profound tragedies. One in particular dramatically changed Jack's standing in the family.

By the late 1930s Rosemary's retardation had caused troubling behavior, probably associated with delayed puberty. Easily frustrated and avid for sexual experience, she became difficult to manage. Once the sweetest-natured of the Kennedys, Rosemary was now the most rebellious. Rose worried that her daughter would run away, be enticed and flattered by someone, and end up sexually assaulted or kidnapped.

Always impressed by innovations and modern technology, Joe Kennedy thought he had discovered the solution to Rosemary's problems—a lobotomy. With hindsight it is clear that performing a lobotomy on Rosemary, who was only mildly retarded and had ill-defined emotional problems, was extremely risky. At the time, though, Joe convinced himself that a lobotomy was a progressive innovation, sanctioned by the medical community and perfectly suited for his daughter. In the fall of 1941, therefore, he decided to go ahead, persuading doctors that his daughter would be an ideal candidate.

The operation was an unqualified disaster. Rosemary emerged far more unstable than she had been before. After the failed operation, Joe told Rose it was time to place their daughter in an institution, and chose St. Coletta's in Jefferson, Wisconsin. Friends and relatives were mystified. For a long while they were told nothing about the operation. Not until John Kennedy's presidential campaign in 1960 did the Kennedy family openly acknowledge that Rosemary was retarded and living at St. Coletta's. (They said nothing about the lobotomy.)

A second tragedy involved Joe and Rose's oldest son. Jack worried about his brother. He carefully watched the news from Europe, and noted with alarm the experience of Joe Jr.'s squadron. "Heard from Joe a while back," he wrote Billings. "They have had heavy casualties in his squadron. I hope to hell he gets through OK."

In August 1944 Joe Jr. volunteered for an extraordinary mission that involved flying a navy Liberator bomber—loaded with ten tons of high-explosive TNT—from England to within a few miles of a purported German V-bomb base where he would eject and let the plane guide itself the rest of the way to the target by remote control. Shortly before 6 p.m. on August 12 he took off. His plane was in the air only twenty minutes when two huge explosions disintegrated his aircraft. Not even a particle of young Joe's body, or the body of his copilot, was ever found.

Deciding that the best way to memorialize Joe Jr. was to collect information for a book honoring him, Jack set about writing and phoning people, gathering tributes and reminiscences from family members, friends, classmates, former teachers, his commanding officer, and his girlfriend.

The result was a slim but moving book, *As We Remember Joe*. Five hundred copies were privately printed and distributed. Early in life, Jack wrote in the introduction, Joe Jr. had "acquired a sense of responsibility towards his brothers and sisters, and I do not think that he ever forgot it. Towards me who was nearly his own age, this responsibility consisted in setting a standard that was uniformly high." Young Joe was an excellent role model. "I think that if the Kennedy children amount to anything now or ever amount to anything, it will be due more to Joe's behavior and his constant example than to any other factor."

A few years later, after leaving Sunday Mass, Jack startled a friend by saying, "Will you wait a minute? I want to go up and light a candle for Joe."

On the heels of young Joe's death came a third tragedy, the culmination of a heartbreaking struggle within the family for the soul of Kathleen Kennedy. Living in London during the war, Kathleen married William "Billy" Cavendish, the Marquess of Hartington. Wealthy and prominent, the Cavendish family had an impeccable lineage dating to the seventeenth century. Upon the death of his father, Billy would become the Duke of Devonshire. The marriage, though, caused no end of pain for Rose Kennedy because Billy came from a prominent Protestant family.

After the marriage, Billy, an officer in Britain's Coldstream Guards, returned to his battalion to prepare for the D-day invasion. On September 9, 1944, a month after Joe Jr.'s death, Billy was killed, a bullet through his heart. "Life is so cruel," Kathleen wrote in her diary.

*

In April 1945, through his friend William Randolph Hearst, Joseph Kennedy secured Jack a temporary assignment as a Hearst reporter. The position would give him something stimulating to do, keep his name before the public, probably grant him credentials to travel in Europe, and expose him to journalism as a possible career.

Kennedy's first assignment was to report on the founding of the United Nations in San Francisco, covering the charter conference, according to his byline, from a GI's viewpoint. His initial articles, published in the first two weeks of May 1945, were cliché-ridden, inconsequential, and boring. But he noticeably improved. By the end of May he was writing with more confidence and skill.

After Prime Minister Winston Churchill decided to call a general election in Britain for July 6, 1945, before the defeat of Japan, Kennedy was assigned to fly to London to cover the campaign. In June he interviewed scores of British politicians, sampled public opinion, listened to Churchill's speeches, and hosted intimate political gatherings. Kennedy had his own opinions, but he wanted to understand everyone else's. "He always asked an enormous number of questions," said a British political friend. "For every one question I asked him he asked two, at least. . . . He had an inquisitive mind."

Kennedy's brief journalism career, from May to August 1945, was an extraordinary experience for a twenty-eight-year-old. He closely observed several international leaders. Afterward, though, Kennedy told friends that while he enjoyed journalism, he often felt frustrated. Reporting was too passive. "Instead of doing things," he said, "you were writing about people who did things. . . . I really would like to weigh in a little heavier." Politics offered that opportunity.

4

Congress and the 1952 Senate Election

AS THE WAR drew to a close, Joe Kennedy focused on the political future of his two oldest sons. The father assumed that Jack's potential would lie in public service while young Joe would be primed to run for political office.

After Joe Jr.'s death, Jack and his father eyed a possible congressional race. When James Curley, congressman from the Eleventh District in Massachusetts, won election for mayor of Boston, the primary contest to fill his vacant seat was set for June 18, 1946. Overwhelmingly Democratic, the Eleventh District included businessmen and Harvard intellectuals, but overall the district was one of the state's poorest.

The Kennedys had deep roots in the Eleventh Congressional District. The area included the birthplaces of Joe Kennedy, John F. Fitzgerald, and Rose Kennedy. The district encompassed Cambridge, where the Kennedys had gone to Harvard. Although Joe Kennedy's reputation had diminished outside Massachusetts, Boston still regarded him as the patriarch of a legendary family whose triumphs and sorrows were well known.

Since the Democratic party barely functioned in the district, to win office Jack needed to create a loyal personal organization. He and his father constructed one that blended seasoned professionals with energetic amateurs. One professional recruit, the clever Joe Kane, became Joe Kennedy's primary consultant and had the ambassador's ear anytime he wanted it.

Many politicians attempted to climb aboard the Kennedy gravy train. When Billy Sutton first saw Jack Kennedy, he said to himself, "150 lbs. of pure cash!" A student of politics, Sutton became a paid staff member for the campaign and often guided Jack around the district.

But more than Joe Kennedy's money attracted people to Jack's campaign. Because he was amiable, fair, and a war hero who seemed to have a great political future, Jack motivated people to work for him. Together with the savvy Boston professionals, a large contingent of amateur enthusiasts energized the campaign. Dave Powers served as campaign manager in Charlestown and directed a voter registration drive for Jack among returning veterans. An exceptionally funny storyteller, Powers remained a close friend and supporter for the rest of Kennedy's life. Family members, college chums, and other friends also came to work on Kennedy's behalf.

Arrayed against Kennedy for the congressional seat were nine other candidates, a few of them prominent. Among veteran politicians, Mike Neville was the best liked and seemed the most capable candidate.

The anti-Kennedy forces accused Jack of being too young and inexperienced, a carpetbagger, a rich Harvard graduate. But overall his critics made little headway. Because the Kennedy family was so prominent and admired throughout the district, voters treated the carpetbagger accusation as sheer nonsense. Of course Jack was a local boy. His father and grandfathers had all been local boys. Voters were proud to have a charming young returning war hero run as a candidate in their district.

To win political office, Joe Kane maintained, three things were necessary: "The first is money and the second is money and the third is money." Joe Kennedy provided all three. He spent about $300,000 on the campaign, far more than the combined expenditure of all of Jack's opponents.

Altogether Kennedy made about 450 speeches during the campaign. At first his delivery was hesitant and self-conscious. In his standard speech he described the sinking of his PT-109, focusing attention on the grim heroism of crew member Patrick McMahon and on his own heroism only by indirection. Gradually the Kennedy team helped Jack develop a new speech focused on bread-and-butter issues—more jobs, better housing, tougher price and rent controls, and a higher minimum wage. Slowly, Jack developed a comfortable style—simple, direct, and informal—avoiding bombastic rhetoric. Although he sometimes stumbled over his words, audiences responded warmly to his determination, his self-deprecating humor, and his sincerity.

The ambassador insisted that his son run primarily as a veteran and war hero. Thus the Kennedy organization mailed a condensation of Hersey's *New Yorker* article to almost every home in the district. Advertisements and nearly every press release stressed the veteran-hero angle.

Organized by Eunice Kennedy, a team of volunteers arranged a huge reception three days before the June primary. Thousands of women in the congressional district received engraved invitations. On the evening of the reception, held at the Commander Hotel in Cambridge, the Kennedys and the volunteers arrived early to arrange flowers, stack dainty sandwiches, and fill silver urns with tea—like a wedding reception.

The election results were a landslide for Kennedy. He collected 22,183 votes, almost doubling the vote for Neville. In the ten-person race his share of the vote was an impressive 42 percent. As expected, on November 5, 1946, he easily defeated Republican Lester A. Bowen, 69,093 to 26,007 in the general election for the seat in Congress.

In different ways, both Joe Kennedy and Jack contributed roughly equally to the victory. The father masterminded the campaign from afar, funded it abundantly, recruited excellent professional assistance, and constantly encouraged his son.

But Jack wasn't merely a puppet, manipulated by his father. During the campaign he displayed persistence and dedication, reflecting a deeper ambition and drive than early observers thought he possessed.

One thing is certain: his victory transformed him into a major force in Massachusetts politics.

*

Kennedy enjoyed the luxury of having others care for most of his practical needs, which allowed him a charmed life in Washington. He didn't have to worry about money because all of his personal expenses were paid by his father's accountants in New York. Domestic help cooked his meals, did his laundry, made his bed, sent out his dry cleaning, and packed his bags. His office staff arranged his travel and picked up his tickets; often he was chauffeured from place to place.

Jack's primary leisure was pursuing beautiful women. And there were many of them. Ralph Horton recalled visiting Congressman Kennedy in Georgetown:

> We went to his house for dinner and shortly after dinner, a lovely looking blonde from West Palm Beach joined us to go to a movie. After the movie, we went back to the house and I remember Jack saying something about, well, I want to shake this one. She has ideas. Shortly thereafter, another girl walked in. . . . I went to bed figuring this was the girl for the night. The next morning a completely different girl came wandering down for breakfast. They were a dime a dozen.

Because of the needs of his urban constituents, his campaign promises, the social welfare tradition in the Kennedy-Fitzgerald family, and his own Democratic views, Jack chose to fight for social-welfare programs. After World War II, millions of returning soldiers, plus the shortage of building materials during the war, made the housing shortage acute and fueled a huge demand for inexpensive housing. Jack thought his constituents needed low-cost public accommodations.

He also became involved in debate on a major new labor law. The Taft-Hartley Act of 1947, passed over President Truman's veto, amended the pro-union Wagner Act of 1935. Among its harsh provisions was one that reduced the political and economic power of unions by outlawing the closed shop (the practice of hiring only union workers) and specifying unfair labor practices. Labor leaders denounced the act as the "slave labor" bill. Like most Northern Democrats, Kennedy voted against the measure, but he wasn't entirely impressed with labor's lament.

Kennedy's approach to his legislative duties impressed Esther Peterson, a legislative lobbyist for the Amalgamated Clothing Workers of America. She met him in 1947 while both worked on minimum-wage issues. He asked intelligent questions, she thought. "He didn't pretend to know what he didn't know, and you knew always that he'd make up his mind for himself on a lot of these issues. He was not well versed in the labor field at that time, but he was certainly learning."

Kennedy's record in the House is not easily defined. On some issues he appeared conservative, on others liberal. What is usually overlooked, however, is that on most *important* issues he voted with President Truman and with liberal Northern Democrats for New Deal–Fair Deal domestic policies. Jack supported the Truman Doctrine, the Marshall Plan, NATO, and the policy of containing communism.

Some historians later claimed that his liberalism conveyed "no passion, no heart, no force," but this critique misrepresents his intentions. He associated political passion with demagogues who exploited the public's fears and prejudices. The responsible politician, he thought, should be wary of passion and strive for reasonableness. In fact he conveyed his views on most issues with considerable sincerity and force.

For the most part Jack was rarely criticized in public in his home state. The *Worcester Sunday Telegram* reported that Democrats loved him:

> A great many Democrats will tell you that young Mr. Kennedy is the grand hope of the Democrats in this state. . . . He "has everything," they will tell you. He is young, able, of high integrity, personally attractive, and modest. He has never been an exhibitionist or a prima donna. . . . He is sanely progressive and wisely cautious.

After only seven months as a congressman, John Kennedy had become a political phenomenon in Massachusetts, a refreshing change from the stodgy leadership in the state. By late 1947 newspapers continually speculated whether he would run for mayor of Boston, for governor, or for senator.

Although Kennedy usually sided with the positions taken by the Truman administration, Northern Democrats, and organized labor, in some ways he was a maverick. He was decidedly not a "wheeler-dealer" who prided himself on hammering out compromises to get bills passed. He struck veteran Democratic legislators as a lone wolf.

His reputation as a maverick, though, was more a matter of style and attitude than voting record. Traditionalists in the House disdained his informality and his casual dress, as when he appeared in the House wearing old khaki pants and addressed the chamber with his shirttail out. He enjoyed three-or-four-day, fun-filled weekends, especially trips to Florida. These long weekends, together with his illness and his extensive campaigning throughout Massachusetts, resulted in a high absentee rate in the House.

Kennedy found most of his fellow congressmen boring, preoccupied only with advancing their careers and their narrow political agendas. The arcane House rules and customs that slowed legislation exasperated him. Even when he was not sick, he appeared underwhelmed by his position. "We are just worms here," he told a friend, as if to suggest his insignificance.

"You can't get anywhere," he often said privately. "You have to be here twenty years." He was too impatient, too unwilling to wait the twenty years to gain any influence in the House.

"I was quite brash [and] independent," Kennedy mused to the biographer James MacGregor Burns in 1959, seven years after he had completed his House career. Being independent at times was fine, but he thought he had made a mistake by not being more friendly with the Democratic leadership in the House and by not following their lead.

On August 1, 1947, Kennedy announced that he would travel to Ireland in September to make a personal study of food and fuel shortages there. Another reason for going was to search for his Irish relatives. "I'm going to find out where the Kennedys and the Fitzgeralds came from," he said. This was not a congressional junket; Jack took the trip on his own initiative and paid for it himself.

He arrived at Shannon airport on September 1 and spent most of his three weeks in Ireland with his sister Kathleen at Lismore Castle in County Waterford in southern Ireland, a spot owned by the Devonshires, the parents of Kathleen's late husband. Kathleen had organized a month-long house party, including among her guests several writers, conservative British politicians, and her friend Pamela Digby Churchill, the beautiful ex-wife of Randolph Churchill, Winston's son.

Only Jack's persistent and mysterious illness marred the idyllic holiday. One morning, when he felt well enough, he quietly asked Pamela to accompany him on an expedition to find the original Kennedys. She agreed, and the two of them spent several hours driving to Dunganstown in Kathleen's new station wagon.

He was directed down the road to the thatched cottage of Mary Ryan, who lived in the original Kennedy home. Mary, the granddaughter of Patrick Kennedy's brother James, had married her second cousin, James Ryan, a grandson of another brother, John. They treated Jack to fresh butter and eggs, partly because their visitor appeared in need of nourishment. "He didn't look well at all," Mary later said. Kennedy peppered the Ryans with questions about ancestors who had gone to America. He couldn't find a definite link, but he and the Ryans decided they were third cousins. He left in a glow of nostalgia.

On September 21 Kennedy arrived in London, accompanied by Pamela Churchill. On the same day he became so ill he couldn't get out of his hotel bed. He phoned Pamela and asked if she knew of a London doctor. She called Sir Daniel Davis, a prominent semi-retired physician, who diagnosed Kennedy as suffering from Addison's disease. Shortly after, Dr. Davis told Pamela, "That young American friend of yours, he hasn't got a year to live."

Back home Rose and Joe decided to withhold information about the true nature of Jack's illness. The media were told that he had suffered from a bout with malaria, a much less ominous disease than Addison's. A common symptom of both diseases is a brownish-yellow skin, making the cover-up easier to sell.

In 1855 the English physician Thomas Addison first described the disease that impaired Jack's life. He studied patients who were thin and weak, and who suffered from low blood pressure, anemia, and a brownish pigmentation of the skin. After autopsies he found that the size of their adrenals had been greatly reduced.

The two adrenal glands, one sitting atop each kidney, produce more than half a dozen hormones, the most important being cortisol and aldosterone. Cortisol ensures that the bloodstream has enough glucose, a form of sugar essential to brain function, while aldosterone averts the loss of large quantities of sodium, a mineral necessary to maintain blood pressure. Modern scientists presume that Addison's is the result of autoimmune disease in which antibodies attack and destroy the glands.

Addison's disease remains incurable, and before 1930, 90 percent of victims died within five years. In the late 1930s scientists developed a synthetic substance, desoxycorticosterone acetate (DOCA), a weak adrenal hormone, which substantially reduced the mortality rate.

"Kennedy was not in the crisis stage when I saw him," said endocrinologist Elmer Bartels, who cared for him at the Lahey Clinic. Before the advent of adrenal replacement, the patient usually died by infection, often by simply having a tooth pulled. "That's the way most Addison's patients used to die, by way of minor dental things," said Bartels.

In 1947, when Kennedy was diagnosed, treatment was still cumbersome and limited in its benefits. A pellet containing DOCA was implanted through an incision into his thigh. This allowed slow absorption of the compound, but a new pellet had to be inserted approximately four times a year. The treatment could not stave off death but could extend life expectancy from about six months to between five and ten years. The prospect that he would almost certainly be dead by 1957 must have haunted Kennedy.

Bartels's treatment helped him overcome his Addison's crisis, but he suffered emotionally and in his performance in the House of Representatives. Was there any point to beating his brains out in Washington if he would soon be dead? Could he ever hope to realize his own and his father's ambitions for him? What about a family and children?

After the onset of the disease, Kennedy had one of the highest absentee rates of any member in Congress. He sponsored no major legislation and gained little press coverage for his congressional work. Later, political commentators, even those sympathetic to him, claimed that his performance in the House was "unspectacular," "lackluster," or "undistinguished." But it stemmed partly from his illness.

Eight months after Kennedy learned he had Addison's disease, another family tragedy sent him and the other Kennedys into a tailspin. In May 1948 Kathleen died in a private airplane crash in France. Her death was potentially scandalous as well, because she was in the company of her not yet divorced Protestant lover, the dashing millionaire playboy Earl Fitzwilliam, who also died in the crash.

Kathleen's death remained a "closed subject" within the Kennedy household. The explanation put out by the Kennedys and reported in newspapers was that Kathleen had "casually encountered" her "friend" Fitzwilliam, and he had offered to fly her to the south of France. A chance meeting became the official explanation for Kathleen's flight with her married lover.

For some time after Kathleen's death, Jack suffered severe insomnia, and his thoughts often morbidly turned to death, which seemed ever-present. It had taken young Joe and Kathleen, and it awaited him. Gradually he adjusted, accepting the fact that he was the only survivor of the golden trio. "Slowly," Billings recalled, "he began to fight back, knowing that to stand still was to stay in sorrow, that to live he had to move forward. . . . Once he focused on what *he* really wanted to do with his life, he realized that it really might be politics after all."

After 1948 Kennedy focused most of his efforts on advancing the liberal domestic agenda on bread-and-butter issues. On one foreign policy issue, though, he joined Republicans in harsh criticism of the Roosevelt-Truman policies. Following a twenty-year civil war in China, in December 1949 Chiang Kai-shek's Nationalist forces fled to the island of Formosa, leaving mainland China to Mao Tse-tung's Communists. In the aftermath, Republicans castigated the Truman administration for "losing" China to the Communists. Kennedy joined the chorus of the Republican opposition, charging that blame for Chiang's defeat should fall squarely on the shoulders of the Truman administration. "The continued insistence that aid would not be forthcoming, unless a coalition government with the Communists were formed, was a crippling blow to the National Government," he charged. "So concerned were our diplomats and their advisers . . . with the imperfection of the democratic system in China after 20 years of war and the tales of corruption in high places that they lost sight of our tremendous stake in a non-Communist China."

Kennedy's outburst was irrational; the blame in fact lay with the Chiang Kai-shek government. Corrupt, inefficient, and obtuse, it had ignored the just aspirations of the Chinese masses. Nothing the United States could have done within the reasonable limits of its capacities would have altered the result. Still, China was lost, and its Communist leaders and those of the Soviet Union now ruled more than a quarter of the world's people.

Meanwhile new treatment for Addison's disease proved enormously encouraging for Kennedy. In 1949, two years after he had been diagnosed, scientists discovered cortisone, and new hope suddenly blossomed for victims of Addison's. By 1951, when cortisone could be taken orally, Kennedy ingested 25 milligrams daily. He also continued to receive periodic implants of 150 milligrams of DOCA pellets in his thighs.

With this new treatment nearly simulating the natural function of the adrenal glands, Kennedy's health and stamina improved dramatically—so did his emotional outlook and his ambition, leading him to consider running for the Senate in 1952.

In 1951 Jack took two major trips abroad, primarily to establish his credentials to address foreign policy issues if he decided to seek the Senate the following year. In January, accompanied by his Harvard classmate Torbert Macdonald, Kennedy visited England, Turkey, Italy, Spain, Yugoslavia, and France, and had a private audience with Pope Pius XII. Far more important was his second trip. In the fall of 1951 the Kennedy party, which included Jack, his brother Robert, and his sister Patricia, flew about 25,000 miles in seven weeks— to Israel, Iran, Pakistan, India, Singapore, and Thailand, to embattled Indochina, and then north to war-torn South Korea. Jack talked with scores of national leaders, ambassadors, ministers, consuls, businessmen, journalists, Communists, and people on the street. On October 19, 1951, the Kennedy party arrived in Saigon. Taking seriously his role as inquiring congressman, he was determined to gain a better understanding of the Indochina situation.

After Japan surrendered in August 1945 and pulled its troops out of Indochina, Communist and nationalist forces led by Ho Chi Minh filled the vacuum. But the French, who had controlled Indochina for more than half a century, fatefully decided to resume their colonial empire that had been interrupted by World War II. War broke out in 1946 between the French and Ho's Vietminh forces, and the fighting continued until 1954.

Each year of the war, the French military position grew weaker. In 1949 Paris tried to undermine its enemy politically by forming native governments in Laos, Cambodia, and Vietnam, giving them the status of "free states" within the French Union. In Vietnam the French selected the incompetent Bao Dai to rule. Nationalists of any stature refused to support him, but the Truman administration recognized the Bao Dai government because by doing so it at least avoided the appearance of endorsing blatant French colonialism.

By early 1950 Washington had embraced the "domino theory," the belief that the fall of Indochina would lead to the rapid collapse of other nations in the region. In March 1950 the United States began furnishing France with military and economic assistance to help defeat the Vietminh. Unfortunately Ho had captured the standard of Vietnamese nationalism, and by supporting France the United States attached itself to colonialism and to a losing cause.

While Kennedy listened to French officials and soldiers in Vietnam, he also sought out newspaper reporters and others with informed judgments. He showed up at the flat of Seymour Topping, an Associated Press reporter in Saigon, and cornered him for hours of searching questions. "He really wanted to know," recalled Topping, impressed by Kennedy's attitude.

What Kennedy learned left him deeply pessimistic. The Vietminh were winning the war, and the French had granted no real independence to the Vietnamese. He detested the callousness and vulgarity of French colonialism, the harshness of its regime, and its attempt to hold on to an empire in a world that had already changed.

When he returned home, Kennedy found himself bored by his insignificance in the House, stymied by the body's rigid seniority system, and motivated by ingrained self-expectation. He decided to abandon his congressional seat and seek higher office in 1952.

*

Before Kennedy could run for any higher office, he needed statewide recognition. Beginning in 1949 he delivered so many speeches throughout Massachusetts that in three years he visited almost all the state's 351 cities and towns. On his tours he quietly evaluated potential Kennedy loyalists. At communion breakfasts or testimonial dinners he took notes on key officials who were present ("good speaker" or "active in electrical workers' union").

Both Kennedy and his opponent in the Senate race, Henry Cabot Lodge, Jr., were tall, handsome, self-assured graduates of Harvard and veterans of World War II. Both possessed noted isolationist forebears. Lodge was more polished and mature, Kennedy more frail-looking, genteelly rumpled, and boyish.

The Kennedy campaign in 1952, observed journalist Ralph Martin, "was the most methodical, the most scientific, the most thoroughly detailed, the most intricate, the most disciplined and smoothly working state-wide campaign in Massachusetts history."

Joe Kennedy worked tirelessly on Jack's behalf, hiring talented speechwriters and advisers, consulting businessmen and politicians, and studying reports. A troubleshooter, he meshed a thousand and one details into a unified and energetic campaign. Joe intuitively understood that the new medium of television could project his telegenic son into people's living rooms.

Despite Joe Kennedy's major role in 1952, the Senate campaign marked a transition between the ambassador's dominance of Jack's campaigns, and Jack's insertion of his own people on his staff. One of the newcomers was Kenneth O'Donnell, a native of Worcester, Massachusetts. After World War II he and Robert Kennedy had been teammates on Harvard's football squad. When Robert asked O'Donnell to help Jack, he joined the campaign in 1951. Another addition was burly, crew-cut Larry O'Brien. A friendly but tough Irishman, O'Brien had worked in advertising and public relations, and had been administrative assistant to Massachusetts congressman Foster Furcolo. Politically astute, O'Brien's genius lay in voter registration and precinct organization.

The most critical new recruit was Jack's own brother Robert. Twenty-six years old, Bobby had graduated from Harvard in 1948 and had received his law degree in 1951 from the University of Virginia. For five months he worked every day on the campaign, laboring longer and harder than anyone else. From the time he assumed control, the campaign hummed. Bobby unleashed his ferocious energy, tapped his dormant organizational genius, and motivated thousands of volunteers.

The campaign again exploited Jack's war heroism. Workers distributed about 900,000 copies of an eight-page tabloid featuring a series of artist's conceptions of Kennedy rescuing his shipmates after the PT-109 sinking. The Kennedy organization also worked hard to create a statewide network of 286 local Kennedy "secretaries"—political novices and people well respected in the community—businessmen, lawyers, doctors, accountants, insurance agents. Eventually they recruited 21,000 volunteers to work under the secretaries' direction.

Besides this elaborate system of secretaries, the campaign organization formed clusters of various occupations and ethnic groups. Doctors, dentists, lawyers, and taxi drivers each had a committee; so did Italians, Canadians, Frenchmen, and Greeks. One Sunday Jack went from an Albanian-American picnic to a Greek-American picnic to a Polish-American meeting to a Portuguese-American banquet to an Italian-American banquet, ending the day at an Irish-American dinner at a country club.

While Dwight Eisenhower remained in Europe, Lodge led the pro-Eisenhower forces back home in the fight for the Republican presidential nomination. At the Republican convention in Chicago in the summer of 1952, Senator Robert Taft thought he had a firm hold on the Southern delegations. Through a complex parliamentary maneuver, Lodge arranged for the convention to adopt a rule that allowed Eisenhower to sweep to the nomination on the first ballot.

Afterward, bitter over the tactics used to defeat their hero, Taft supporters in Massachusetts vented their wrath on Lodge. Joe Kennedy worked behind the scenes to exploit their resentment, allowing Jack to inherit many of the votes of the disaffected Taft supporters. At the same time Joe Kennedy mobilized the rest of the Kennedy clan, intending to turn the campaign into a family crusade. By late May 1952 the far-flung Kennedys began to gather: a reporter observed that when an outsider threatened to thwart the ambition of a Kennedy, "the whole family forms a close-packed ring, horns lowered, like a herd of bison beset by wolves."

The Kennedy campaign hosted thirty-three formal receptions. The ornate gatherings, complete with lace tablecloths and candelabras, resembled exclusive parties. The turnouts were exceptional—a thousand women in Brockton, two thousand in Springfield, a thousand in Salem, seventeen hundred in Fitchburg.

In the campaign Jack Kennedy preferred to avoid one issue: the question of Joe McCarthy was too awkward, too sensitive for him to handle. On February 9, 1950, at Wheeling, West Virginia, Senator Joseph McCarthy of Wisconsin had charged that 205 individuals, known to the secretary of state to be members of the Communist party, were still working in the State Department and shaping American foreign policy. The cold war atmosphere of the time made McCarthy's sensational accusation seem believable. In the paranoid world of McCarthyism, the mistakes and failures of U.S. foreign policy were due chiefly to deliberate disloyalty—or at least the willingness to tolerate deliberate disloyalty—not to misjudgment, error, or unforeseen events.

Senator Millard Tydings, a Democrat from Maryland, chaired the subcommittee of the Senate Committee on Foreign Relations that conducted an inquiry into McCarthy's accusations and eventually branded them a "fraud and a hoax." But in the 1950 congressional elections the media mistakenly credited McCarthy's campaign efforts with the defeat of Senator Tydings and other Democratic senators, thereby turning the Wisconsin senator into a giant-killer.

McCarthy described the five terms of Democratic presidents Roosevelt and Truman as "twenty years of treason." Secretary of State Dean Acheson, he charged, was a Kremlin lackey who should seek asylum in the Soviet Union. McCarthy's attack on Gen. George C. Marshall was the most seditious of his career. A man of enormous stature and prestige, noted for his integrity and public service, Marshall had coordinated the Normandy invasion in 1944, served as secretary of state, and devised the Marshall Plan for postwar aid to Europe.

Liberal Democrats denounced McCarthy's ethics and tactics. Before he became the nation's preeminent anti-Communist, McCarthy had been censured twice by the Wisconsin Supreme Court for judicial misconduct, had distorted his military record in World War II to advance his political career, and had failed to pay his Wisconsin taxes. In Massachusetts, though, many Catholics revered him. Devoted to his every cause, the *Boston Post* printed most of his accusations and treated him with the reverence of a saint.

Kennedy's own family was close to the Wisconsin senator. In Chicago, McCarthy had become social friends with Eunice Kennedy and Sargent Shriver. Both Eunice and Pat Kennedy had had friendly chats with the senator in his Washington office; McCarthy dated Pat. Robert Kennedy was also enamored with McCarthy and would later briefly join the senator's staff. Joe Kennedy, though, was McCarthy's most ardent supporter. Since his falling out with Franklin Roosevelt, Joe Kennedy had grown increasingly cranky, conservative, and prone to suspicions of conspiracy.

Jack made no speeches supporting McCarthy and didn't attempt to appease the passions of the McCarthyites in his state. But he made no speeches attacking McCarthy either. As an Irish Catholic with an excellent war record, he could have been an influential critic of McCarthy.

The thorny McCarthy problem placed both Lodge and Kennedy in an awkward predicament. Lodge disliked McCarthy and opposed his tactics, but McCarthy was a Republican colleague, and most Republican leaders and partisans backed his anti-Communist crusade. With pro-McCarthy sentiment strong in Massachusetts, especially among Irish Catholics, Lodge had to be careful. He hoped that McCarthy would not campaign in Massachusetts.

In effect the Kennedy campaign decided that only when Lodge took a stand on McCarthy would Kennedy take his own position on the Wisconsin senator. And since Lodge issued no public statement on McCarthy, neither did Kennedy. In the end, McCarthy did not speak or intervene in the Massachusetts Senate campaign, and both Kennedy and Lodge pretended he didn't exist. The prickly issue, though, would haunt Kennedy in later years.

The two candidates seldom differed on issues. Slogans dominated billboards and advertisements: "Kennedy Will Do *More* for Massachusetts," "Lodge Has Done—and Will Do—the *Most* for Massachusetts."

Kennedy won the Senate seat, 1,211,984 to 1,141,247 votes, a margin of more than 70,000. Eisenhower won the presidency and in Massachusetts defeated Adlai Stevenson by 208,800 votes.

During the campaign Larry O'Brien spent a few days at the Kennedy home in Hyannis Port. At breakfast one morning Joe Kennedy looked O'Brien in the eye and said, "Larry, Jack is a man of destiny. He is going to defeat Lodge and serve with distinction in the Senate and eventually he is going to be President of the United States."

5

Senate Years

IN JOHN KENNEDY'S TRANSITION from congressman to senator, his staff underwent two major changes. Evelyn Lincoln became his personal secretary and remained in that role for the next eleven years. More important, Jack hired Theodore Sorensen as his legislative assistant, beginning one of the most momentous political partnerships in modern American history. The product of a progressive political family in Nebraska, Sorensen had graduated first in his class at the University of Nebraska law school. Although he performed many functions for the new senator, his primary task was to paint in words. Until 1953 Kennedy's speeches were workmanlike efforts but lacked flair. Sorensen provided it.

Kennedy's bachelor days ended too. In 1951, at a small dinner party, he had met Jacqueline Bouvier, daughter of Jack Bouvier, a stockbroker who had lost most of his money in the Wall Street crash, and Janet, his society-conscious wife. After divorcing her husband, Janet married Hugh D. Auchincloss, who was much wealthier and more successful than Jack Bouvier. Well educated, fluent in French and Spanish, Jackie cultivated tastes for ballet, opera, fine art, and expensive furniture and antiques. She married Jack on September 12, 1953.

LeMoyne Billings immediately discerned that Jackie was different from the other women Jack had dated—she was more intelligent, and literary. "Joe Kennedy not only condoned the marriage, he ordained it," Billings said. A politician needed a wife, and a Catholic politician needed a Catholic wife. She should have class, and Joe Kennedy thought Jackie had more class than any of Jack's earlier girlfriends.

At the Capitol, Kennedy's difficulty with the McCarthy dilemma resurfaced after the 1952 election. On Friday evening, July 30, 1954, Republican senator Ralph Flanders of Vermont introduced a resolution to censure McCarthy. Ninety senators were assembled; the galleries were packed. Kennedy was present with a speech ready for delivery. Because questions arose about orderly procedure and the absence of formal charges, the Senate established a special committee headed by Republican senator Arthur Watkins to study the McCarthy censure issue. After the Senate changed its approach, Kennedy took his undelivered speech back to his office and filed it.

On October 21, he underwent spinal surgery in New York, and didn't resume his Senate duties until May 24, 1955. On December 2, 1954, five weeks after he entered the hospital, the Senate voted 67 to 22 to censure McCarthy for obstructing the Senate's business, impairing its dignity, and bringing the body into dishonor and disrepute. Forty-four Democrats voted "yea." Recuperating from his back surgery, Kennedy was the only Democrat not present or recorded.

Ted Sorensen later took the blame for not recording Kennedy on the censure vote, insisting that the senator's failure to be recorded was not due to his indifference. Had he been present, Sorensen said, Kennedy would have voted for censure.

Two years after McCarthy's censure, Kennedy's undelivered speech resurfaced. Given to reporters, Kennedy's office used it to prove that he was ready to vote for censure. But the speech did not get Kennedy off the hook with critics of McCarthy. "It may hang him even higher," said a reporter in the *Progressive*. Kennedy had based his stand for censure on a narrow technical point. He contended that evidence brought out during the Army-McCarthy hearings showed that Mc-

Carthy condoned the improper conduct of his staff members, Roy Cohn and G. David Schine. Therefore Kennedy favored censure. The ghost of Joe McCarthy, though, would continue to plague his career.

Kennedy's back pain had become excruciating after his election to the Senate. Early in 1954, when he participated in floor debate, he leaned on crutches. He decided to go ahead with surgery under the care of two prominent New York physicians. Dr. Ephraim Shorr, an endocrinologist, would mastermind the management of the Addison's disease during his surgery, which would be performed by Dr. Philip D. Wilson of the New York Hospital for Special Surgery.

On October 21 doctors performed a lumbosacral fusion and a sacroiliac fusion at the same time. Dr. Wilson was a respected orthopedic surgeon, but his operation on Kennedy was an experimental procedure with a low success rate. To stabilize Kennedy's lower back, Wilson used three screws to bolt a plate onto bone. Friends and family reported that Jack was critically ill on the third day following surgery.

On December 21 Kennedy left the hospital to recuperate at his father's home in Palm Beach. In mid-February 1955 he was flown back to New York where Dr. Wilson performed another operation to remove the infected metal plate installed initially. After Wilson's operations, the problem of explaining Kennedy's continuing back pain is complicated by his experience of surgical trauma, scarring, and back wound infection, all of which caused mechanical vulnerability of the lower lumbar spine and no doubt contributed to ongoing chronic recurrent low back and leg symptoms.

Meanwhile, in 1954 and 1955 Kennedy worked on *Profiles in Courage,* in which he presented the stories of eight American political leaders whose courage at critical moments had led them to resist their constituents and defy their legislative peers in order to serve a broader national good. When published, the book received prominent and favorable reviews and became a smashing popular success. *Profiles* rose to the top of the best-seller lists and remained there for several months. The book proved more politically valuable than Kennedy could ever have imagined. It boosted his stature considerably within the Democratic party, making him the spokesman for the politics of integrity and enhancing his image as an insightful student of American history and democratic theory.

*

In 1957 Jack and Jackie purchased for $78,000 a red-brick townhouse at 3307 N Street NW in Georgetown. Earlier, in October 1956, the young Kennedys had become Cape Cod taxpayers after purchasing the Irving Avenue property in Hyannis Port destined to become the "Summer White House." The home was within the same compound as Joe and Rose's home, only a few hundred feet away.

The marriage of Jack and Jackie was loving, but distant and sometimes strained. Few ever saw Jack kiss or embrace his wife. Jacqueline's world had not included politics; she had not even bothered to vote. Since Jack seldom discussed political matters with her, she couldn't appreciate his work. She wanted her husband to become more cultivated, a person with superior taste, style, and manners. She only partially succeeded in her goals, but friends and observers noticed an improvement. Jackie helped refine Jack. He now wore sharply cut and perfectly pressed suits.

The early years of their marriage were difficult for Jackie because her ambitious husband led such an active life. The pain of separation was most acute on weekends when Jack spoke at engagements throughout the country while she remained alone. "I was alone almost every weekend," she said of the first year of marriage. "We had no home life whatsoever."

Then too, there were many other women in Jack's life. Kennedy's cohort in philandering was George Smathers, a ruggedly handsome Democratic congressman from Florida who had risen to the Senate in 1950. Although married with two children, Smathers behaved like a bachelor—his friendship with Kennedy was based mainly on their acquisition of women together. Kennedy's sexual adventurism frequently led him into orgies at the Carroll Arms Hotel, across the street from the Senate Office Building. There he amused himself with several women. "That kind of thing was probably his favorite pastime," Smathers said.

"Jack had the most active libido of any man I've ever known," Smathers observed. "He was really unbelievable—absolutely incredible in that regard, and he got more so the longer he was married." Smathers added that his friend "was like a rooster getting on top of a chicken real fast and then the poor little hen ruffles her feathers and wonders what the hell happened to her. . . . Just in terms of the time he spent with a woman, though, he was a lousy lover. He went in more for quantity than quality."

Smathers introduced his disreputable friend Bill Thompson to Senator Kennedy in the mid-1950s. Thompson was a railroad lobbyist from Florida and a notorious seducer of women. Kennedy and Thompson developed a "very special relationship," reflected Thompson's daughter Gail Laird. "I think it was somewhat on the sleazy side. My father was a terrible womanizer." Thompson "was a pimp for Jack," Charles Bartlett contended, adding that Jack "was a lousy husband." "Jack would never intentionally hurt anyone, most of all Jackie," Smathers thought. "I just don't think he was capable of being monogamous, and he handled it the best way he could."

*

In 1956 the race for the Democratic presidential nomination matched Senator Estes Kefauver of Tennessee against Adlai Stevenson. Kefauver, an independent liberal, a supporter of labor, civil liberties, and—most unusual for a Southern senator—civil rights, had waged an intense battle for the presidential nomination in 1952 but had finally lost to Stevenson.

Discerning, eloquent, and witty, Stevenson had served as governor of Illinois for four years before carrying the Democratic standard against Eisenhower in 1952. On the eve of the Democratic convention in Chicago in August 1956, Stevenson was in firm control. The only drama left was who would be his running mate. Some pundits judged Kennedy a possible choice. "As a Catholic, he would offset the disadvantage of Stevenson's divorce," *Newsweek* reported; "moreover, he's from the industrial East and would therefore appeal to the big-city labor and minority vote."

After his easy nomination, Stevenson made an unexpected announcement that electrified the convention, providing its most suspenseful moments. Without a hint of his own personal preference, he broke precedent and left the nomination of his running mate entirely up to the will of the convention delegates.

Kefauver had a marked advantage in an open contest because so many delegates from his presidential bid were still in attendance, ready to vote him the consolation prize. After Stevenson's announcement, Kennedy's brothers and sisters, in-laws and friends, advisers and staff gathered in his room, where he decided to contend for the vice-presidential nomination. Soon the suite was filled with confused, chaotic action as Kennedy's supporters burst forth with amateurish enthusiasm.

At the end of the first ballot, Kennedy and Kefauver seemed to be the only two major contenders: Kefauver 483-1/2; Kennedy 304.

The second ballot turned into a nail-biting duel as the lead seesawed. At the end of the second ballot, with all states recorded, Kennedy led Kefauver, 618 to 551-1/2. The senator from Massachusetts was only 69 votes away from 687, the magic number that would win the nomination. When Kentucky switched its 30 votes to Kennedy, only 39 votes separated him from a majority.

But now, in rapid order, other states switched their votes to Kefauver. The final vote stood at Kefauver 755-1/2, Kennedy 589.

The Democratic convention in Chicago was the critical turning point in Kennedy's national ambitions. He passed through a kind of "political sound barrier," observed biographer James MacGregor Burns, indelibly registering his name on the nation's consciousness. "In this moment of triumphant defeat, his campaign for the presidency was born."

Meanwhile, nothing clicked in Stevenson's campaign for the presidency. On election day he was trounced by Eisenhower, winning only Missouri and six Southern states. Of all the Democrats in 1956, Kennedy emerged the biggest winner. He had leaped to prominence while being spared the handicap of association with the embarrassing Stevenson-Kefauver defeat.

*

After the election Kennedy began planning his run for president in 1960. In the first six months of 1957 he delivered eighty-five speeches in thirty states. From memory he gave his advisers a complete rundown on every state he visited, rattling off the names of local politicians who were friendly, hostile, or neutral.

There were problems to overcome, skeptics to convert. Kennedy's father, his ambiguous stand on civil rights, his silence on the McCarthy issue, his youth, and his Catholicism all concerned Democrats. Why was he in such a rush? "If I were his father," said James Reston in the *New York Times* in 1957, "I would tell him to slow down. . . . His age is against him now; in another few years it won't be. He has time."

Still, the media and the public found him captivating. His youth, war heroism, handsome features, large energetic family, great wealth, and stunning wife made excellent copy. In the summer of 1957, *Look* magazine featured Jack and

Bobby in an eight-page article complete with sixteen photographs of the two brothers at work, with their families, and meeting the public. Other popular magazines ran stories on Jack, or Jackie, or the entire Kennedy family. Jack Gould, the *New York Times'* television columnist, called Jack "the most telegenic personality of our times."

On May 7, 1957, when the Pulitzer Prize Committee announced its winners in the field of letters, it awarded the prize in biography to John F. Kennedy for *Profiles in Courage*—marvelous publicity for its author. Some observers contend that the Kennedy circle lobbied for the award, pulling strings to secure him the prize. Several years after Kennedy's honor, Arthur Krock boasted that he had lobbied committee members, implying that his role was decisive in convincing members to grant the award to Kennedy.

In fact that was not the case. John Hohenberg, professor of journalism at Columbia University and from 1954 to 1976 administrator of the Pulitzer Prizes, confirmed that Krock had promoted Kennedy but stressed that Krock's advocacy was not instrumental. Krock had such a well-known reputation as a "drumbeater" that his efforts may have been counterproductive. Nor was there any sign that Ambassador Kennedy had intervened. Joseph Pulitzer, Jr., later emphatically declared that there was "not a chance in a million" that the ambassador could have had any influence even if he had tried.

Did Kennedy actually write the book? On December 7, 1957, during ABC television's *Mike Wallace Show*, Wallace interviewed Drew Pearson, one of the country's most popular political columnists. On the program Pearson claimed that Kennedy's book was ghostwritten, and subsequently named Sorensen as the author.

The following Monday morning, December 9, Kennedy phoned attorney Clark Clifford and asked to meet with him immediately. When Kennedy arrived, very dejected, he described Pearson's comments. "I cannot let this stand," he told Clifford. "It is a direct attack on my integrity and my honesty."

The best solution, Clifford thought, was to obtain an immediate retraction from ABC and Pearson before the story spread and generated a life of its own. Clifford quickly arranged a meeting with executives and lawyers at ABC, who contacted Pearson. Brilliantly prepared for Pearson's charge, Clifford pointed out that in the book's preface Kennedy had acknowledged his "greatest debt" to his "research associate, Theodore C. Sorensen." The crafty Clifford had stashed Sorensen in a nearby hotel, waiting to be called. When ABC asked to interrogate Sorensen, the senator's assistant arrived momentarily and expertly rebutted efforts by ABC's lawyers to break down his story. Shortly after, Sorensen signed an affidavit disclaiming authorship, which Clifford sent to ABC.

Despite Kennedy's efforts, and despite a retraction by ABC, doubts and rumors persisted. The crucial question remains: Was Kennedy the real author of *Profiles in Courage,* or was it ghostwritten? Did he manufacture a writing talent to enhance his image?

Plenty of people witnessed Kennedy working on the project. Gloria Sitrin, Sorensen's secretary, later said, "I personally took dictation from Senator Kennedy on the book . . . in Florida."

Sorensen's letters to the senator convey the impression that Kennedy was a major contributor. "All of the corrections which you have suggested in your various letters . . . have been incorporated," Sorensen wrote on September 12, 1955.

The foremost expert on the writing of *Profiles in Courage* is Herbert Parmet, who closely studied the controversy for his book *Jack: The Struggles of John F. Kennedy.* Because Parmet's book is well researched, thoughtful, and usually evenhanded, his judgment on *Profiles* has influenced a generation of students of Kennedy's life. Parmet's conclusion? *Profiles* was essentially ghostwritten, mostly by Theodore Sorensen.

The chronology of Kennedy's life in 1954 and 1955, and the materials accumulated in the preparation of the book, "do not even come close to supporting the contention that

Jack could have been or was its major author," Parmet writes. Besides his work in the Senate, Kennedy underwent two major spinal operations, and when not convalescing he frequently made appearances throughout the country to advance his political career. From August to October 1955 he also made an extensive European tour.

In his close inspection of files Parmet found that what Kennedy personally wrote were "very rough passages without paragraphing, without any shape, largely ideas jotted down as possible sections, obviously necessitating editing." For practical reasons—limitations of time, health, and appropriate talent—Kennedy served "principally as an overseer or, more charitably, as a sponsor and editor, one whose final approval was as important for its publication as for its birth," Parmet writes. The burdens of time and literary craftsmanship, Parmet concludes, "were clearly Sorensen's, and he gave the book both the drama and flow that made for readability."

Influenced by Parmet's analysis, most students of Kennedy's life have referred to him as the author only in a limited sense. Kennedy authorized the book, observes Garry Wills, but Theodore Sorensen and others "wrote" *Profiles in Courage.*

History, however, may have cast too harsh a judgment on Kennedy's role in writing *Profiles*. Although Parmet's research was extensive, it was not exhaustive. Evidence seems to have disappeared, evidence that might have shown additional Kennedy contributions. New tape recordings were made on top of old recordings, Parmet concedes, "so that the existing reels do not represent the full extent of [Kennedy's] dictation."

Missing are the notebooks to which Kennedy often referred, which convinced several people that he did write major portions of the book. In Sorensen's correspondence at the time and in later interviews, he repeatedly referred to letters and phone calls from the senator concerning the book. Yet none of these sources appear in Parmet's analysis.

It is incorrect to assume that the chronology of Kennedy's life in 1954–1955 made it unlikely that he could substantially contribute. In fact, while convalescing from his two surgeries he had little else to do *except* work on the book.

Even if additional information shows that Kennedy deserves more credit for writing the book, historians may still conclude that Sorensen actually wrote most of *Profiles in Courage*. Nonetheless, one thing is clear: Kennedy deeply believed he wrote enough of *Profiles* to claim real authorship. He may have been wrong in his judgment, but there is no evidence he tried to deceive. He could accept the Pulitzer Prize with a clear conscience.

The difficult process of writing the book created remarkable synergy between Kennedy and Sorensen, a dynamic working relationship that resulted in the strikingly memorable speeches Kennedy later delivered. In the end, that creative working partnership may have been the most important consequence of *Profiles in Courage*.

*

In the fall of 1957, as Senator Kennedy crisscrossed the country giving speeches, Jackie awaited the birth of their much-anticipated first child. On November 27 she gave birth to a seven-pound baby girl, Caroline Bouvier Kennedy. Jack seemed more emotional about Caroline's birth than anything his friends had ever seen. "His voice cracked when he called to tell the news," said Lem Billings.

From May 1955 until October 1957, Jack Kennedy spent forty-five days in hospitals, all while he was campaigning for the vice presidency and planning his campaign for the presidency in 1960. Back miseries, abdominal pain, and problems in managing his Addison's disease accounted for most of his confinements. Managing his illnesses was becoming a pharmaceutical nightmare. Historian Robert Dallek describes the various treatments he was receiving:

> Ingested and implanted DOCA for the Addison's, and large doses of penicillin and other antibiotics to combat the pros-

tatitis and the abscess. He also received injections of procaine at "trigger points" to relieve back pain; anti-spasmodics—principally Lomotil and trasentine—to control the colitis; testosterone to keep up his weight (which fell with each bout of colitis and diarrhea); and Nembutal to help him sleep.

Joe and Rose taught their children to be self-reliant, tough, and stoic. "Kennedys don't cry," the children were taught. "Be as good as the spirit is." Indomitable, with astonishing willpower, John Kennedy refused to surrender to his own debilities. "He could withstand pain about as well as anybody I ever saw in my life," said George Smathers. "He never would complain about it and yet [when] that poor guy would get out of the chair, he couldn't even straighten up for thirty minutes or so."

In the Senate, Kennedy pondered several dilemmas of U.S. foreign policy. One involved Vietnam. After his tour of Vietnam in 1951, he stepped up his brash but clear-sighted criticism of U.S. policy in the Far East. He rebuked the French for their colonialism and urged the United States not to involve itself in the Vietnam quagmire.

In the spring of 1954, as the French tried to fend off Vietminh forces at Dienbienphu, Adm. Arthur Radford, chairman of the Joint Chiefs of Staff, advocated U.S. intervention in Indochina, and Secretary of State John Foster Dulles talked of "united action" with allies to assist the French.

Kennedy dissented. On April 6, 1954, in a major Senate speech, he declared that "to pour money, material, and men into the jungles of Indochina without at least a remote prospect of victory would be dangerously futile and self-destructive." After the battered French forces at Dienbienphu surrendered to the Vietminh in July 1954, France relinquished its colony and signed the Geneva Accords, ending the Indochina war. What happened during the next two years had a profound impact on the future of Southeast Asia, on the policies of United States, and on the career and reputation of John F. Kennedy.

The Geneva Accords imposed a cease-fire and divided Vietnam at the seventeenth parallel. To separate the forces, the French withdrew from the northern part of Vietnam and the Vietminh from the southern part. The temporary division, the agreement said, should not be "interpreted as constituting a political or territorial boundary." Free democratic elections were to take place in 1956 to reunify the two parts of Vietnam.

As the French were leaving Vietnam, the Eisenhower administration adopted a momentous change in policy. The United States would replace the departing French as the defender of Laos, Cambodia, and the southern part of Vietnam—which Washington now recognized as the independent nation of South Vietnam, with its capital in Saigon. The administration committed itself to the fragile government, using its economic and military resources to construct in South Vietnam a strong non-Communist nation.

The Eisenhower administration and other U.S. leaders, including Kennedy, helped maneuver Ngo Dinh Diem into power in South Vietnam. In 1955 Diem became the president of the Republic of Vietnam. From the U.S. standpoint, he had two major strengths: he was anti-Communist and, as a nationalist, had opposed the French. Unfortunately he had several major shortcomings as well, weaknesses that U.S. policymakers badly underestimated. An elitist, he was insensitive to the needs and problems of the Vietnamese people; and he had no blueprint for building a modern nation. "Introverted and absorbed in himself, he lacked the charisma of Ho Chi Minh," writes historian George Herring. Nor did Diem believe in democracy. A Confucian mandarin, he thought of himself as an enlightened sovereign with the "mandate of heaven" to govern.

Diem crushed his opponents, but he successfully restored order, earning American praise. In 1956 Kennedy's speeches revealed how quickly he had lost touch with conditions in Vietnam. He now called South Vietnam the "cornerstone of the Free World in Southeast Asia, the keystone to the arch, the finger in the dike." He accepted the new domino theory: Burma, Thailand, India, Japan, the Philippines, Laos, Cambodia—all would be threatened "if the Red Tide of Communism overflowed into [South] Vietnam." Diem's government was a "democratic experiment," Kennedy said.

His view left several serious problems unanalyzed. By asserting U.S. power and influence in Vietnam, wouldn't the United States be perceived as colonial imperialists in the same way as the recently ousted French? Could Diem lead a "democratic experiment" in South Vietnam when he lacked key leadership traits and didn't believe in democracy? Was Western-style democracy a priority for impoverished Vietnamese peasants?

Kennedy didn't anticipate the quagmire the United States might be entering. Earlier, while keenly perceiving the French mistakes, he had argued that pouring money and material into Indochina was a hopeless attempt to save for the French a land that did not wish to be saved, in a war in which the enemy was "everywhere and nowhere at the same time." Perhaps the United States too was now entering a conflict in which the enemy would be everywhere and nowhere at the same time.

Ho Chi Minh believed that the first Indochina war had been a political war in which his Vietminh forces outlasted the French. Perhaps he could outlast the Americans too.

*

The demeaning, usually racist portrayal of blacks in American history influenced John Kennedy just as it influenced millions of other white Americans. His views made him hesitant to force racial change in the South.

As a congressman and a senator, Kennedy favored civil rights legislation as a matter of course rather than from deep conviction. Along with a growing number of Northern Democrats, he had supported a strong Federal Employment Practices Commission (FEPC), abolition of the poll tax, antilynching legislation, and restrictions on filibusters. (Because Senate rules traditionally allowed almost unlimited debate, a minority could frustrate a majority by talking or threatening to talk a bill to death. For years a small group of Southern senators had adroitly used the filibuster rule to block any civil rights legislation.)

Those who discussed civil rights with Kennedy were impressed with his honesty and sincerity, but unlike many Northern liberals he kept a low profile on civil rights, and his position on racial matters was not well known. In the Senate his efforts were overshadowed by dynamic civil rights advocates like Senators Hubert Humphrey of Minnesota and Paul Douglas of Illinois. Kennedy led on other issues.

By the late 1950s civil rights had become a serious political dilemma for Kennedy. How could a Democratic presidential candidate capture black voters—and their supporters in the North—without writing off all prospects for Southern white support? Civil rights strained the Democratic party after World War II. Conservative white Southerners demanded the status quo; Negroes, liberals, and organized labor in the North insisted on fundamental improvements for blacks.

By the late 1950s many in Congress had become more responsive to civil rights advocates, and legislators were more sensitive to the damage that segregation inflicted on blacks and on the U.S. image abroad. In early 1957 President Dwight Eisenhower urged Congress to pass a civil rights act. In its tortuously slow and winding path through Congress, the bill was considerably weakened. It weathered conflicts between Northerners and Southerners, amendments and counteramendments, divisions between House and Senate, ambiguous administration policy, and complex backstage maneuvers.

The debate was a nightmare for Kennedy. No matter what position he took, he was sure to antagonize one wing of his party. So he maneuvered independently, standing apart from both factions. Still, he supported major features of the bill and worked for a compromise to salvage some improvement for

Negroes. Nonetheless, two of his votes outraged civil rights advocates.

The heart of Eisenhower's bill, approved by the House on June 18, 1957, was Title III, which would enable the attorney general to protect through injunction *all* civil rights, including integrated schools, not just voting rights.

After the legislation passed the House, it met an uproar in the Senate. On July 2 Democratic senator Richard Russell of Georgia described the bill as "a cunning device" to force a "commingling of white and Negro children." Southern opponents tried to delay, defeat, or weaken the legislation. The longer they could prevent consideration, the more effective would be the South's ultimate weapon—the Senate filibuster.

Kennedy took almost no part in the Senate debate, but two of his votes won him unwelcome notice. Civil rights advocates hoped to save the bill from almost certain death in the Senate Judiciary Committee, where James Eastland, Democrat from Mississippi, a cigar-chomping segregationist, ruled with an iron hand. Under Eastland's control the Judiciary Committee had buried civil rights legislation.

When the House bill arrived in the Senate, Republicans used a novel and controversial parliamentary maneuver to save it from death in the Judiciary Committee. They proposed to bypass Eastland's committee entirely and place the bill on the Senate calendar, where it could be called up for consideration by majority vote at any time. Opponents might still filibuster, but at least the legislation avoided Eastland's dreaded clutches. Many Democratic senators opposed the move—including Senate majority leader Lyndon Johnson, Kennedy, and several liberal Northern senators—but enough Northern Democrats joined the Republicans to approve it. This was the first of Kennedy's votes to which civil rights advocates objected.

Under pressure from Southern senators, Lyndon Johnson now maneuvered to eliminate Title III, the heart of Eisenhower's proposal. On July 24, 1957, by a vote of 52 to 38, the provision was struck, dealing a near-fatal blow to the legislation. Kennedy favored Title III and voted with civil rights forces.

Title IV applied only to voting rights. Eisenhower's proposal would have allowed a federal judge to issue a criminal contempt citation if a white Southern registrar, found to be denying voting rights, disobeyed a court injunction to stop.

Even the modest provisions in the remaining bill were too strong for Southern senators, who objected to the provision that anyone who violated a federal court order enforcing civil rights could be cited for criminal contempt. If that were so, surely the accused should be granted a jury trial. Brilliantly the South seized on a jury-trial amendment to confound the Northerners. They argued that the Constitution ensures a private citizen a jury trial when charged with a crime.

Having already lost Title III, most civil rights advocates insisted that the jury-trial amendment would cripple the remaining bill. No Southern white jury would ever convict a white registrar for refusing to allow a Negro to register to vote. There was no clear right to a trial by jury in such contempt cases anyway.

The right of an accused to trial by jury, however, was so deeply ingrained in the American tradition that the amendment attracted support from such Northern liberals as Joseph O'Mahoney of Wyoming and Frank Church of Idaho.

With the threat of a filibuster hanging over the Senate, Kennedy consulted two eminent legal scholars at Harvard, who advised him that the jury-trial amendment was a minor issue. Armed with his legal advice, Kennedy announced that he favored the jury-trial amendment—again alienating civil rights advocates.

In the end Kennedy backed a compromise amendment which became part of the final bill. The "O'Mahoney amendment" upheld the right of a judge to rule without a jury in a case of *civil* contempt—that is when the judge had tried to secure compliance with or prevent obstruction of the court's rulings. Under certain conditions jury trials would be allowed in *criminal* contempt cases—those involving willful disobedience of the law on the part of the defendant.

Finally a persistent coalition of liberal Republicans and Northern Democrats salvaged a bill that Kennedy supported. On September 9, 1957, President Eisenhower signed the first civil rights act in eighty-two years. Besides Title IV, the law created a six-person Federal Commission on Civil Rights with the power to hold hearings and subpoena witnesses and documents.

The new law brought meager results. Civil rights champions, deeply disappointed, had questioned whether they should even support the final bill. Senator Paul Douglas thought the law had as much substance as "soup made from the shadow of a crow which had starved to death." The new law did little to increase black voting and did nothing to protect other civil rights. Despite the act's mild features, though, it did reverse the federal government's traditional hands-off policy in the civil rights field. No evidence later appeared that the jury-trial amendment weakened the bill in any way.

Under severe pressure throughout the lengthy debate, had Kennedy acted cowardly? His support for Section III, his insistence that Eastland's committee report the bill, and his vote for final passage suggested otherwise. "Certainly, however, he showed a profile in caution and moderation," concluded James MacGregor Burns.

Constituent mail from Boston's Negro leaders, columns and editorials in Negro newspapers, and remarks by leaders of the National Association for the Advancement of Colored People (NAACP) castigated Kennedy's willingness to send the legislation to Eastland's committee and his support for the jury-trial amendment. Cunningly political, they charged, Kennedy was attempting to convince Southerners that he was safe on civil rights while simultaneously trying not to antagonize Northerners. The *Chicago Defender* charged that the "cat got his tongue" during the civil rights debate. He "cast his vote with the Southern bloc as the first installment toward Dix-iecrat support come 1960." Negroes in Massachusetts also rebuked their senator. The *Quincy Ledger* condemned his "sorry performance," motivated by his political ambition.

Kennedy was understandably upset that many of his de-tractors failed to credit his support for the key feature of the original bill, Title III, "certainly the section most repugnant to the South," he wrote. Frustrated with one letter-writing critic, Kennedy replied curtly: "Thank you for your letter of September twenty-ninth, which has reference to a statement I did not make, political allies I do not have and a Presidential nomination I do not seek."

The battle over the 1957 Civil Rights Act taught a sober-ing lesson. If he ever won the presidency, Kennedy thought he would have to find alternative means, besides new federal legislation, to advance the cause of civil rights. The legisla-tive route was too perilous and unproductive. New legislative initiatives would merely cause another uproar in Congress, aggravate tensions within his own party, risk a long filibuster, block the president's entire legislative program, and proceed glacially toward enactment. Then, most likely, after oppo-nents had emasculated the legislation, it would end up with little substance. Other approaches—executive action and en-forcement of existing federal laws—he saw as the only real-istic ways for the federal government to improve the lives of Negroes.

In 1958 Kennedy stood for reelection to the Senate. Every-one knew he would win. The only question was, could he win an overwhelming victory, one that would "send a message" to skeptics about his presidential chances in 1960? He not only needed to defeat his opponent, he needed to overwhelm him.

On election night Kennedy won a huge victory, winning by 874,000 votes, a 4-to-1 margin over his Republican chal-lenger Vincent Celeste. These were figures that impressed po-litical prognosticators. During a roaring celebration at his downtown Boston headquarters, Kennedy was repeatedly hailed as "our next president."

*

"John Kennedy was not one of the Senate's great leaders," Theodore Sorensen later wrote in assessing Kennedy's eight-year Senate career. No law of national importance bore Kennedy's name; some called him lazy because of his absenteeism.

Laziness wasn't the problem. Kennedy's national campaigning after 1956 caused many of his absences. His back surgery and other health problems kept him away from the Senate for more than seven months. In addition, his womanizing adventures with George Smathers, Bill Thompson, and others distracted him from his Senate duties.

Kennedy did have solid legislative achievements to his credit. He sponsored an aid bill for India, tried to use foreign economic assistance to divide the Soviet Union from its satellites, fought for expanded unemployment compensation and an increase in the minimum wage, spearheaded an economic program for New England, delivered several forceful speeches on foreign policy, and made a sterling effort on behalf of labor reform.

"He was a well-respected, well-liked man," said colleague Mike Mansfield. "A little cool, a little reserved on the surface, but very friendly and warm-hearted, kind, generous, understanding and tolerant underneath." Yet he wasn't part of the Senate's inner circle. He didn't run with the liberals, the moderates, or the conservatives. Most of the time he stood by himself.

Kennedy did not fit the mold of a traditional senator who concentrated primarily on legislation. He viewed himself, as historian Alonzo Hamby noted, "as a public leader, concerned with campaigning, getting elected, educating the people on the issues, and exercising his informed, independent judgment on important matters." He understood issues far better than he had as a congressman. He was more self-confident, a better public speaker, and better organized in his Senate duties. He read far more than most senators, knew more history, and was more candid and informal. Whether these were qualities that would make him an effective presidential candidate remained to be seen.

6

Running for President

LIKE THE REST of his family, young John Kennedy recited grace at every meal, said the Rosary with the family, and prayed on his knees before bed at night. He was present when Rose taught her children the meaning of Shrove Tuesday and Palm Sunday. During World War II, however, Kennedy seemed on the verge of abandoning his Catholic faith. "He had kind of lost his religion," his friend Johnny Iles recalled. Politics in America, however, require deference to God. After the war spiritual symbols and stories occasionally crept into Kennedy's political statements and speeches. He consistently attended Mass each Sunday, even in the midst of exhausting campaign trips when the public or the media wouldn't know if he had attended or not.

Having a Catholic in the White House seemed subversive to many Americans because of the Protestant roots of the nation's democracy. Al Smith was the only Catholic ever nominated for president; when he lost to Herbert Hoover in 1928, he left a major challenge for any Catholic presidential candidate to follow. During Smith's campaign, anti-Catholic zealots distributed millions of handbills, leaflets, and posters with such titles as "Popery in the Public Schools," "Convent Life Unveiled," and "Crimes of the Pope."

Kennedy didn't look like the stereotype of the Irish Catholic politician, wrote Catholic writer John Cogley. "The pugnacious, priest-ridden representative of an embittered, embattled minority, simply does not fit the poised, urbane, cosmopolitan young socialite from Harvard."

When Kennedy entered Congress, he hadn't developed well-defined views on church-state issues. As a young congressman he supported federal aid to education programs in which parochial school students would share in funds for bus transportation, nonreligious textbooks, and health services. But a decade later he had changed his mind. In 1958 he introduced a bill for federal aid to education limited to public schools.

On March 3, 1959, *Look* magazine published Fletcher Knebel's article "Democratic Forecast: A Catholic in 1960." In expressing his candid views, Kennedy had sparked full-blown controversy about his religion. He opposed the appointment of an ambassador to the Vatican and reiterated his position against aid to parochial schools. His statement on conscience and the officeholder caused an unexpected uproar.

> Whatever one's religion in his private life may be, for the office holder nothing takes precedence over his oath to uphold the Constitution in all its parts, including the First Amendment and the strict separation of church and state. . . . I believe that the separation of church and state is fundamental to our American concept and heritage, and should remain so.

In trying to allay Protestant fears about his potential candidacy, Kennedy had raised the ire of zealous Catholic critics who objected to his argument that *nothing* took precedence over the officeholder's oath to uphold the Constitution. The Jesuit weekly *America* thought Kennedy "doesn't really believe that. No religious man, be he Catholic, Protestant or Jew, holds such an opinion. A man's conscience has a bearing on his public as well as his private life." "No man may rightfully act against his conscience," *Ave Maria* agreed. Some friendly Protestant leaders argued that the senator had gone too far in the direction of secularism.

Kennedy responded that he had not intended his remarks in *Look* as a full exposition of his views on the role of conscience. "I should have thought it self-evident that all men regard conscience as an essential element in all human decisions."

Kennedy enjoyed jokes at the expense of the clergy. Speaking at a dinner in New York, he related: "I sat next to Cardinal Spellman at dinner the other evening, and asked him what I should say when voters question me about the doctrine of the pope's infallibility. 'I don't know, Senator,' the Cardinal told me. 'All I know is he keeps calling me Spillman.'"

Kennedy's humor was applauded and often quoted, but in his drive for the presidency he worried about the thorny problem posed by his religion. Working through his anxiety, though, stimulated his thinking and resulted in a fresh and powerful public expression of his views.

*

Kennedy's goal was a first-ballot victory at the Democratic convention, to be held in Los Angeles in July 1960; he couldn't see himself winning the nomination any other way. "I'll be the last guy to come out of a smoke-filled room," he said.

During 1959, while Larry O'Brien traveled about half the time, he discovered that Kennedy had the presidential field almost entirely to himself. No one representing other candidates preceded O'Brien to the statehouses and union halls. Kennedy campaigned unopposed for many months while his opponents underestimated him.

Three Democratic opponents eventually emerged as Kennedy's most likely challengers. A fiery liberal, ebullient personality, and outstanding orator, Minnesota Democrat Hubert Humphrey, forty-eight, supported organized labor, civil rights, and programs for the less privileged. But he had two liabilities: he was too liberal to win in the conservative South, and he lacked strong financial backing.

Lyndon Baines Johnson, fifty-two years old in 1960, had been elected to the Senate from Texas in 1948. Because of his hard work and genius for persuasion and compromise, in 1953 Democrats elected him their floor leader. As a moderate Democrat and consensus builder, he thought he could most effectively unify the nation. His style in the Senate, though, led critics to label him autocratic. Johnson couldn't decide whether to run; he authorized a campaign headquarters, then refused to allow it to do anything.

After his second defeat by Eisenhower in 1956, Adlai Stevenson declared that he had no intention of actively soliciting a third Democratic nomination, nor did most Democrats want him to. Still, his renunciation of a third nomination was partly a tactical maneuver, a strategy of capturing the nomination without actively seeking it. He would remain aloof but keep himself in the public eye, waiting—secretly hoping—for Democrats to turn to him again.

On January 2, 1960, Kennedy announced his candidacy. His first big test would take place in April when Hubert Humphrey planned to challenge him in Wisconsin's primary. In three years, from 1957 to 1959, Kennedy had visited Wisconsin about ten times, establishing his organization and making many speeches and appearances. Humphrey could staff only two offices in Wisconsin; Kennedy staffed eight. Nor was the Kennedy staffing primarily paid personnel; most were volunteers and family members.

That one-third of Wisconsin residents who identified with a church were Catholic was simply too intriguing a circumstance for the media to ignore. On April 5, election night, Kennedy defeated Humphrey 476,024 to 366,753, winning slightly more than 56 percent of the vote. He carried six of the state's ten congressional districts.

Four of the six districts Kennedy won contained significant Catholic populations, making it appear that Protestants had simply voted for the Protestant Humphrey, and Catholics for the Catholic Kennedy. Pundits claimed that Kennedy hadn't proved that he could attract non-Catholic voters. In fact, the religious voting pattern was exaggerated in the postelection analysis. Three "Protestant" districts that Humphrey carried shared a common border with Minnesota, were influenced by the pro-Humphrey media centered in the Twin Cities, and were rural areas that supported Humphrey's farm record. Kennedy did not lose these districts simply because he was a Catholic. State historian Robert Thompson concluded that "religion was only one of many factors, and not necessarily the most important one."

Because Kennedy won only six of the ten districts, analysts judged the Wisconsin results indecisive. Kennedy badly needed a victory over Humphrey in West Virginia on May 10 to prove that he could win without the aid of a Catholic crossover. A victory could eliminate Humphrey as a rival and demonstrate that Kennedy was "a winner," ending speculation that his religion was an insurmountable obstacle.

The media reported that Kennedy's religion might severely damage him in West Virginia, where Catholics comprised only 5 percent of the population. Except for politely answering hundreds of questions about his religion, Kennedy hadn't emphasized the religious issue in Wisconsin; now he felt he had to modify his approach. First, he changed the topic of an upcoming speech at a national meeting of newspaper editors to the subject of religion. Second, instead of trying to avoid the issue as he had mostly done in Wisconsin, he would face the issue directly and openly in West Virginia, and call for fair play.

On April 21, 1960, he addressed the American Society of Newspaper Editors in Washington. "There is no religious *issue*," he told the editors. The media had not created the religious issue, but reporters and editors "will largely determine whether or not it does become dominant—whether it is kept in perspective—whether it is considered objectively—whether needless fears and suspicions are aroused." To that date the issue had *not* been kept in perspective.

Four days later on April 25, before a crowd of 350 people gathered around the post office steps in Charleston, West Virginia, someone in the crowd asked him about the religious issue. He replied differently than he ever had before. "I am a Catholic," he responded, "but the fact that I was born a Catholic, does that mean that I can't be the President of the United States? I'm able to serve in Congress, and my brother was able to give his life, but we can't be president?"

The Kennedy campaign stressed his war record because in West Virginia, with its reverence for war heroes, the courage of Kennedy in the Solomon Islands struck a responsive chord. One way the Kennedy camp hoped to arouse apathetic lower-income groups was to portray Kennedy as a dedicated New Deal Democrat. To foster this strategy Franklin D. Roosevelt, Jr., was recruited to stir memories of his popular father. Wherever he campaigned in West Virginia, FDR's namesake drew large crowds and received the greatest applause when he mentioned "my father."

As the May 10 primary approached, most of the media assumed that the results would derail Kennedy's nomination bid or at least severely damage his chances. The *New York Times* saw evidence of "conflicting political trends" but remained certain of Kennedy's defeat. Humphrey was "setting the pace," wrote *Time* magazine. The *New Republic* assumed "Humphrey's style of campaigning would overcome Kennedy's organization."

On election day Kennedy won by 236,510 to Humphrey's 152,187. Humphrey thereupon withdrew from the presidential race.

Kennedy won for several reasons: an efficient and well-funded organization, an extensive television campaign, his success in addressing the religious issue, his war record, the support of Franklin D. Roosevelt, Jr., and Kennedy's pledge to help the distressed areas of the state.

Several writers have charged that the Mafia helped Kennedy in West Virginia. Mafia funds were supposedly channeled through Skinny D'Amato, a shadowy underworld figure with ties to gambling in West Virginia. But no link has ever been established between D'Amato and the 1960 West Virginia primary; he has never been interviewed or even located. Soon after the primary, Republicans, sensing an explosive issue with which to attack Kennedy in the general election, investigated allegations of illegal campaign contributions; the FBI searched for violations of federal voting laws; and West Virginia's attorney general also investigated, as did the *Charleston Gazette*. None of these probes uncovered any noteworthy evidence of wrongdoing by Kennedy's campaign.

Despite his primary victories, Kennedy's youth remained a persistent problem—until he lanced it with a deft blow. Shortly before the Democratic convention opened, former President Truman lashed out at Kennedy. "Senator," he asked in his public statement, "are you certain you are quite ready for the country, or that the country is ready for you in the role of President in January 1961?" Democrats needed to nominate "someone with the greatest possible maturity and experience."

At a crowded televised news conference two days after Truman's challenge, Kennedy brilliantly rebutted the former president. Courteous and serene, Kennedy defended the contributions made by Americans under forty-four years of age: "To exclude from positions of trust and command all those below the age of 44 would have kept Jefferson from writing the Declaration of Independence, Washington from commanding the Continental Army, Madison from fathering the Constitution, Hamilton from serving as Secretary of the Treasury, Clay from being elected Speaker of the House and Christopher Columbus from even discovering America."

The Democratic convention opened on Monday, July 11. Kennedy needed 761 votes to secure the nomination. When Wyoming came through with enough votes to surpass the mark, Kennedy threw his score sheet in the air in celebration. Bewildering confusion marked the selection of the vice-presidential nominee, but eventually Lyndon Johnson was chosen because he bolstered the ticket with farmers, Southerners, and the state of Texas.

In winning the nomination, the Kennedy-for-President organization—a blend of intellectuals, relatives, friends, politicians, and technicians—had produced a highly professional performance. Kennedy's wealth had been a huge advantage in his drive for the nomination. Money bought radio, television, and newspaper ads, financed his staff, and provided an airplane to convey him quickly to campaign stops. Jack's handsome features, charm, and intelligence all contributed to his success. But his dogged, unrelenting effort was the heart of his long campaign.

*

As vice president under Eisenhower, the Republican candidate Richard Nixon was compelled to defend the administration's record; Kennedy was free to exploit its shortcomings. He charged that under Ike the nation had failed to keep pace with the Soviets in education, technology, and the production of ballistic missiles. America's prestige had declined in the world, particularly among the newly emerging nations of Africa and Asia, and the administration had lost Cuba to the Communists.

Kennedy's nomination rekindled anti-Catholic agitation, which peaked on September 7 with a formidable attack by a new group of prominent clergymen, the National Council of Citizens for Religious Freedom. The group represented mostly evangelical conservative Protestants organized primarily in the National Association of Evangelicals. The most notable member of the group was Dr. Norman Vincent Peale, sixty-two, a longtime Republican, friend of Vice President Nixon, and the best-selling author of *The Power of Positive Thinking*.

Kennedy was unacceptable as president, the group's manifesto said, because no Catholic could be free of the church hierarchy's "determined efforts . . . to breach the wall of separation of church and state." It was inconceivable "that a Roman Catholic President would not be under extreme pressure by the hierarchy." The group's pronouncement largely discounted Kennedy's legislative record and public statements and ascribed to him the political positions of the Catholic church (positions the manifesto often distorted).

An avalanche of criticism descended on the Peale group, but Kennedy saw it as an opportunity. On the heels of the controversy came one of Kennedy's most dramatic campaign appearances. On Monday evening, September 12, he sat down on the dais in the ballroom of the Rice Hotel in Houston, Texas, as three hundred evangelical clergymen waited for his 9 p.m. speech to be broadcast on Texas television.

In his opening remarks, Kennedy pointed out that far more critical issues than his religion should be emphasized in the campaign. Nonetheless, with all the controversy he needed to state again "not what kind of church I believe in, for that should be important only to me—but what kind of America I believe in."

> I believe in an America where the separation of church and state is absolute—where no Catholic prelate would tell the President (should he be Catholic) how to act, and no Protestant minister would tell his parishioners for whom to vote—where no church or church school is granted any public funds or political preference.

The finger of suspicion was currently aimed at Catholics, Kennedy said, but some day it might be pointed at Jews, Quakers, Unitarians, or Baptists. "Today I may be the victim—but tomorrow it may be you."

> Finally, I believe in an America where religious intolerance will someday end—where all men and all churches are treated as equal—where every man has the same right to attend or not attend the church of his choice—where there is no Catholic vote, no anti-Catholic vote, no bloc voting of any kind. . . .
>
> This is the kind of America I believe in—and this is the kind I fought for in the South Pacific, and the kind my brother died for in Europe. No one suggested then that we might have a "divided loyalty," that we did "not believe in liberty,"

or that we belonged to a disloyal group that threatened the "freedoms for which our forefathers died."

He wanted to be judged on the basis of his record during fourteen years in Congress, on his declared stands against a U.S. ambassador to the Vatican, and against aid to parochial schools, not on the basis of scurrilous publications. These were his own views, he stressed,

> for, contrary to common newspaper usages I am not the Catholic candidate for President. I am the Democratic Party's candidate for President who happens also to be a Catholic. I do not speak for my church on public matters—and the Church does not speak for me.
>
> Whatever issue may come before me as President—on birth control, divorce, censorship, gambling, or any other subject—I will make my decision in accordance with these views, in accordance with what my conscience tells me to be the national interest, and without regard to outside religious pressures or dictates.

The speech was powerful and eloquent, his best of the 1960 campaign and one of the most important in his political career. "I didn't take an actual poll of the correspondents," said journalist Edward P. Morgan of the Houston appearance, "but I didn't need to. We were all so enormously struck and impressed." For the next seven weeks the Kennedy campaign organization saturated the nation with edited television tapes of the speech. The program played in forty states.

After intense negotiations, both presidential candidates agreed to four one-hour debates to air simultaneously on the three television networks and all four radio networks. The first of these unprecedented encounters would be held in Chicago on September 26.

At the debate Kennedy aggressively carried the fight, correcting a questioner's assertion, taking time effectively to refute earlier Nixon statements. Many TV viewers wondered why Nixon looked so haggard, so worn, so grim. His facial muscles tensed, sweat appeared on his brow and cheeks; sometimes he forced a smile unrelated to his words. His eyes shifted and darted.

Seventy-five million viewers watched the first debate. The next day few could recall what the candidates had said. But Kennedy had greatly enhanced his image—and image won out over content. Newspaper editorials mostly gave Kennedy the edge, as did public opinion polls. Overnight, it appeared to Theodore White, crowds "seethed with enthusiasm and multiplied in numbers, as if the sight of him [on TV] . . . had given him a 'star quality' reserved only for television and movie idols." The final three debates were anti-climactic. All three were judged to be close, but they had less impact. The debates as a whole, said most poll surveys, were won by Kennedy.

The Democratic platform had staked out an advanced liberal position on civil rights, emphasizing the need for new legislation and implying that previous laws passed by Congress were insufficient. Early in the general election campaign Kennedy advocated new civil rights legislation. By the beginning of October, though, he had clearly shifted his emphasis away from legislation to the potential for executive action. He must have realized that he was promising too much, that Congress would undoubtedly block civil rights legislation in the next session. Replying to a question in Minneapolis on October 1, he said, "There is a great deal that can be done by the executive branch without legislation. For example, the President could sign an executive order ending discrimination in housing tomorrow."

On one dramatic occasion late in the campaign, when Kennedy displayed his personal concern for racial injustice, his symbolic action helped carry him to victory. Nixon had expected sizable support from blacks. He had developed a good relationship with Martin Luther King, Jr.—better than Kennedy's. King had voted Republican in 1956, and his father had endorsed Nixon in 1960. But Nixon abandoned King at a critical moment, and Kennedy seized the opportunity.

On October 19, 1960, police arrested King for picketing an Atlanta department store. Three days later he was released from jail but immediately rearrested for violation of a parole agreement growing out of a trumped-up charge—driving with an Alabama license while a Georgia resident. For this offense he was sent to a remote Georgia prison for a four-month term at hard labor. Coretta Scott King, having every reason to believe that her husband was in mortal danger, called her friend Harris Wofford and, crying, said, "They're going to kill him. I know they are going to kill him." Wofford immediately phoned Sargent Shriver in Chicago, where Kennedy was campaigning, and told Shriver of the near-hysteria of the pregnant Mrs. King.

The two concocted a plan. Shriver would rush to O'Hare Airport and try to persuade Kennedy to make a reassuring telephone call to Mrs. King. When Shriver found him, Kennedy listened intently and replied, "That's a good idea. Why not? Do you have her number? Get her on the phone." Afterward she phoned Wofford and expressed her gratitude. She quoted Kennedy as saying, "I want to express to you my concern about your husband. I know this must be very hard for you. I understand you are expecting a baby, and I just wanted you to know that I was thinking about you and Dr. King. If there is anything I can do to help, please feel free to call on me." Robert Kennedy then phoned the judge and bawled him out, and the judge agreed to release King.

After this episode, Martin Luther King's father, an influential Baptist preacher, publicly changed his endorsement from Nixon to Kennedy. Negro newspapers in the North picked up the story and lavished praise on the Democratic candidate. They quoted Martin Luther King, Jr., as saying that "it took a lot of courage for Kennedy to do this, especially in Georgia. For him to be that courageous shows that he is really acting upon principle and not expediency."

Ultimately two million pamphlets describing the incident were distributed at black churches and bars in the North. The pamphlet, *The Case of Martin Luther King, Jr.*, featured on the cover page, "'No Comment' Nixon versus a Candidate with a Heart, Senator Kennedy." This improvised public relations offensive helped tip the balance in the election.

For eight years President Eisenhower, despite passage of civil rights legislation, had practiced a steady indifference to Negroes and to civil rights. Because blacks were desperate for attention and consideration, Kennedy's symbolic act, his expression of personal concern, fulfilled an important need in the black community.

*

At about 2 a.m. on October 14, arriving at the University of Michigan at Ann Arbor, Kennedy was dumbfounded to discover ten thousand students waiting for him in the middle of the night. In his little-noticed, extemporaneous remarks, he focused on the essence of what later became the Peace Corps. "How many of you are willing to spend two years in Africa or Latin America or Asia working for the United States and working for freedom?" he asked. "How many of you [who] are going to be doctors are willing to spend your days in Ghana?" Kennedy did not actually mention a "Peace Corps" at Michigan, but his remarks embraced the spirit of the idea.

A week later he spoke in San Francisco's Cow Palace auditorium before a huge crowd of 35,000 people. The main theme of his address was the impact that talented young Americans could have in the Third World, "building goodwill, building the peace." He advocated a new government organization, a Peace Corps, that would help impoverished nations help themselves. It would recruit talented young men "willing and able to serve their country in this fashion for three years as an alternative to peacetime selective service— well-qualified through rigorous standards; well-trained in the language, skills, and customs they will need to know."

The following day the *New York Times* prominently headlined: "Kennedy Favors U.S. 'Peace Corps' to Work Abroad."

The national media followed suit, praising the concept. By the end of 1960 Kennedy had received more letters on his proposal for a Peace Corps than on any other subject.

＊

Nixon and Kennedy vied for the honor of being the most aggressive cold warrior. They concentrated on the best policy toward Castro's Cuba, but neither candidate enlightened voters on the subject.

In 1959 Fidel Castro had overthrown the Cuban government of Fulgencio Batista, one of the most corrupt dictators in Latin America. At first Americans sympathized with Castro, hoping for a more democratic leader, but sentiment turned against him when he exacted brutal vengeance on Batista's followers and drifted into the Soviet orbit in foreign policy.

At first Kennedy tried to outflank rather than confront Nixon's tough position on Cuba. He aimed his salvos at past Republican policy, calling Castro's Cuba another clear symbol of American decline under Eisenhower. He reminded voters that "In 1952 the Republicans ran on a program of rolling back the Iron Curtain in Eastern Europe. Today the Iron Curtain is 90 miles off the coast of the United States."

The issue of Cuba failed to have a crucial impact on the election, historian Kent Beck concluded, "because the campaign produced no clear-cut difference between Kennedy and Nixon." There was no strong sentiment for American intervention in Cuba in 1960, and the candidates avoided a serious discussion of policy toward the island.

In the November election, Kennedy won comfortably in the electoral college, capturing 303 votes to Nixon's 219. But in the razor-thin popular vote, he barely edged Nixon, winning by less than 120,000 votes out of more than 68 million cast. Kennedy earned 49.7 percent of the total to Nixon's 49.6 percent, the smallest popular-vote margin of any presidential contest in the twentieth century.

Several factors explained Kennedy's victory. Winning the first debate was important. So was his personal attractiveness, effective campaign style, and the phone call to Mrs. King. President Eisenhower's tepid efforts on behalf of his vice president hurt Nixon's campaign. Lyndon Johnson's presence on the ticket probably inched Texas and its electoral votes into the Democratic column.

The Negro vote was a major reason that Kennedy carried the crucial states of Illinois, Michigan, New Jersey, New York, and Pennsylvania. In 1956 Adlai Stevenson had won 60 percent of the black vote; in 1960 Kennedy captured 80 percent.

Kennedy's religion helped elect him and very nearly defeated him. He collected 78 percent of Catholic votes, propelling him to victory in urbanized Northeastern states with large electoral votes. But he won only 38 percent of the votes of Protestants. The religious issue hurt Kennedy most in the South, where about 17 percent of the normal Democratic vote defected.

Nowhere was the vote closer than in Illinois, which Kennedy carried by a mere 8,858 votes out of more than 4.6 million cast. In Chicago, Kennedy won by the overwhelming margin of 456,000. The powerful and notoriously efficient Cook County Democratic machine, directed by Chicago mayor Richard Daley, threw its potent resources behind the candidate. Critics contend that a bargain arranged by Joe Kennedy gained the election for his son in Chicago. Behind the scenes, Joe Kennedy had promoted Jack's candidacy as old Democratic pols like Jim Farley and Ed Flynn had for Franklin Roosevelt.

One of the bosses Joe Kennedy may have contacted was Chicago's crime boss, Sam ("Mooney") Giancana, one of America's leading criminals. According to Seymour Hersh's investigation, the senior Kennedy made an agreement with Giancana to ensure victory in Illinois and in other states where the syndicate had influence. "The deal," Hersh claimed, "included an assurance that Giancana's men would get out the Kennedy vote among the rank and file in the mob-controlled unions in Chicago and elsewhere, and a commitment for campaign contributions from the corrupt Teamsters Union pension fund." When John Kennedy assumed the presidency, so the story goes, he was therefore indebted to organized crime and to Giancana for securing the victory in Chicago.

What are we to make of this allegation? Along with his virtues, Joe Kennedy had infinite capacity for poor judgment and immoral, unethical activity. Perhaps Hersh's description of their meeting is correct, because similar meetings were taking place elsewhere. Joe Kennedy met with scores of big-city bosses in his attempt to elect his son. What's most important, though, is the lack of evidence of any campaign activity directed by Giancana to elect Kennedy. The mob boss commanded few votes. Mayor Daley, not Giancana, managed the huge and potent Democratic organization in Chicago.

Giancana controlled only two wards, both of them heavily Democratic anyway. Chicago's First and Twenty-eighth wards, the crime syndicate's strongholds in the city, produced *low* recorded vote counts for Kennedy compared to the maximum turnout in nine other automatically Democratic wards. In other words, if Giancana and the crime syndicate campaigned for Kennedy, they did a poor job of turning out their voters. John Kennedy felt no obligation to return a favor to Sam Giancana. Edmund Kallina, the preeminent authority on the Chicago election in 1960, concluded that Hersh's "hearsay" evidence was not convincing.

If Daley and the Cook County Democratic machine did steal the election for Kennedy, it would not, by itself, have changed the national results. Kennedy would have won in the electoral college even if Illinois had gone Republican.

Kennedy ran behind the Democratic ticket more often than he ran ahead of it. "Senator Kennedy's lack of a personal mandate will make it more difficult for him to strike out for the new frontiers he has pledged himself to reach," concluded columnist Richard Rovere.

7

The Bay of Pigs and Berlin

AS PRESIDENT, Kennedy wanted a "ministry of talent," but his political career left him with limited options in his search for the best. Shortly after the election he confided in Dean Acheson about possible cabinet appointments. He told Truman's secretary of state that he had spent so much time in the past few years coming to know people who could help *elect* him president that he now found he knew few people who could help him *be* president. Acheson judged Kennedy's dilemma "both true and touching."

Kennedy devoted far more effort to his appointments to the State, Defense, Justice, and Treasury departments than he did to other cabinet officers. Robert Lovett provided the best advice on three of the major posts. A Republican and an international investment banker on Wall Street, Lovett had nonetheless served as undersecretary of state and as secretary of defense under Truman. Because of poor health, he declined to accept any appointment from Kennedy, making him unbiased and magnifying his influence.

For Treasury, Kennedy settled on Douglas Dillon, the board chairman of a prominent Wall Street brokerage firm. He expected Dillon to provide public assurance that the administration would be fiscally responsible.

Kennedy knew that he didn't want Adlai Stevenson as his secretary of state. Kennedy no longer liked him and judged him as indecisive; neither Lovett nor Acheson endorsed Stevenson. Instead, Kennedy named Stevenson to a lesser diplomatic post—U.S. representative to the United Nations.

After Acheson and Lovett both endorsed the little-known Dean Rusk, Kennedy appointed the Georgia native as secretary of state. A Rhodes scholar and professor of government, Rusk had joined the State Department in 1946, working as an aide to Acheson and Lovett until 1953.

For secretary of defense Kennedy selected Robert McNamara, the new president of the Ford Motor Company. McNamara immediately delighted his new boss. "He was dazzled by McNamara's toughness, quickness, fluency, competence, incorruptibility, freedom from political cant, and force of personality," observed Michael Beschloss. Kennedy noted that McNamara would "come in with his twenty options and then say, 'Mr. President, I think we should do this.' I like that. Makes the job easier."

The most controversial cabinet appointment turned out to be that of attorney general. Joe Kennedy insisted that Jack's brother Robert be given the post, but the president-elect resisted. Not that he didn't think his brother had major attributes. "I don't even have to think about organization," he had remarked about Robert during the campaign. "He's the hardest worker. He's the greatest organizer." But appointing his brother invited charges of nepotism. Pressured and convinced by his father, Jack changed his mind. He needed an absolutely reliable attorney general, he decided, and "I can count on [Bobby] completely."

The major positions on the White House staff all went to longtime, loyal members of Kennedy's Senate and campaign staff—with one exception. Initially Kennedy barely knew his special assistant for national security affairs, McGeorge Bundy, frequently calling him "McBundy." A descendant of two of Boston's first families, the Lowells and the Bundys, the national security adviser was self-confident and, above all, possessed dazzling clarity and speed of mind. Bundy, remarked

George Ball, had an "extraordinary facility to grasp an idea, summarize or analyze it, and produce an orderly response as fast as a computer."

Kennedy appointed his former legislative secretary Evelyn Lincoln as his White House secretary. As press secretary Kennedy selected Pierre Salinger, who had functioned in that capacity during the campaign. Kennedy had great confidence in his longtime aide, the hardworking Larry O'Brien, and named him as special assistant to the president for congressional relations. O'Brien had the difficult task of mobilizing the resources of the White House to persuade Congress to enact the legislative program of the so-called New Frontier.

Ted Sorensen's duties included preparing the legislative program, planning domestic policy, and writing speeches, which gave him important entreé into foreign policy as well. Ken O'Donnell became one of the president's most trusted advisers. Officially O'Donnell was appointments secretary to the president, but his real duties were far-ranging. He planned the president's White House schedule, mapped out trips, and served as a sounding board for Kennedy's ideas.

Ebullient and elfish, Dave Powers, forty-nine, became Kennedy's constant companion during the White House years. Powers also assumed a very private role during Kennedy's presidency: he was the key person who procured women for the president's sexual satisfaction.

Arthur Schlesinger was asked to join the administration because Kennedy intended to be a great president and thought it prudent to have a great historian in attendance.

Kennedy expected that his inaugural on January 20, 1961, would set the tone for his presidency. He hoped to heal the lingering wounds inflicted during the 1960 campaign, to remind Americans of their common heritage and purpose, and to set forth generally the policies and objectives of his administration.

At 12:51 p.m. on the steps of the Capitol, Kennedy stepped forward and took the oath of office. Then, hatless, in a clear, crisp voice on a cold day, with his characteristic jabbing finger, he delivered his inaugural oration.

> Now the trumpet summons us again—not as a call to bear arms, though arms we need—not as a call to battle, though embattled we are—but as a call to bear the burden of a long twilight struggle, year in and year out, "rejoicing in hope, patient in tribulation"—a struggle against the common enemies of man: tyranny, poverty, disease, and war itself. . . .
>
> And so, my fellow Americans: ask not what your country can do for you—ask what you can do for your country.
>
> My fellow citizens of the world: ask not what America will do for you, but what together we can do for the freedom of man.

"Reaction to the speech was immediate," *Time* wrote. "From all shades of political outlook . . . came a surge of congratulations. . . . The speech set forth few concrete proposals, but its broad, general imperatives stirred the heart."

In mid-February the public gave Kennedy a 72 percent favorable approval rating. Die-hard Republicans were still waiting for the first "real Kennedy blooper." One was right around the corner, but even that didn't dampen the new president's popularity.

*

As Fidel Castro became more stridently anti-American and cozied up to the Soviets, a benevolent approach to Castro's Cuba became impossible for any American political leader. In the later months of 1960 Kennedy had adopted the standard U.S. view that Castro was a Communist who had "betrayed the ideals of the Cuban revolution" and transformed Cuba "into a hostile and militant Communist satellite."

In January 1960 the Eisenhower administration had made a top-secret decision to overthrow Castro. By the following March the Central Intelligence Agency had devised a plan. The CIA's model was a successful 1954 coup in Guatemala. In just one week the agency had helped to overthrow the leftist government of Jacobo Arbenz Guzmán using a force of 150 exiles and a few World War II P-47 fighters flown by American pilots. The CIA had won a reputation as the government's covert-action experts, the agency that arranged quick fixes for awkward foreign difficulties.

Allen Dulles, the elderly CIA director, was the amiable and scholarly younger brother of John Foster Dulles, Eisenhower's secretary of state. His deputy, Richard Bissell, the CIA official directly in charge of the Cuban operation, had been at the center of the CIA's most exciting adventures.

Originally the plan called for a long, slow, clandestine buildup of guerrilla forces in Cuba, all recruited, trained, and infiltrated into Cuba by the CIA. Thirteen months later the agency had drastically changed its plan, advocating an overt amphibious landing of fourteen hundred combat-trained, heavily armed, Cuban-exile soldiers. Eisenhower backed the plan.

Unfortunately for Kennedy, the supposedly covert plan became an open secret. On January 10, 1961, the *New York Times* exposed it on the front page. "U.S. Helps Train an Anti-Castro Force at Secret Guatemalan Air-Ground Base" screamed a three-column headline.

Meanwhile Allen Dulles told senators privately that Cuba was rapidly falling into the Soviet bloc. Making decided progress in controlling the entire Cuban population, Castro was creating a Communist totalitarian state and might influence nearby countries.

President Kennedy's first official briefing on the Cuban plan took place on January 28, 1961. If he was to endorse it, he hoped to oust Castro without suffering serious political consequences. With the United States a champion of the world's emerging nations, he didn't wish to begin his presidency by openly destroying Castro's government, casting himself and the United States as the traditional imperialist. Committing full American military force to a Cuban invasion would be a propaganda disaster—comparable to the Russian invasion of Hungary in 1956—with horrifying pictures of Cuban bodies in the streets of Havana. What's more, a full-scale U.S. invasion might spark Soviet retaliation against West Berlin. Yet if Kennedy didn't do something about Castro, Republicans would accuse him of being soft on communism, a weakling.

The CIA's intelligence claimed broad anti-Castro resistance in Cuba: as many as three thousand rebels, supported by twenty thousand sympathizers.

On March 11 the first of two critical meetings took place in the Cabinet Room. Sounding an ominous note of urgency, Allen Dulles warned that the United States had a "disposal problem" with the U.S.-trained Cuban Brigade. "If we have to take these men out of Guatemala, we will have to transfer them to the United States, and we can't have them wandering around the country telling everyone what they have been doing." The surly, bridled invasion force would spread the word that the United States had turned tail. Republicans would call Kennedy a chicken.

At the meeting Richard Bissell presented his plan, code-named Operation Trinidad. He recommended an amphibious/airborne assault with tactical air support. The Trinidad landing site (a city in Cuba, not the island of Trinidad) had several advantages: it was far from Castro's known troop locations, permitted changeover to guerrilla operations in the Escambray Mountains if the invasion failed, and had a local population that had shown past antipathy toward Castro.

After lengthy discussion the president said he would go ahead but could not endorse a plan that "put us in so openly, in view of the world situation." Trinidad was "too spectacular," too much like a "World War Two invasion."

Kennedy told Bissell to revise the plan in two ways. The invasion must be an unspectacular landing at night in an area with a minimum likelihood of opposition. And, if ultimate success depended on tactical air support, that support must appear to come from a Cuban air base, meaning the landing site must have an existing airfield nearby.

From March 13 to 15 the CIA's paramilitary staff worked feverishly to devise a plan that addressed Kennedy's concerns. On March 15 Bissell presented his revised plan: an attack at the Bay of Pigs (Bahía de Cochinos), a site also known as Zapata. As Kennedy had requested, near the beachhead was an airstrip—possibly two—adequate to handle B-26s. No one questioned the extraordinary fact that in only a few days Bissell had made major changes in the plan. The Kennedy team was impressed when they should have been skeptical.

The Zapata plan had been prepared so hastily that the Joint Chiefs could give it only perfunctory evaluation. Nonetheless they endorsed it as the best alternative, never indicating at the meeting that they still preferred the Trinidad plan. The Chiefs assumed that the new plan included air support and accepted the CIA's assurances that thousands of Cuban insurgents would immediately join the invasion forces and that, in the event the landing failed, the invaders would at once "go guerrilla" and take to the hills. The endorsement by the Joint Chiefs, Dean Rusk later observed, "tended to encourage President Kennedy to make the decision to go ahead with it."

While considering the Zapata plan, at no time was Kennedy or Bundy or McNamara or the Joint Chiefs made to understand that, unlike the Trinidad plan, the new one had lost a feature that Kennedy considered vital: the guerrilla option for the invaders. The president and his team still believed the invasion force could "melt into the mountains"; the mountains, however, were now too far away.

To control the political risks, Kennedy had insisted, above all else, that the invasion carefully allow the United States to claim deniability. The CIA should not involve U.S. planes, ships, weapons, facilities, or personnel. It must use nothing that could serve, if captured, as proof of a U.S. role. Bissell agreed but neglected to tell the president that the need for deniability might affect the viability of the project. It might be impossible to disguise U.S. involvement in an invasion of the size now contemplated.

Opposition to the Cuban venture emerged in the president's councils, but supporters of the invasion muffled the voices of critics. On the evening of April 4 Kennedy met at the Department of State with senior officials involved in planning the Zapata operation. He invited Senator William Fulbright, chairman of the Senate's Foreign Relations Committee. After listening to Bissell describe the operation, Fulbright realized the seriousness of the situation.

Angry and defiant, Fulbright denounced the entire operation. If it succeeded, Cuba would inevitably become dependent on the United States, and the world would brand the United States as brutal imperialists. If it failed, America would look weak and ineffective. In any case, an invasion clearly violated America's treaty obligations and compromised the nation's moral position in the world. Despite Fulbright's eloquent plea, most of the meeting's participants remained unshaken. His comments did not even elicit discussion.

The president asked everyone, "What do you think?" He wanted "yes" or "no" answers. The consensus was to move ahead with the operation.

"I really thought they had a good chance," Kennedy told Sorensen afterward. Ideally the Cuban exiles, without overt U.S. participation, would establish themselves on the island, proclaim a new non-Communist government, and rally the Cuban people to their cause. If they could oust Castro, all Latin America would feel more secure. Already armed and trained, the Cuban exiles could not be contained much longer—they yearned to return to Cuba. If the invasion failed, the exiles could always flee to the mountains and fight as guerrillas, still a net gain. The CIA and the Joint Chiefs had the experience, the know-how. Evidently Eisenhower trusted them. Why shouldn't the new president? The invasion plan must be feasible—it had worked in Guatemala.

The invasion began on April 15. In a communiqué issued in Havana on that Saturday, Castro charged that at 6 a.m. that morning B-26 bombers from the United States had simultaneously bombed several Cuban cities. The air assault, actually carried out from a secret CIA airbase in Nicaragua, had begun. On the afternoon of April 15 the UN General Assembly began debating the conflict developing in Cuba. Castro's UN delegate, Raul Roa, accused the United States of aggression against Cuba, and the Soviet representative, Valerian A. Zorin, warned that "Cuba has many friends in the world who were ready to come to its aid, including the Soviet Union."

Early on Monday morning, April 17, the fourteen-hundred-man Cuban Brigade landed at the Bay of Pigs. Although tactically surprised, Castro's forces reacted quickly and powerfully. At dawn Cuban aircraft attacked the beaches and shipping, sinking two freighters which together carried a critical ten-day supply of ammunition for the brigade plus medical supplies, food, and communications equipment.

Almost everything went awry for the invaders. Their landing craft foundered among the unanticipated coral reefs. When portable radios got soaked, they didn't function. Men landed at the wrong locations, several miles from comrades, and others reached shore without adequate supplies. On the morning of April 18 the outlook was gloomy. That evening the president left a White House reception to meet with his key advisers.

Several people in the room assumed that the brigade could still escape "into the hills." It was "time for this outfit to go guerrilla," said Gen. Lyman Lemnitzer. Bissell shocked them when he explained that the invaders couldn't "go guerrilla" and were captives of the swamp.

After three days of fighting, the battle ended with the surrender of brigade forces. In the end, 1,189 men were taken prisoner; 140 died. Soviet premier Khrushchev denounced the invasion as "fraught with danger to world peace." He promised the Cuban people and their government "all necessary assistance in beating back the armed attack."

"I have had two full days of hell," Kennedy said to Clark Clifford as the invasion force surrendered. "I haven't slept— this has been the most excruciating period of my life. I doubt my Presidency could survive another catastrophe like this."

The debacle distressed friends of the United States. "Bad show," reported the *London Daily Mail*, "a shocking blow to American prestige." At a press conference on April 21, Kennedy took full personal responsibility. "There's an old saying, that victory has a hundred fathers and defeat is an orphan."

The Bay of Pigs invasion has been aptly described as "the perfect failure." What had gone wrong? To begin with, everything about the operation was marginal or inadequate. The landing force was too small to control the thirty-six-mile beachhead or repulse the enemy counterattack. Air support over the beaches did not include enough high-quality planes and pilots; too many restrictions hampered bombing runs against the Castro airfields; and the invaders had no fighters to fend off Castro's planes. An amphibious landing against a hostile enemy shore is one of the most difficult of all military maneuvers, requiring surprise, air superiority, and exceptionally good logistics.

Everything was small in relation to needs, so that the operation had to work perfectly to ensure success. But the CIA had planned the project without adequate boats, bases, training facilities, and Spanish speakers. It had no disaster plan and only vague directions for action following the landings.

Several crucial misunderstandings between the White House and the CIA also damaged the operation. The president clearly stated that he wouldn't permit the invasion to turn into an American operation. But CIA officials didn't believe him. They assumed that if the invasion was about to fail, Kennedy would change his mind and insert American forces. The military and the CIA *assumed* the president would order American intervention; the president *assumed* they knew he would refuse to exceed his original limitation.

In case of failure, the president assumed the guerrilla option was still available to the exiles. The CIA never informed him that most of the exiles were untrained for guerrilla warfare, or that the eighty-mile escape route to the Escambrays was too far away and blocked by swamps and Castro's troops.

The greatest CIA failure was its incompetent intelligence. It overestimated domestic discontent in Cuba and the number of potential dissidents. All allied intelligence reports showed Castro completely in control and supported by most Cubans.

The Joint Chiefs, entrusted with the responsibility of evaluating the military feasibility of the operation, did not oppose the final plan, and their mild assent gave others the impression of approval. Kennedy's subsequent bitter feelings toward the Joint Chiefs, however, were misguided. It wasn't their plan. The Chiefs' advice had assumed the accuracy of the CIA's intelligence estimates.

All the key officials involved in the Bay of Pigs operation were unfamiliar working with Kennedy and with one another, hampering communications and circumscribing responses. McNamara's inexperience and deference to the CIA led him to accept the plan uncritically. "The truth is I did not understand the plan very well and did not know the facts," McNamara reflected. "I had let myself become a passive bystander."

As is often the case, the disaster became the foundation for future success. Kennedy no longer accepted conventional wisdom or bureaucratic momentum without intense scrutiny. Robert McNamara, disenchanted with the military advice he had received, insisted on examining the facts himself before he passed on his advice to the president. "We all learned from it," said McNamara. "It was a horribly expensive lesson, however."

Afterward Kennedy reorganized his staff. The distinguished Gen. Maxwell Taylor was persuaded to come out of retirement to be Kennedy's military adviser; later Kennedy appointed him chairman of the Joint Chiefs. Kennedy quietly asked both Dulles and Bissell to leave, though he did not reprimand either one. Bundy moved his operation from the Executive Office Building into the basement of the west wing of the White House, where he established a communications center and took on added responsibility for security matters. Neither Robert Kennedy nor Ted Sorensen had taken part in the meetings on the Bay of Pigs; afterward Kennedy gave both a broad mandate to advise him on foreign policy.

When a Gallup poll, conducted two weeks after the failed invasion, showed that support for the president had gone *up* to an unprecedented 82 percent, Kennedy dismissed it. "It's just like Eisenhower. The worse I do, the more popular I get."

*

More than other foreign policy dilemmas, historical circumstances conditioned and restricted Kennedy's policy toward troubled Berlin. At the end of World War II the victorious allies had agreed temporarily to divide Germany into four zones—controlled by the British, French, Americans, and Soviets—and to establish four-power control over the city of Berlin. At the start of the cold war the Americans, French, and British converted their zones into West Germany (the Federal Republic of Germany), and the Soviet Union transformed its zone into East Germany (the German Democratic Republic, GDR). Berlin was left as an enclave far inside East Germany, 110 miles from West Germany. Independent West Berlin was now the "last democratic outpost on the communist side of the Iron Curtain," noted Arthur Schlesinger.

The West wanted an undivided Berlin with open access, and an undivided Germany. "The East feared the reunification of Germany under capitalism," noted Lawrence Freedman; "the West feared the reunification of Berlin under communism." Public opinion in the United States overwhelmingly supported the defense of West Berlin.

The Soviets held the initiative in Berlin as the Western powers had no realistic way to prevent the Soviets from asserting their control. The only hope was to threaten them with nuclear weapons if they tried to change the status quo. But the nuclear threat did not seem entirely believable. Would the United States actually risk nuclear war to save West Berlin? Kennedy had to make the nuclear threat credible while simultaneously doing everything possible to avoid unleashing a nuclear war.

In May 1961 Kennedy and Khrushchev agreed to meet at a summit in Vienna early the following month. Their meeting was to be informal and agenda-free. The atmosphere would not be promising for an important agreement, but Kennedy felt he needed to size up Khrushchev, and establish a rapport that might later prove valuable. "I would rather meet him the first time at the summit, not the brink," the president said.

Kennedy prepared meticulously, looking for clues to understanding Khrushchev. He studied the Soviet premier's speeches and read the minutes of earlier summits between Eisenhower and Khrushchev. He consulted with journalists and sought the guidance of former ambassador Chip Bohlen, Secretary of State Dean Rusk, and former secretary of state Dean Acheson.

On June 3 and 4, 1961, the two leaders engaged in their only face-to-face confrontation. The first session began on June 3 at 12:45 p.m. at the American ambassador's residence. Kennedy told the Soviet leader he wanted to avoid any "miscalculation" by either country, replacing it with "precision in judgments." But Khrushchev rejected the way Kennedy used the word "miscalculation," and wouldn't concede that he might ever miscalculate. The premier briefly turned the session into an ideological harangue, putting Kennedy at a disadvantage. Kennedy urged the Soviet Union to stop supporting nationalist movements. The United States supported "free choice," the president said. The United States, retorted the Soviet leader, did not appreciate the aspirations of people to overthrow their oppressors. He lectured Kennedy about communism and Marxism, going as far back as the French

Revolution. Conflicts were inevitable; ideas belonged to no one nation. Once born, ideas should be cultivated:

> If Communist ideas should spread in other countries, the USSR would be happy, just as the US would be glad if capitalist ideas were to spread. In any event, the spread of ideas should depend on peoples alone. Ideas should not be borne on bayonets or on missile warheads.

When Kennedy lamely interjected that "Mao Tse Tung had said that power was at the end of the rifle," Khrushchev accused him of misunderstanding the Chinese leader. "Mao Tse Tung is a Marxist and Marxists have always been against war."

In the afternoon session, Kennedy improved his dialogue. When Khrushchev remarked that the United States supported undemocratic governments, specifically Spain and Iran, the president brought up Soviet-dominated Poland. If given a free choice, the people of Poland probably would not endorse the current Communist government.

The president then zeroed in on the crisis in Laos. He suggested that the two superpowers use their influence to create a cease-fire and an independent neutral Laos; Khrushchev, surprisingly, agreed.

Several times during the summit Kennedy backed Khrushchev into a corner, forcing the Soviet premier to change the subject. Kennedy's immersion in previous American-Soviet discussions and his meticulous preparation allowed him to weather some of Khrushchev's bluster. Khrushchev demanded the withdrawal of Allied troops from Germany, noting that President Roosevelt had promised to make such a withdrawal within two to four years after the war ended. "President Roosevelt said we would withdraw our troops if Germany was reunited under one government," Kennedy countered. Khrushchev had no response.

At another point in a heated debate, Kennedy asked, "Do you ever admit a mistake?"

"Certainly," Khrushchev replied. "In a speech before the Twentieth Party Congress, I admitted all of Stalin's mistakes."

"Those were Stalin's mistakes," Kennedy countered. "Not your mistakes." Again Khrushchev did not respond.

The third session, held at the Soviet embassy, began at 10:15 a.m. on June 4. Khrushchev steered the subject to disarmament. Referring to the U.S. demand for twenty annual on-site inspections of underground nuclear tests, Khrushchev insisted that the Soviet Union would accept only three; any more would threaten Soviet sovereignty and make it easier for the United States to engage in espionage. Khrushchev linked the issue of nuclear tests with disarmament. He had repeatedly argued that the USSR wanted general and complete disarmament.

The president couldn't agree to only three inspections. The U.S. Senate, he said, would never accept a test ban without a foolproof control system to prevent cheating. The test ban alone was not very important, Khrushchev contended; what was needed was general and complete disarmament. If the two countries failed to reach agreement on a nuclear test ban, other countries would probably launch a nuclear weapons program, the president replied.

With general and complete disarmament, Khrushchev said, nuclear weapons would be eliminated altogether. If both sides accepted general and complete disarmament, the president inquired, would the Soviet Union accept inspection any place in the USSR? Contradicting his earlier expression of fear of espionage, Khrushchev replied in the affirmative, saying "absolutely."

When the discussion turned to Berlin, the crucial issue, Khrushchev displayed intense animation. He confronted Kennedy with an ultimatum and a dilemma: the two sides could sign a treaty accepting the existence of two Germanys, or Khrushchev would be forced to sign a separate treaty with East Germany no later than December 1961. He wanted to reach agreement with the West on a treaty, Khrushchev said, but if the United States refused, the Soviet Union would sign a treaty with East Germany by itself.

Kennedy understood that a treaty acknowledging two Germanys would cancel all existing commitments—occupation rights, administrative institutions, and rights of access. The German Democratic Republic would control West Berlin's communications, and agreement on access would have to be reached with the Democratic Republic, an intolerable situation for the West. West Berlin, in effect, would gradually be gobbled up by Communist East Germany.

Every U.S. president since World War II had been committed to West Berlin by treaty and other contractual rights, Kennedy pointed out.

> If we were expelled from that area and if we accepted the loss of our rights no one would have any confidence in U.S. commitments and pledges. U.S. national security is involved in this matter because if we were to accept the Soviet proposal U.S. commitments would be regarded as a mere scrap of paper.

The Soviet leader responded that he "was very sorry but he had to assure the President that no force in the world would prevent the USSR from signing a peace treaty."

Khrushchev's argument was transparently insincere. If only the Berlin issue could be resolved, he suggested, mutual relations would improve. Why didn't the president accept the Soviet Union's "good intentions and motivations"? It was one thing for the Soviets to transfer their rights to the German Democratic Republic, Kennedy retorted; it was an altogether different matter for the USSR to give away U.S. rights.

The Soviet Union would probably sign a peace treaty at the end of the year, Khrushchev insisted, with all the ensuing consequences. It wasn't the United States that precipitated the new crisis, Kennedy declared; Khrushchev was aggravating the situation by seeking to change the status quo. Simply signing a peace treaty was not the crucial issue, the president repeated. The matter of a peace treaty with East Germany was a matter for Khrushchev's judgment and was not a belligerent act. "What is a belligerent act is transfer of our rights to East Germany."

After the last scheduled session, Kennedy insisted on one more chance to reach an understanding with Khrushchev. "We're not going on time," he barked at his staff. "I'm not going to leave until I know more."

In their extra session, Kennedy reiterated that it was the chairman, not he, who wanted to force a change. Khrushchev replied that a peace treaty would involve no change in boundaries—avoiding reference to the change in control of West Berlin. His decision to sign a peace treaty was firm and irrevocable; the Soviet Union would sign it in December if the United States refused an interim agreement. "If that is true," Kennedy responded, "it is going to be a cold winter."

"He just beat hell out of me," the stunned president told James Reston shortly after the last session. "I've got a terrible problem. If he thinks I'm inexperienced and have no guts, until we remove those ideas we won't get anywhere with him. So we have to act."

Arthur Schlesinger judged that the president "had never encountered any leader with whom he could not exchange ideas—anyone so impervious to reasoned argument or so apparently indifferent to the prospective obliteration of mankind. . . . Berlin held the threat, if not the certitude, of war."

Kennedy made an obvious mistake at the summit by allowing himself to be drawn into an abstract ideological debate on Marxist theory and the role of historical inevitability. His shallow understanding of Marxism played to Khrushchev's advantage. Kennedy did much better by staying with his pragmatic arguments.

How did Kennedy perform at the summit? Yuri Barsukov, Washington correspondent for the Soviet newspaper *Izvestia*, contended the Soviet leader was surprised to find "in John Kennedy such an inexperienced politician." Viktor Sukhodrev, Khrushchev's interpreter, thought the Soviet leader came away from Vienna with a poor impression of Kennedy, a feeling that "the guy was inexperienced, perhaps not up to the task of properly running a country such as the United States." "I think Khrushchev . . . thought that he'd gotten away with many of these talking points; that he had placed President Kennedy in a state of confusion where he had nothing to say in return," said George Kennan.

The notion that Kennedy was weak, confused, and humiliated at Vienna is incorrect. "That judgment comes mostly from Kennedy's own gloomy view of the meeting, and the way he backgrounded James Reston instantly after the meeting and the way [Reston] reported that," McGeorge Bundy explained. Kennedy was upset because the Soviet leader refused to budge. Their conversation didn't suggest weakness or humiliation; nor did the premier confuse or intimidate. Kennedy did what he always did and did well: he listened.

Most of the time Kennedy was in good form—precise, logical, and informed. Both men were unyielding and vigorous in argument. "Kennedy carried the conversational initiative, introducing topics, keeping them specific, bringing straying discussions back to the question and pressing Khrushchev for answers," Sorensen accurately summarized. "Khrushchev usually talked at much greater length. Kennedy usually talked with much greater precision." "I think the President handled the thing exceedingly well. I think he made a great impression on Mr. Khrushchev," the diplomat Llewellyn Thompson concluded.

Kennedy himself insisted that the confrontation had been "invaluable," providing him "a clearer idea of the intensity of the struggle we are in." What's more, despite their differences, the leaders established rapport, making it easier to communicate in their future correspondence.

For weeks afterward the Vienna confrontation preoccupied Kennedy. He took personal charge of the planning discussions to meet the Berlin crisis. At times the work consumed him. When Kennedy asked veteran diplomat Dean Acheson to present his recommendations for handling the crisis, the former secretary of state argued that Khrushchev was testing American resolve: Berlin was "not a problem but a pretext." The Soviets would interpret any attempt to negotiate as a sign of American weakness. They hoped "to neutralize Berlin as a first step and prepare for its eventual takeover by the German Democratic Republic." In addition, the Kremlin hoped "to weaken if not break up the NATO Alliance." Finally, Khrushchev wanted "to discredit the United States or at least seriously damage its prestige," allowing the Soviets to extend their influence throughout Europe. The United States must be willing to use nuclear weapons rather than allow Khrushchev to get away with his demands. Acheson urged the president to call up reserves, move more troops and aircraft to Europe, increase defense appropriations, resume nuclear testing, and declare a state of national emergency.

In the end, Kennedy overruled Acheson on several points. "We have nothing to fear from negotiations," he said, "and nothing to gain by refusing to take part in them." Nor would he declare a state of national emergency. That was too drastic and could be effective only once. Better to wait and see if the Soviets actually signed a treaty or blocked access to West Berlin.

Nonetheless, to impress the Soviets with America's determination, Kennedy called for a significant military buildup. The United States would send six new divisions to Europe by the end of the year, and the president would ask Congress for standby authority to triple draft calls and to call up reserves.

On July 25, in a nationally televised address from the Oval Office, Kennedy delivered a strong and urgent message but steered clear of threats. The United States would combine military proposals with diplomatic measures. It wished to negotiate, to talk, to listen, but only about reasonable proposals. The freedom of Berlin was not negotiable:

We cannot negotiate with those who say, "What's mine is mine and what's yours is negotiable.". . . The source of world trouble and tension is Moscow, not Berlin. And if war begins, it will have begun in Moscow and not Berlin.

A Gallup poll showed that 85 percent of Americans were ready to risk war to keep U.S. troops in Berlin. On July 28 the Senate unanimously approved Kennedy's defense buildup.

After Vienna, events turned sour for Khrushchev. Instead of retreating, Kennedy held firm. Meanwhile the Soviets were spending a fortune subsidizing the collapsing East German economy. The GDR's Walter Ulbricht had few options as refugees fled to the West, including physicians, engineers, teachers, and other professionals. Between 1945 and 1960 nearly 4.3 million Germans took flight from the German Democratic Republic, and the problem was growing worse.

Because East Germany was hemorrhaging, Khrushchev fell back on Ulbricht's earlier suggestion to erect a wall. On August 13, 1961, the East Germans constructed a physical barrier along the boundary with West Berlin using obstacles and barbed wire; construction of a concrete wall began six days later.

Kennedy quickly realized that the wall was less a problem than a solution. "Why would Khrushchev put up a wall if he really intended to seize West Berlin?" he said privately to his aides. "There wouldn't be any need of a wall if he occupied the whole city. This is his way out of his predicament. It's not a very nice solution, but a wall is a hell of a lot better than a war."

On August 14 Kennedy urged Rusk "to exploit politically propagandawise" the closing of the border:

This seems to me to show how hollow is the phrase "free city" and how despised is the East German government, which the Soviet Union seeks to make respectable. . . . It offers us a very good propaganda stick which if the situation were reversed would be well used in beating us. It seems to me this requires decisions at the highest level.

The Berlin Wall, viewed as a crisis in West Berlin and West Germany, did not turn into a crisis for Kennedy. Republicans were not critical, nor were the media, and hard-line columnists mostly supported the president.

As Kennedy and his advisers discreetly reconciled themselves to the benefits of the Berlin Wall, American policy on Germany broke loose "from what was, in effect, West Germany's domination of it," noted historian John Gaddis. The wall changed the cold war. "From this point on it is possible to trace the start of the European détente, based upon a shift in West Germany's foreign policy to a tolerance of the territorial status quo and a readiness to open up lines of communication to the East," wrote Lawrence Freedman.

Kennedy narrowly defined American goals in Germany: the presence of Allied forces in West Berlin, physical access and security for the city, and the security of West Germany against attacks from the East. He would not use force to end the "de facto division of Germany" or the "de facto absorption of East Berlin into East Germany."

Kennedy continued to monitor events in West Berlin, always trying to put the problem into cold storage. Stave off a crisis for ten years until the world situation changed, he believed.

For the most part, Kennedy's statecraft during the Berlin crisis was successful. Unlike his handling of the Bay of Pigs misadventure, he wisely managed the crisis by combining power with creative negotiations. He had been tempered and measured in the way he used the nation's nuclear capacity as a diplomatic weapon. His combination of firmness and negotiations helped resolve the Berlin crisis, put it on ice, and reduce its explosive potential.

8

Domestic Affairs and the Economy

ALTHOUGH KENNEDY had promised to provide dynamic leadership in dealing with Congress, as it turned out he had precious little political capital when he came into office. The close margin of his election victory did not convey a mandate for any of his initiatives.

The Eisenhower administration had created the White House Office of Congressional Relations, but Larry O'Brien centralized the operation and made it systematic and aggressive. The amiable O'Brien was the primary lobbyist for the White House on Capitol Hill, and well liked. Some judged him the ablest man in the administration. Yet the Kennedy-O'Brien operation encountered nearly insurmountable obstacles. With no national depression, no mass unemployment prompting constituents to demand government action, the New Frontier operated in a milieu vastly different from Roosevelt's New Deal. Senate Majority Leader Mike Mansfield blamed the "strangely quiescent" mood of the country: "It isn't stirred to any degree."

Since Republican support was negligible on nondefense issues, Kennedy needed to win at least fifty conservative Southern Democrats in the House in order to enact administration bills. He flattered Southern legislators, channeled patronage southward, and kept civil rights legislation off his agenda for two years.

"Of our defeats, none was more bitter than our inability to pass the bill to provide federal aid to elementary and secondary education," O'Brien reflected. Three days before Kennedy's inauguration, Francis Cardinal Spellman of New York savaged the recommendations of Kennedy's task force on education, which had urged federal aid only to the public schools. The proposal was "unfair," "blatantly discriminating," and "unthinkable"; it made Catholic children "second-class citizens."

On February 20, 1961, Kennedy recommended $2.3 billion over three years for general federal aid for public elementary and secondary classroom construction and teachers' salaries, but he did not include parochial schools because of "the clear prohibition of the Constitution." In early March Kennedy proposed two major programs for higher education: $2.8 billion in loans over five years for academic facilities, and $892 million for more than 200,000 four-year college scholarships, based on merit and need.

Negotiations with Congress and attempts at compromise followed. In July 1961, while the House Rules Committee was considering Kennedy's education bills, a single congressman became crucial: Democrat Jim Delaney, a Catholic from Queens, New York, who had a large Catholic constituency. Delaney normally voted with the administration, but he decided on principle that he could not support aid to public schools and not to Catholic schools as well. On July 18 the Rules Committee, with Delaney joining the opposition, voted 8 to 7 to table all the education bills, destroying Kennedy's education program.

Kennedy had no intention of bludgeoning or punishing members of Congress. "Had [Delaney] been bargaining, holding out for some patronage plum, we might have done business, but the only thing he wanted was the one thing Kennedy could not give—federal aid to Catholic schools," said O'Brien.

Medical care for the aged—Medicare, as it was later called—was another major domestic goal. Throughout the 1950s Congress had debated the issue. Organized labor, a few Republicans, liberal Democrats (including Kennedy), Northern urban legislators, and the liberal lobby Americans for Democratic Action supported a compulsory health insurance program for people over sixty-five, financed through the Social Security payroll tax. Opponents included most Republicans and Southern Democrats in Congress, business and insurance groups, and the influential American Medical Association (AMA)—they pushed for a voluntary system and a narrower federal role. In 1960 Congress enacted the limited Kerr-Mills Medical Assistance for the Aged (MAA) program. When Eisenhower left office, health insurance remained a major political issue, largely because the Kerr-Mills solution was piecemeal and ineffective.

On February 9, 1961, Kennedy sent Congress a message calling for the extension of Social Security benefits for fourteen million Americans over sixty-five to cover hospital and nursing-home costs. A small increase in Social Security taxes would finance the benefits. "The program," Kennedy stated, "is not socialized medicine. . . . It is a program of prepayment for health costs with absolute freedom of choice guaranteed. Every person will choose his own doctor and hospital."

The AMA discovered that the most effective technique to combat the administration's bill, known as King-Anderson, was to label it "socialized medicine," and to link socialized medicine with poor-quality health care, impersonal service, overcrowded hospitals, and the specter of the Soviet Union.

The fate of the Medicare proposal lay with the House Ways and Means Committee, chaired by Democrat Wilbur Mills of Arkansas, who had co-sponsored Kerr-Mills. The influence of Mills within Ways and Means was crucial, and the administration's lobbyists concentrated on persuading him to support the president's program. If convinced, he could carry the committee with him.

But in 1962 the administration still did not have a majority in Ways and Means to report out its bill. Only eleven members out of twenty-five favored the legislation. The impasse continued. The Senate too failed to pass Kennedy's medical bill. In 1963 the president put Medicare on hold; he told the media that he would get a bill out in 1964.

Congress did endorse Kennedy's call for a major new space program. In 1958, reacting to the Soviet's success with *Sputnik* the year before, President Eisenhower approved the creation of the National Aeronautics and Space Administration (NASA), an agency that began to organize resources for the U.S. space program.

On April 12, 1961, three months after Kennedy's inauguration, Moscow announced that Cosmonaut Yuri Gagarin had executed an orbital flight around the earth, becoming the first human in space. Jubilant Soviet leaders used Gagarin's flight to promote themselves and the Communist system to the world's peoples.

Gagarin's achievement ignited the president's intense competitive spirit. In the six weeks after the Soviet success he gathered recommendations, then presented his case to a joint session of Congress on May 25: "I believe we should go to the moon . . . before this decade is out."

The president's goal struck a responsive chord. Within a few months Congress increased NASA's budget enormously. "Between 1961 and 1963 NASA's payroll swelled from 16,500 people to more than 28,000, and the number of contractors working on the space program grew from less than 60,000 to more than 200,000," observed historians John Logsdon and Alain Dupas.

Liberal critics contended that the space program drained money from housing, education, and other domestic programs. Senator William Fulbright urged the president to spend less on the space race and more on education and urban renewal. "Bill,

I completely agree with you," the president responded. "But you and I know that Congress would never pass that much money for education. They'll spend it on a space program, and we need those billions of dollars in the economy to create jobs."

The space program boosted America's prestige. "It harnessed American technological and organization skill, showed what government could do, and harmed nothing," noted historian Carl Brauer. "Some people argued that it drained funds from more pressing objectives, but Kennedy was almost certainly right to observe that Congress would not have appropriated funds for *those* objectives."

A Peace Corps was on Kennedy's mind the day after his inauguration, when he phoned Sargent Shriver and asked him to form a presidential task force on the feasibility of such a program. Shriver recommended that Kennedy issue an executive order granting the new organization life through its first year while awaiting congressional approval. Kennedy agreed and signed the order on March 1.

After four months of brilliant lobbying, Shriver succeeded in convincing Congress to establish permanently an independent Peace Corps. Kennedy praised Shriver's astonishing success with Congress, calling him "the most effective lobbyist on the Washington scene."

Because of his other responsibilities and Shriver's competence, Kennedy seldom focused on the Peace Corps. Shriver used the president mainly to publicize the agency. Kennedy cared about the Peace Corps and never turned down Shriver's requests. When Ambassador John Kenneth Galbraith returned from his post in India, Kennedy asked, "How are Sarge's kids doing?"

Although the Peace Corps failed to stimulate economic growth in host countries, it succeeded in other ways. It brought an understanding of Third World nations, improved the lives of poor people, and showed America's idealistic side.

Two other important programs initiated modestly during the Kennedy administration bore fruit after the president's death. In September 1962, in an article in the *Saturday Evening Post*, Eunice Kennedy Shriver candidly wrote about her sister Rosemary's retardation, exposing for the first time Rosemary's real condition. "It was a historic moment in the history of mental retardation in America," observed Lawrence Leamer. "By any measure, the article represented the Kennedys at their most exemplary."

At the request of his sister, the president attended receptions and spoke to several groups interested in the issue. He appointed a 26-member President's Panel on Mental Retardation. After reviewing the panel's report, with its 112 recommendations, he addressed Congress on February 5, 1963, clearly outlining the challenge:

> We as a Nation have long neglected the mentally ill and the mentally retarded. This neglect must end, if our Nation is to live up to its own standards of compassion and dignity and achieve the maximum use of its manpower.

Over the next 20 years Congress passed 116 laws or amendments providing support for the mentally retarded and their families. By 1976 federal agencies administered 135 special funding programs.

During the 1960 campaign Kennedy had made only a few references to poverty, referring instead to the need to find jobs for the unemployed. Nor did he focus on poverty during the first two years of his presidency, partly because there was no strong public concern for an anti-poverty program. Yet the problem had attracted the attention of academics and social critics. In *The Other America* (1962), Michael Harrington maintained that poverty was hidden, "disguised by inexpensive clothing and concealed by beltways and interstate highways that no longer required driving through decaying inner cities and blighted rural areas." Puerto Ricans in New York, Hispanics in the Southwest, blacks in ghettos, Indians on reservations, the elderly, and many rural people comprised the "other America." In the *New Yorker* in January 1963,

Dwight Macdonald vividly analyzed all the recent literature about poverty.

Kennedy read Harrington's book and Macdonald's essay. He also sensed "a greater public concern because of recent studies on poverty—including a TV documentary—and a spiraling civil rights movement that exposed black deprivation," noted historian James Giglio. And there was another factor: the tax reduction Kennedy pushed would stimulate the entire economy but would not help people too poor to pay income taxes. A poverty program might offset the accusation that the administration's tax cut favored only the middle and upper classes.

In December 1962 the president said to Walter Heller, his chief economic adviser, "Give me facts and figures on the things we still have to do. For example, what about the poverty problem in the United States?" The suggestion stimulated the staff thinking needed to formulate a war on poverty. On November 5, 1963, Heller wrote department heads requesting that they submit proposals for an anti-poverty program. Their recommendations should "concentrate on relatively few groups and areas" where problems were most serious and solutions most feasible. They should minimize handouts, maximize self-help, and emphasize the prevention of poverty.

Kennedy made no final decision to proceed publicly. Before leaving on his trip to Dallas in November 1963, he told Heller to continue his planning. "First, we'll have your tax cut; then we'll have my expenditures program."

In the end Congress failed to pass Medicare or Kennedy's education bills, but Larry O'Brien proudly listed many other legislative successes: a four-year, $451 million Area Redevelopment program; a major trade bill; a tax reform bill; an International Wheat Agreement treaty; the Communications Satellite Act; a $435 million Manpower Development and Training Act, providing job training for the unemployed; and others.

Historians, critics, and frustrated supporters of the Kennedy program emphasize the president's limitations for his failure to pass major liberal proposals. They claim he didn't have his heart in congressional relations, wasn't good at the small talk most congressmen enjoyed, and was too timid. Legislators expected arm twisting and pressure rather than reason and persuasion. Columnist Walter Lippmann accused the president of failing to educate and mobilize the electorate on the importance of his program.

Kennedy did have limitations in dealing with Congress, but he tried hard. Lippmann's accusation riled Kennedy's advisers. They countered that the president sold himself and his policies in a subtle but more effective way. "Everyone yells about the need for more education on the President's program," one Kennedy lieutenant declared. "We feel they are out of touch, not we. Everything the President does sells his program." He was, in fact, an active publicist, discussing his ideas and programs in speeches and press conferences, and in conversations with opinion-makers.

The president made it clear that Larry O'Brien was to have direct and frequent contact with him. He signaled to everyone that O'Brien was his personal representative for legislation and contact with legislators. When anyone, even prominent members of Congress, suggested legislation to him, his reply was, "Have you discussed this with Larry O'Brien?"

The president often invited congressmen in groups of fifteen to the White House to socialize, and the liaison staff brought individual congressmen to visit the president for private chats. On Tuesday mornings Kennedy huddled with Democratic legislative leaders over breakfast. Informal but businesslike, they focused on the president's thoughts about legislation. "He was always courteous to us," said Mansfield. "He asked us for our views, and he gave them consideration."

In 1961 Kennedy hosted thirty-two Tuesday morning leadership breakfasts and held about ninety private conversations with congressional leaders. "All in all, Kennedy had about 2,500 separate contacts with members of Congress during his first year in office," O'Brien recalled. Most of O'Brien's "social" life during Kennedy's presidency involved entertaining members of Congress.

The primary reason the president failed to enact more of his program was simple arithmetic. After the 1960 election Democrats controlled the House, 263 to 174, and the Senate, 64 to 36, but the numbers misled because many of the members were part of the anti–New Deal coalition of conservative Southern Democrats and conservative Republicans. The conservative coalition controlled 285 of the 437 members in the House and 59 of 96 in the Senate. Conservative Southern Democrats controlled two-thirds of Senate committees, including Armed Services, Judiciary, Foreign Relations, and Finance. The same situation existed in the House.

Thus Congress failed to enact Kennedy's major domestic programs primarily because the voters who elected him did not vote in enough members of Congress to support the New Frontier. In 1964 Democrats gained thirty-nine additional seats in the House. The election gave President Lyndon Johnson the luxury of a working majority, enabling him to pass major legislation in the congressional sessions of 1965 and 1966. In the 1966 midterm elections, Johnson lost most of that majority and his Great Society stalled. Had he lived, Kennedy would have had a working majority after the 1964 election as well, and would have been able to enact his program.

"A myth has arisen that [Kennedy] was uninterested in Congress, or that he 'failed' with Congress," Larry O'Brien lamented. O'Brien contended that even when Kennedy's program failed, it was building toward the future. "We could not pass Medicare in 1961–63, but we raised the issue, we forced our opponents to go on record against it, and we paved the way for its eventual passage in 1965," said O'Brien. "I would take nothing from Lyndon Johnson's brilliant and tireless performance with Congress, but I believe that, had Kennedy lived, his record in his second term would have been comparable to the record Johnson established."

*

Sluggish economic growth, slack demand, and high unemployment (6.7 percent) faced Kennedy when he became president. During the Eisenhower era the nation had experienced three recessions in seven years. Yet people seemed complacent and not amenable to changes in economic policy. "The major barrier to getting the country's economy moving again lay in the economic ignorance and stereotypes that prevailed in the land," contended Walter Heller, the new chairman of the Council of Economic Advisers (CEA).

John Maynard Keynes, the brilliant British economist, had convincingly argued during the Great Depression that governments did not have to sit idly by while "imperfect markets inflicted misery on mankind." A government had two methods to control the economy rationally, Keynes suggested. It could regulate the money supply (monetary policy) and had the power to tax and spend (fiscal policy). "Using these tools to manipulate aggregate demand, political leaders could make capitalism work properly," noted author Allen Matusow.

After World War II liberal economists in Europe and in American universities contended that it was not necessary to redistribute the wealth of the rich in order to improve the condition of the poor. By applying proper economic measures, the total amount of wealth could be increased, benefiting everyone. Keynesian ideas, continually updated and modified, became the new academic orthodoxy. Nonetheless, by 1961 few politicians had learned the Keynesian lessons, nor had much of the public been converted.

All the members of Kennedy's Council of Economic Advisers—Heller, James Tobin of Yale, and Kermit Gordon of Williams College—were widely respected Keynesian economists. They hoped to teach the president modern economics. A budget surplus, they contended, though needed to cool down an inflationary economy, was a "fiscal drag" on recovery from a recession and would result in another economic downturn before the country reached full employment. High tax levels drained needed purchasing power and caused expansion to stop short of full employment.

The president, they advised, should concentrate on full employment and willingly accept substantial federal deficits even during an economic recovery. A large pool of potential workers far exceeded the supply of jobs. "Unless the economy grew fast enough to create new jobs as rapidly as the manpower tide increased, there would be no end to recurring recessions, or even to high unemployment in the midst of prosperity," Sorensen reflected. Not overly worried about inflation, Heller and the CEA were confident they could control its consequences if it became a problem.

Kennedy would have liked to stimulate economic expansion by increasing government expenditures, but opposition to new spending programs in Congress blocked this route. The conservative-dominated Congress would support large increases in federal spending only for defense and space programs; it would never support increased spending for federal aid to education, "socialized medicine," or other social measures. And Congress insisted on a balanced budget.

Thus the president and his advisers needed a program that was not only economically workable but politically marketable. Kennedy doubted that tax-cutting was politically marketable. In his inaugural address he had stressed the need to sacrifice; a tax cut was inconsistent with that message. His theme of sacrifice, his narrow victory margin, and the demand for "fiscal responsibility" hemmed him in.

Popular myths about the economy could not be changed overnight, and until people were better informed, Kennedy thought it was political suicide to push the CEA's approach. Nonetheless he showed a willingness to learn. Surrounded by brilliant economists, he soaked up information and asked incisive questions. He insisted on seeing economic reports as quickly as possible; memos and letters from economists should immediately be brought to his attention. "Mr. Heller,"

Evelyn Lincoln informed the economist, "President Kennedy read every memorandum you ever sent him from cover to cover." He wanted facts and perceptive analysis. "We were often amazed at his capacity for understanding a particular set of relationships in economics," said Heller, who added proudly that Kennedy was "the best student" he ever had.

Heller's effort to educate the president was finally rewarded in the summer of 1962. When Treasury Secretary Douglas Dillon also saw the benefit of a massive stimulant for the slack economy, Kennedy agreed to seek a major tax reduction. Although the economy had clearly been improving in 1961, it was doing so only gradually. Again the issue arose: why a tax cut instead of an expenditure program? Liberals such as Galbraith favored the Keynesian alternative to a general tax cut: a large increase in federal spending to improve housing, schools, hospitals, and welfare programs.

Heller conceded that the nation badly needed federal social programs, but there were two problems with Galbraith's approach. Even if Congress agreed to appropriate the added billions for social programs—an unlikely event—how could the money be spent in time? "Attempts to enlarge spending at the rate required to do the economic job would lead to waste, bottlenecks, profiteering, and scandal," Heller argued.

The second problem was political. An expansion of spending would bring charges of "fiscal irresponsibility" in the same way tax cuts would. "But on top of this would be all of the opposition to expansion of government, to over-centralization, to a 'power grab' and a 'take-over' of the cities, the educational system, the housing market." "A vigorous economy, stimulated by tax cuts," Heller concluded, "will provide a broader economic base and an atmosphere of prosperity and flushness in which government programs can vie much more successfully for their fair share of a bigger pie."

Kennedy agreed with Heller and sought to educate the public about the "myths," "truisms," "clichés," and "stale phrases" that obscured truths about U.S. economic life. Privately Kennedy told key advisers: "If this policy is right it will pay off in the long run; that is what interests me, not the ephemeral day-to-day popularity that is readily available. . . . If it works, people will like what the final result is even if it takes two or three years."

In January 1963 Kennedy asked Congress to reduce taxes by $13.5 billion. The tax cut was designed to stimulate the economy as consumers spent more money. Then, explained economist Robert Heilbroner, "tax revenues would also rise, and in the end the budget would be balanced at a higher level of national output than if there had been no cut in the first place."

The tax-cut legislation passed the House on September 25, 1963. The Revenue Act, eventually enacted under President Johnson in 1964, had the effect Kennedy had hoped. The Kennedy "boom," begun unspectacularly in the spring of 1961, became the longest peacetime period of prosperity in modern U.S. history. In 1966 nearly 5.5 million more people were employed than in 1961. Corporate earnings soared; between 1961 and 1965 profits after taxes improved by almost 70 percent. The growth of real per capita income—which had risen 5.9 percent between 1946 and 1950, and another 15.2 percent in the 1950s—in the 1960s rose spectacularly by 31.7 percent.

Kennedy wanted the support of business for all his economic initiatives. Several of the administration's actions were favorable to business—private ownership of the Communications Satellite Corporation, more liberal depreciation allowances, trade expansion, and lower taxes. One issue, though, created severe tension with the business community.

Ideally the interplay of market forces established wages and prices without government intervention. During World War II and the Korean War the federal government had imposed wage and price controls. In the absence of wartime controls the Council of Economic Advisers sought another method to restrain inflation. Economic historian Kim McQuaid observed that Kennedy wanted to control the process "whereby powerful unions forced higher and higher costs upon industry and equally powerful industrial combines then passed such increased costs on to the public in the form of ever higher prices."

Modern economists had designed wage and price guidelines to equate price and productivity levels. They calculated the average annual productivity increase in American industry after World War II, a figure initially set at 3.2 percent per year. McQuaid explained:

> If . . . workers in an industry where productivity had been growing at the average 3.2 percent rate wanted a wage increase, they could obtain up to a 3.2-percent hike without their employer's having to raise prices to recoup the profits lost to increased production costs. In this situation, prices would remain stable and neither management nor labor would lose anything.

In its Annual Report of January 1962, the Council of Economic Advisers for the first time established voluntary informal wage and price guidelines. With these published guidelines, public opinion and presidential persuasion could hopefully counteract the market power of strong unions and strong businesses. To be noninflationary, wage and price decisions had to be geared to productivity increases, and those decisions, the administration hoped, would be measured against the CEA's published guidelines.

The White House stayed in close contact with labor-management talks in several major industries, but one in particular: the steel industry. In late March 1962, when negotiators led by Secretary of Labor Arthur Goldberg managed to convince both sides to agree on a noninflationary pact, Kennedy was delighted. The settlement protected worker job security and cost only 2.5 percent, well within the CEA's wage-price guidelines. Because the agreement seemed to make unnecessary a price increase by steel companies, the settlement was a major victory for collective bargaining and for the president's intense desire to control inflation. Neither side complained about the settlement. The steelworkers' union, which in previous contracts had received wage hikes as high as 8 percent, settled for much less.

Then, on April 10, 1962, during an appointment at the White House, U.S. Steel's chairman Roger Blough handed Kennedy a memo declaring that his company would immediately raise prices on its products by 3.5 percent, or six dollars a ton. Nearly every other major steel company immediately followed suit.

Stunned, Kennedy told Blough he was making a mistake. Dismayed, Arthur Goldberg tendered his resignation, insisting he had lost credibility with labor because of Blough's action. (Kennedy did not accept his resignation.) "You kept silent, and silence is consent," Goldberg told Blough. "One thing you owe a President is candor."

Kennedy viewed Blough's action as a personal affront. Blough's decision would undermine Kennedy's prestige with labor and his program to control inflation. "They kicked us right in the balls," Kennedy angrily told *Washington* Post senior editor Ben Bradlee. "Are we supposed to sit there and take a cold, deliberate fucking. . . . They fucked us, and we've got to try to fuck them."

At his next press conference the president pointed out the simultaneous and identical actions of U.S. Steel and other major steel corporations. Increasing steel prices by six dollars a ton was totally unjustified and an irresponsible defiance of the public interest.

> In this serious hour in our nation's history, when we are confronted with grave crises in Berlin and Southeast Asia, when we are devoting our energies to economic recovery and stability, when we are asking reservists to leave their homes and families for months on end and servicemen to risk their lives . . . and asking union members to hold down their wage increases, at a time when restraint and sacrifice are being asked

of every citizen, the American people will find it hard, as I do, to accept a situation in which a tiny handful of steel executives, whose pursuit of power and profit exceeds their sense of public responsibility, can show such utter contempt for the interests of 185 million Americans.

Attorney General Robert Kennedy immediately convened a grand jury to investigate whether the steel companies had violated the law. "I told the FBI to interview them all—march into their offices the next day. . . . All of them were subpoenaed for their personal records and . . . their company records." The White House produced facts and figures to prove that U.S. Steel did not need to raise prices.

Shortly after, U.S. Steel and the steel companies that followed its lead rescinded their price increases. Kennedy had forced the steel companies to capitulate, but the administration's tactics led critics to scream "Gestapo," "secret police." At a news conference on April 18, Kennedy claimed he harbored "no ill will against any individual, any industry, corporation, or segment of the American economy." A few days later, though, a reliable report circulated that Kennedy had privately remarked that his father had always told him that all businessmen were "sons-of-bitches," but he never believed it until Blough double-crossed him. The story first appeared in the *New York Times* on April 23. Two weeks later, asked about the remark, Kennedy awkwardly declared that his comment was not meant to apply to "all" businessmen, but he did not deny having said it. Once it became public, Kennedy's "son-of-a-bitch" remark further alienated the business community.

In all, the Kennedy administration's "coercion" of the steel companies frightened the business community and severely strained relations. The damage was "irreparable," wrote *Business Week*. A survey of six thousand business executives in June 1962 found that 52 percent described the administration as "strongly anti-business," and 36 percent as "moderately anti-business."

Little could be done to allay the suspicion of business, Sorensen wrote the president. "Businessmen have a natural dislike for the President, his party, his advisers and his program." Nonetheless a few new approaches might alleviate the hostility. Small groups of business leaders should be invited to presidential luncheons or black-tie stag dinners. Each Cabinet member should host similar gatherings for businessmen affected by his operations. Perhaps the Securities and Exchange Commission could tone down its investigations, Sorensen suggested.

Kennedy's friendly gestures toward business did increase after the steel crisis. He invited more businessmen to social events and for private talks at the White House. He asked their help in securing a tax cut. He did not oppose a steel price increase in 1963, and no longer emphasized the guidelines on price and wage policy. "Businessmen who are seeing the President in growing numbers report that he is a sympathetic listener," reported *U.S. News and World Report.*

By early 1963 some business circles looked more favorably on Kennedy. Criticism continued, "but it was neither as pervasive nor as harsh as it had been during the preceding eighteen months," noted historian Jim Heath. A financial columnist wrote, "The Kennedy Administration is cooperating and trusting U.S. business to a degree unprecedented in modern times." Indeed, Kennedy did try to cooperate with business. They needed each other.

9

Civil Rights

INITIALLY President Kennedy's goal was to control the civil rights movement: moderate its tactics, channel its demands toward voting, and limit the social instability it was causing in the South. This proved a daunting task because he underestimated the passion, energy, and idealism of the movement.

Kennedy faced his first civil rights crisis four months after the inauguration. In early May 1961 a band of six whites and seven Negroes set out by bus to ride from Washington to New Orleans. Calling themselves Freedom Riders, the group provoked trouble, hoping to prove that Southern interstate travel remained segregated in fact, though integrated by law.

Near Anniston, Alabama, a white mob hurled an incendiary bomb through a window of the bus, setting it afire. As it filled with black, acrid smoke, the frightened riders tried to escape, only to be beaten up by white toughs.

The bus-burning in Anniston caught the attention of John and Robert Kennedy. Dismayed and exasperated, the White House desperately a wanted to avoid a confrontation with white Southern authorities. The timing was crucial. The president, embarrassed by the disaster at the Bay of Pigs only a few weeks earlier, was about to confront Nikita Khrushchev at the summit conference in Vienna. The violence the Freedom

Riders provoked focused unwanted international attention on U.S. racism.

Although frustrated with the Freedom Riders, Robert Kennedy believed that if Alabama officials shirked their duty to protect the riders in the peaceful pursuit of their constitutional rights to travel and speak, the federal government must ensure those rights. On May 21 he sent a force of four hundred federal marshals to Alabama.

Continuing Freedom Rides forced the administration to take further action. Under heavy pressure from Robert Kennedy, the Interstate Commerce Commission brought an end to all segregation signs in railroad, airport, and bus terminals.

Immediately after his inauguration, Kennedy mobilized the full powers of the executive branch to advance civil rights through executive action: litigation, negotiation, persuasion, appointments, directives, and an executive order—but not new legislation. "Next to Eisenhower, Kennedy seemed a breath of fresh air to many blacks," observes James Giglio. "Symbolic gestures abounded." At the inauguration parade the president noticed the all-white Coast Guard unit. Afterward he pressured the academy to integrate. He also invited more Negroes to White House meetings and social functions than any previous president. The administration filled key positions with supporters of civil rights and appointed forty blacks to prominent administration posts. At his first Cabinet meeting, Kennedy asked all Cabinet members to study the employment and advancement practices in their departments, giving special attention to the status of Negroes.

In his first day in office Robert Kennedy and John Seigenthaler toured the Department of Justice. The dearth of black employees dismayed them. Afterward the attorney general ordered the "thorough integration" of all Justice's offices everywhere in the country. In May 1961 he sent letters to the deans of forty-five law schools requesting that they recommend their most promising Negro graduates but stressing that ability was still the "primary consideration" for appointment. In two years the department added ninety black attorneys to the staff. "Ashamed that his men's club, the Metropolitan, refused to take blacks, he quit in protest," notes Evan Thomas.

On March 6, 1961, President Kennedy issued an executive order establishing the Committee on Equal Employment Opportunity (CEEO) and named Lyndon Johnson as chairman. Kennedy charged the CEEO to end racial discrimination in government employment and in work performed for the government because federal money should encourage the "national goal of equal opportunity." The administration's enforcement placed greater demands on contractors.

When his department had clear legal authority, Robert Kennedy aggressively applied federal power to extend civil rights. He enforced court orders desegregating schools with no prompting by civil rights organizations. Legal authority on voting rights was stronger (though still limited) than in any other civil rights field. Using existing legislation, Kennedy's Department of Justice brought fifty-seven voting suits, thirty of them in Mississippi.

Emphasizing voting rights was primary in Robert Kennedy's view because there the federal government had more legal authority. The effort could accomplish the greatest measure of good and create less civil strife and less opposition. His approach also paid valuable political dividends because most of the new black voters would be Democrats.

Because the voting rights legislation passed in 1957 and 1960 was limited, action based on it had only limited success. Each suit required an enormous effort. "We faced tough judges," said John Doar of the Justice Department. Enforcing voter registration laws was an incrementalist approach, and the lawsuits usually moved at a snail's pace. The South had a genius for delaying the judicial process.

The civil rights movement could get John Kennedy's undivided attention when protests embarrassed the United States in the eyes of other nations. African diplomats, for example, were leery of being assigned to Washington, D.C., a Southern city with a strong Jim Crow tradition. Would they find decent housing or be assaulted on the streets of Washington? Spearheaded by the State Department, the administration initiated a plan to desegregate public facilities in Maryland and Washington, D.C., where African diplomats traveled and lived.

After John Kennedy's death, several of his private comments about civil rights protesters came to light, and their callousness earned condemnation. They were sparked by fear that racial confrontations would cause international embarrassment. During the Freedom Rides the angry president phoned Harris Wofford and yelled, "Stop them! Get your friends off those buses!" The riders embarrassed him just as he entered the world spotlight for his meeting with Khrushchev in Vienna.

When an African ambassador drove Route 40 between Washington and New York, he was refused service, even a glass of water. The incident made headlines in the Washington newspapers and around the world. "Can't you tell them not to do it?" the embarrassed president asked Angier Biddle Duke, the State Department's chief of protocol. "Can't you tell these African ambassadors not to drive on Route 40? It's a hell of a road—I used to drive it years ago, but why would anyone want to drive it today when you can fly? Tell them to fly!"

On these occasions the president seemed impervious to the daily humiliation of racism. Freedom Riders judged their cause to be as important as Kennedy's visit with the Soviet premier; white Americans drove Route 40 without suffering embarrassment.

Many critics, then and now, blame Kennedy for not seeking civil rights legislation during the first two years of his presidency. He vacillated, equivocated, and retreated, they say. Roy Wilkins of the NAACP thought Kennedy made a "tactical error" and was acting with "super-caution."

The president judged that his decision was eminently reasonable given the harsh political realities. Southerners controlled two-thirds of the standing committees in the Senate. Larry O'Brien worried that pushing civil rights legislation would derail the rest of the president's legislative program. "We needed the Southerners to have any majority at all," said O'Brien, "and we would lose them if we pushed for a civil rights bill." The American people were not sufficiently aroused by civil rights, the Kennedys insisted, and were not demanding new legislation. Nor were newspapers, radio, or television.

Kennedy might be excused for not pushing new legislation. Less excusable was his failure to take an executive action he had pledged. Several times during the 1960 election campaign he had promised to sign an executive order ending racial discrimination in federal housing. He would do so, he said, with the "stroke of a pen." Presidents often used the executive order to bypass Congress, as President Truman famously did when he ordered the armed forces integrated.

In office, Kennedy kept delaying his housing order. He needed Southern backing to get Congress to support a new Department of Urban Affairs, and he worried about the economic effects of the housing order; issuing it would damage the economy and, in the process, hurt Negroes. The delay continued through most of 1962 with political considerations paramount. In the end the president issued a low-key announcement after the 1962 midterm elections, hoping to cause as little divisiveness as possible. What's more, because it excluded private financial institutions, the housing order applied to less than 3 percent of existing housing and only 20 percent of new construction.

*

In the 1960 campaign Kennedy had reproached President Eisenhower for allowing the Little Rock crisis to explode in 1957, requiring paratroopers in combat gear with fixed bayonets to integrate the high school there. The incident had humiliated the United States throughout the world and provided ammunition for Soviet propaganda. Expert preparation and behind-the-scenes negotiation would help control a civil rights crisis, Kennedy believed. The Justice Department's civil

rights team acted as the president's civil rights crisis management force, focusing on preserving law and order. When racial confrontations threatened violence, the team first tried to
stabilize the situation. The use—or the threat—of U.S. troops
was a last resort.

The administration had to use all its skills to enroll a single Negro student at an all-white university. In January 1961
James Meredith quietly applied for admission to the University of Mississippi in Oxford. A twenty-eight-year-old air force
veteran, Meredith was transferring to all-white Ole Miss from
all-black Jackson State. After a tortuous legal battle, the NAACP
obtained a federal court ruling in 1962 ordering Meredith's
admission, and a series of subsequent court rulings enjoined
Mississippi officials from interfering. But Mississippi governor
Ross Barnett claimed he would rather go to jail than let "that
boy," backed by the "Communist" NAACP, get into Ole Miss.

Barnett's undisguised defiance presented President Kennedy with a dilemma. Meredith had the legal right to enroll,
and civil rights forces backed his enrollment. But how should
it be accomplished? To arrest and imprison a sitting governor would make Barnett a legend in Mississippi. Yet Kennedy
could not allow him to get away with his defiance.

Barnett's strategy was clear: make Robert Kennedy retreat,
or make him exert extraordinary force to enroll Meredith. Either way the governor would win. Any public conciliation or
public compromise with the Kennedys would bring disaster
for Barnett.

The Kennedys' strategy was also clear, though difficult
to implement successfully. Avoid the approach Eisenhower
followed in the Little Rock imbroglio. Instead, make an extraordinary effort to find a peaceful solution by using quiet
and patient action in the courts, judicious public statements,
personal telephone appeals to the governor, and behind-the-
scenes negotiation.

The world watched as events unfolded in Mississippi. Re-
marking on the rival efforts of the Soviet Union and the United

States to make friends in Africa, a Negro diplomat from a nonaligned African country remarked, "We are waiting to see what President Kennedy will do in Mississippi." The racial barrier "made nonsense of United States claims to be the custodian of the free world in opposition to Communism."

On Sunday afternoon, September 30, the Justice Department sent three hundred deputy marshals to Oxford. The plan was to have Meredith peacefully register at the Lyceum administration building on Monday. At 6:30 p.m. Sunday evening, Meredith picked out a room at deserted Baxter Hall, and federal marshals guarded him.

As word spread that federal marshals were on campus ringing the Lyceum, 2,500 people surged toward them. Some chanted "Go to hell, JFK!" Roughnecks carried clubs, rocks, pipes, bricks, bottles, bats, and rifles.

With Meredith's successful registration imminent, President Kennedy appealed for calm and reason during a special Sunday evening television address. Unknown to the president, while he spoke the situation had deteriorated in Oxford. When he concluded, Robert Kennedy arrived in the Cabinet Room and announced that rioters outside the Lyceum were "throwing iron spikes."

During a riotous night, both Kennedys worried they might be facing disaster. "They're storming where Meredith is," announced Robert, reacting to an incorrect bulletin that rioters had found Meredith in his dormitory. As the grim siege watch continued, the president, anguish on his face, paced impatiently. He slept only three hours.

Shortly after midnight the Pentagon was ordered to airlift a force of MPs from Memphis to Oxford. Army officials promised that they could complete the operation in two hours and suppress the riot, but it actually took them four and a half hours. "Damn army!" exclaimed Robert Kennedy at about 1 a.m. The troops finally arrived on the campus at 4:30 a.m. and quickly restored order. Two died in the rioting and 375 were injured, including 166 federal marshals.

"Scorned by classmates and surrounded by marshals, Meredith attended classes and ate in lonely isolation," notes Evan Thomas. Officials throughout Mississippi echoed their governor in blaming "trigger-happy marshals" and federal intruders for the riot.

Most of the public approved the administration's actions. It made a "deep impression" on Negro diplomats in Washington, Dean Rusk reported. "The Mississippi affair seemed from here to have been superbly handled," Ambassador John Kenneth Galbraith wrote from India. "President Kennedy's handling of the crisis has impressed the capital," James Reston wrote in the *New York Times*. "He struck a good balance between conciliation and force."

For all the Kennedys' good intentions and executive actions, their efforts in 1961–1962 disappointed most civil rights supporters and, later, most historians. They had refused to call for much-needed legislation, had engaged in interminable litigation over voting rights, and had postponed—and finally limited—the stroke of the pen. Critics accused the Kennedys of refusing to abandon their strict-constructionist views of federal power. They wouldn't concede Southern electoral votes in 1964 and failed to develop empathy for the victims of Southern racism. Kennedy's campaign promises on civil rights, and his promise to be an assertive executive, willing to do the right thing even at the risk of incurring momentary displeasure, appeared hollow.

The president should have embarked on a public education crusade to arouse the nation to the need for civil rights, critics said, much as President Franklin Roosevelt had reassured Americans with his fireside chats during the depression. Despite the unlikely possibility of success, critics argued, Kennedy should have pushed for the legislation anyway as a matter of principle.

Despite their differences with Kennedy, many civil rights leaders respected the president, enjoyed his personality, and believed he was committed to their cause. He was accessible, candidly explained his strategy, assured them of his long-term commitment, and, as a civil rights leader commented, "won them with charm." Kennedy's supporters contend that he did not promise as much on civil rights in the 1960 election as critics claim he did. What's more, they insist his assumption that Congress would block civil rights legislation in 1961–1962 was absolutely correct.

It is naive to assume that Roosevelt-style fireside chats could have generated public support for civil rights. "The sense of urgency that accompanied the New Deal was missing from the New Frontier and that made the public appeal over the heads of Congress a much less viable tool of Presidential leadership," observes civil rights historian John Hart.

Critics underestimate the significance of the Kennedy administration's executive action and often ignore the depth of white Southern opposition and hatred of the Kennedys for promoting civil rights. "Some political jokes and slogans that developed across the South are not heard today and not read in anything that is written, and the depth of hostility for the administration somehow has been missed as a result of what I call revisionist history," John Seigenthaler has reflected.

In August 1962, as Harris Wofford was leaving the administration for a position with the Peace Corps, Kennedy said to him very seriously, with unusual gentleness and warmth, "It will take some more time, but I want you to know that we are going to do all these things," referring to the agenda of civil rights proposals. "As we parted," Wofford recalled, "he smiled reassuringly and repeated, 'You will see, with time I'm going to do them all.'"

1963

WHEN CONGRESS met early in 1963, no one foresaw that within a few months the nation's racial crisis would become America's most urgent domestic issue. Kennedy hadn't intended to offer major proposals on civil rights; the issue remained dormant in order to retain the backing of Southern Democrats for the President's major tax bill.

In the spring the administration's attitude changed. Beginning on April 3, 1963, Martin Luther King led a series of demonstrations in Birmingham, Alabama, hoping to break the city's wall of racial segregation. During April and May hundreds of blacks marched through downtown Birmingham and staged sit-ins to protest discrimination at lunch counters, in department stores, and in hiring practices.

For twenty-three years the city's arch-segregationist public safety commissioner Eugene ("Bull") Connor had cowed Negroes with loud threats and club-swinging police. On May 2 hundreds of Negro schoolchildren staged protest marches and were arrested and jailed. During the next few days Bull Connor countered the demonstrations with fire hoses and police dogs. "The dogs, held on long leashes, lunged at those who retreated slowly," *Time* reported. They were "chased by snarling dogs and club-waving cops." "Look at those niggers run," shouted the delighted Connor.

"We're through with tokenism and gradualism and see-how-far-you've-comism," King thundered during the protest. "We're through with we've-done-more-for-your-people-than-anyone-elseism. We can't wait any longer. Now is the time."

The injustice, lack of opportunity, and meanness of Birmingham's response shocked the president. He also viewed the struggle in a worldwide context. Battered and bloody Negro children in the streets badly tarnished the nation's image. Donald Wilson, acting director of the United States Information Agency, wrote the president that "Most [world] attention was given to the use of brutality and especially dogs against the Negro demonstrators." The administration swung into action, organizing a behind-the-scenes campaign to convince Alabama business executives to push for a settlement.

Another crisis emerged simultaneously. During his 1962 election campaign Governor George Wallace had promised "to stand in the schoolhouse door" to bar any black students from entering the University of Alabama. Two Negro students, Vivian Malone and James Hood, both twenty, intended to register at the university on June 11, 1963. By detailed planning, the Kennedy administration sought to avoid the tragic violence that had occurred the preceding fall when James Meredith enrolled at the University of Mississippi. President Kennedy hoped to enroll the students without using armed force and without arresting Wallace and making him a martyr. To resolve the crisis peacefully, the Justice Department worked secretly with the university president, the faculty, and the state attorney general.

To avoid the problems that had occurred at Ole Miss, where Mississippians bitterly resented the presence of "Yankee" troops on Southern soil, President Kennedy planned to federalize the Alabama National Guard if Wallace refused to step aside. "Because the guard commander and his troops were Alabamians, Kennedy believed it more likely that Wallace would peacefully capitulate," James Hilty writes.

On June 11 Wallace arrived at the university campus at 10 a.m. and stood in the doorway of Foster Hall where the students were to register. In Washington, Robert Kennedy had rolled up his sleeves and turned his office into a command post. With him were his aides and a telephone line linking him with his team in Tuscaloosa: a group of U.S. marshals and Justice Department officials headed by Deputy Attorney General Nicholas Katzenbach. At Fort Benning, Georgia, four hundred army riot-trained troops sat in helicopters, ready to respond to any emergency.

There were two separate confrontations with Wallace during the day. At their first meeting late in the morning, Katzenbach asked Wallace to step aside. The Governor refused. Katzenbach then telephoned Robert Kennedy, who called the president. At 1:34 p.m. President Kennedy signed an order federalizing the Alabama National Guard.

At the second confrontation in mid-afternoon, Brig. Gen. Henry Graham of the Alabama Guard asked Wallace to stand aside "so that the order of the court may be accomplished." After a brief statement protesting the "trend toward military dictatorship," Wallace stepped back. The federal officials escorted the two Negro students into the building where they registered.

The culmination of the incident was exactly what the Kennedys had hoped—no riot, no violence, and no need for troops. The only opposition was Wallace's empty gesture of defiance. When Wallace stepped aside, Robert Kennedy breathed a sign of relief and lit his cigar.

On the evening of June 11 President Kennedy threw his prestige and the weight of his office behind the civil rights cause he had once tried to avoid. His speech to the nation was blunt, eloquent, idealistic, and one of the most emotional he ever delivered.

> We are confronted primarily with a moral issue. It is as old as the Scriptures and is as clear as the American Constitution.
>
> The heart of the question is whether all Americans are to be afforded equal rights and equal opportunities, whether we are going to treat our fellow Americans as we want to be treated. If an American, because his skin is dark, cannot eat lunch in a restaurant open to the public, if he cannot send his children to the best public school available, if he cannot vote for the public officials who represent him, if, in short, he cannot enjoy the full and free life which all of us want, then who among us would be content to have the color of his skin changed and stand in his place? Who among us would then be content with the counsels of patience and delay?

It was time for Congress to face the issue, and therefore the president would shortly be asking for new legislation, including the right of all Americans to be served in facilities that were open to the public—hotels, restaurants, theaters, retail stores, and similar establishments.

To many, Kennedy appeared bold and statesmanlike. Martin Luther King told reporters the speech was a masterpiece.

In *Newsweek* Walter Lippmann lauded his "momentous and irrevocable step. No President . . . has ever staked his personal prestige and has brought to bear all the powers of the Presidency on the Negro cause. . . . I count very high the speed, the intelligence, the imagination, and the courage of the Kennedy reaction."

The Kennedys now did what they did best: meticulously organized and promoted. The president held intense consultations with members of Congress. "The attorney general and I," said Burke Marshall, "met personally with every senator, including senators who were going to be dead set against this bill, and [nearly] every member of the House." To arouse public support for the new legislation the White House invited influential citizens—groups of businessmen, women, educators, labor officials, lawyers, religious leaders—to meetings at the White House. About 250 people attended each session; the president or his designate—usually Robert Kennedy or Lyndon Johnson—addressed the group, then turned it over to the floor for questions and comments.

Before the meeting with religious leaders on June 17, domestic adviser Ralph Dungan reminded the president "to underscore again the moral position of the churches on the question of racial equality." Kennedy didn't need the reminder. During the meeting he stressed that the civil rights movement would no longer tolerate being "second class" citizens. "I would hope each religious group would . . . underscore the moral position of racial equality."

A group of fifteen Negro physicians requested an audience with the president while Congress considered the civil rights legislation. They shocked him with their stories of discrimination, particularly in the South but in Northern communities as well. Hospitals would not permit Negro physicians to use their facilities, they explained. Often the rule required that only members of the local medical society could use the hospitals and admit patients, and the local medical society itself was the one that restricted Negro membership. The president was aghast and said he wanted to meet with leaders from the American Medical Association.

The president planned to introduce his civil rights bill into the House of Representatives rather than the Senate because James Eastland chaired the Senate Judiciary Committee. The chairman of the House Judiciary Committee, however, was Emanuel Celler, a liberal and longtime champion of civil rights. Celler also presided over the House Judiciary Committee's Subcommittee No. 5, where the administration's bill would begin its legislative journey. Because Celler's subcommittee was dominated by liberal Democrats, the bill would receive more favorable treatment than anywhere else in Congress.

Although all the supporters of the new legislation agreed the bill must start in the House, the huge obstacle of a future Senate filibuster had to be considered long before the bill made its way to the Senate. Southerners were certain to filibuster, and the Senate had never imposed cloture against a civil rights talkathon. For the two-thirds vote (sixty-seven members) required for cloture, the administration would need the support of at least twenty Republicans.

On June 18 Senate Majority Leader Mike Mansfield advised the president that there was only one practical way to assure passage of the legislation in the Senate: count sixty-seven votes on cloture for whatever House bill was pushed. "Any phraseology in the legislation, any parliamentary tactic or political statement which subtracts from the total of votes obtainable for cloture is to be avoided. As it now stands, the short-side of 67 lies in the public accommodations title." Mansfield advised that the needed sixty-seven votes for cloture required "complete cooperation and good faith" with influential Republican Senate leader Everett Dirksen. Bipartisan cooperation was crucial. Kennedy agreed.

Of the eight provisions in Kennedy's bill, one was at its heart. Title II prohibited discrimination in public accommodations, including all places of lodging, eating, and amusement, and other retail or service establishments. The focal point of the Birmingham campaign had been the exclusion of Negroes from lunch counters, restaurants, amusement parks, theaters, hotels, and other public places. Several times Senator Mansfield discussed with the president the difficulty of securing passage of the public accommodations section. "You've got to get it done," Mansfield recalled the president responding. "It's the heart of the matter. These people are entitled to this consideration."

At a meeting with civil rights leaders on June 22, the president's commitment impressed the group. "I liked the way he talked about what *we* are getting," said King. "It wasn't something that he was getting for you Negroes. You knew you had an ally."

In a series of votes on October 29, the administration's bill won approval. By 20 to 14 the House Judiciary Committee accepted Kennedy's version. It was a compromise—a bipartisan "unity bill." It forbade discrimination in hotels, motels, filling stations, movie houses, and restaurants. An equal employment opportunities commission would outlaw discrimination in industries employing twenty-five or more people and engaged in interstate commerce. The bill granted the attorney general greater power to intervene in discrimination against black voters and to move against segregated public facilities. Kennedy's bill had cleared its first big hurdle.

*

Kennedy damaged his political fortunes with his stand on civil rights. In a major poll reported by *Newsweek* in late October 1963, the political impact of the racial upheaval was clear: "it has hurt John F. Kennedy, and it may have hurt him badly." The president had picked up one million Negro votes since 1960, but the *Newsweek* poll indicated that the racial issue had driven about 4.5 million white voters away from Kennedy. Nonetheless the resulting net loss of 3.5 million voters was something he could currently afford because of his commanding lead over potential challengers in 1964. Still, no Democratic president in the twentieth century was so widely disliked in the South.

The *Newsweek* poll concluded that the 1964 election would be a landslide for Kennedy were it not for the racial issue. Civil rights held little opportunity and great danger. "The civil-rights issue represents a definite, distinct loss for Mr. Kennedy in 1964, and, if it grows into the overriding issue, it might just cost him the election."

Dr. King came to believe that the Kennedys had responded "to creative pressure," that their actions were not just political calculation and crisis management. Kennedy "frankly acknowledged that he was responding to mass demands," but he had done so, said King, "because he thought it was right to do so. This is the secret of the deep affection he evoked. He was responsive, sensitive, humble before the people, and bold on their behalf."

10

The Cuban Missile Crisis

"MONGOOSE was poorly conceived and wretchedly executed," concluded Arthur Schlesinger, normally a champion of Robert Kennedy. "It deserved greatly to fail. It was Robert Kennedy's most conspicuous folly." Operation Mongoose proved to be folly for President Kennedy as well.

In 1975 the Senate formed the Select Committee to Study Government Operations with Respect to Intelligence Activities, commonly known as the Church Committee, which investigated illegal and improper activities by the CIA and FBI. In the course of the probe, sensational evidence emerged about Kennedy's presidency, including reports on assassination plots and covert operations to overthrow Fidel Castro.

Because Eisenhower had used covert operations, Kennedy probably assumed that the secret approach was acceptable presidential conduct. Unlike his traumatic public failure at the Bay of Pigs, covert action permitted Kennedy to act without being held accountable. If covert action failed against Castro, nobody would know, and it wouldn't hurt him politically. Nobody could blame the president.

After the Bay of Pigs, Kennedy established a secret committee—the Special Group—to bring order and discipline to decision-making in intelligence matters. He soon authorized two other powerful secret committees: the Special Group (CI) focused on counterinsurgency while the Special

Group Augmented (SGA) planned specifically to subvert Castro's rule in Cuba.

SGA acted like a circuit breaker so that developments did not explode in the president's face. Robert Kennedy played an active role in all three committees. The SGA designated its secret war on Castro as Operation Mongoose, named for the ferret-sized mammal known for its ability to kill rats and other small animals.

At the weekly meetings of SGA, Robert Kennedy was the driving force, demonstrating, in the words of Evan Thomas, "his scorn for the bureaucracy, his zest for covert action, his misplaced idealism and identification with the underdog, his restless insistence on action as well as his carelessness about the consequences." Getting rid of Castro was Robert Kennedy's priority.

The SGA gathered intelligence data on possible Cuban targets, infiltrated the island with guerrilla teams, recruited agents, arranged to sabotage a large Cuban copper mine, and blew up bridges and production plants. Nonetheless, little was accomplished.

Operation Mongoose had one exceptionally sensitive feature: between 1960 and 1965 the CIA concocted eight plots to assassinate Castro. A few did not advance beyond planning and preparation; one used Mafia figures to recruit Cubans with the intention of poisoning the Cuban dictator; others intended to use bizarre assassination devices. Debate has raged for several decades about whether President Kennedy knew about the plots. Did he authorize them? What was the role of Robert Kennedy?

The key CIA figure in the assassination plots was Richard Helms. He testified before the Church Committee that the extraordinary pressure forced on him by the Kennedy administration to overthrow Castro had led him to conclude that the CIA was acting within its authority by trying to assassinate the Cuban leader, even though assassination was never directly authorized. Helms claimed he never informed the SGA or any of its members of the attempts to kill Castro. Nor did he tell officials in the White House or, amazingly, even his own boss, CIA director John McCone.

Was President Kennedy informed of any assassination plots? Helms averted a direct answer. "I think any of us would have found it very difficult to discuss assassinations with a President of the U.S.," he testified. "We all had the feeling that we're hired out to keep these things out of the Oval Office." Nobody wanted to embarrass the president "by discussing the assassination of foreign leaders in his presence."

Every major surviving member of the Kennedy administration swore under oath that assassinating Castro was improper without a direct order from the president, and that assassination was outside the range of the anti-Castro program. What's more, they were sure the president never gave such an order.

Still, two incidents reveal that the assassination of Castro was on President Kennedy's mind. According to Senator George Smathers, in late March 1961, during a stroll on the White House grounds, Kennedy asked him how South America would react if Fidel Castro were assassinated. Smathers rejected the idea because the United States would be blamed throughout Central and South America. "I disapproved of it, and [Kennedy] completely disapproved of the idea," Smathers recalled.

Then on November 9, 1961, the president discussed the Cuban situation in the Oval Office with journalist Tad Szulc of the *New York Times*. An expert on Cuba, Szulc had interviewed Castro several times after the Bay of Pigs. The president asked Szulc, "What would you think if I ordered Castro to be assassinated?" It wouldn't work, said Szulc, and besides, the United States should not engage in such an action. Kennedy replied that he and his brother agreed, but that he was under "terrific pressure."

Was the president merely sending up a trial balloon with Szulc to see how the media would react? Szulc's notation that the president was being pressured puzzled the Church Committee. Who was pressuring him? Everyone else questioned by the committee denied ever discussing assassination with the president, let alone having pressured him to consider it.

The Church Committee never discovered a written order to kill Castro, but just because there was no paper trail did not necessarily mean that the two brothers were not involved. As James Hilty has observed, covert action could have been initiated by a "nod of the head or with vague verbal instructions that later could be refuted under the doctrine of plausible deniability."

In the final analysis, circumstantial evidence leans toward the fact that the Kennedys did in fact authorize the CIA to kill Castro. The conversations the president had with Smathers and Szulc are telltale. "Why would [the president] discuss the possibility of the assassination of Castro with two friends if such a possibility did not in fact exist?" notes one critic.

If Helms lied before the Church Committee, the entire controversy becomes clear. Robert Kennedy met secretly with Helms, verbally ordered him to try to assassinate Castro, and both of them maintained the secret. Helms had a record of lying. In 1973, during testimony before the Senate Foreign Relations Committee, Helms had sworn under oath that the CIA had never tried to overthrow the government of Marxist president Salvador Allende of Chile, or that it had funneled money to political enemies of Allende. Later, Senate investigators discovered that the CIA had run a secret operation in Chile that gave more than $8 million to Allende's opponents. Allende died in 1973 during a military coup.

"I had found myself in a position of conflict," Helms explained to a federal judge during his trial for perjury. "I had sworn my oath to protect certain secrets. . . . I didn't want to lie. I was simply trying to find my way through a difficult situation in which I found myself." The judge found Helms guilty of two misdemeanor charges of perjury.

Helms probably lied to the Church Committee as well, finding himself in a "position of conflict," trying to find his way through "a difficult situation." The pressure on Helms, particularly from Robert Kennedy, had been intense. Several times Helms had said privately, "My God, these Kennedys keep the pressure on about Castro." It was "white heat." Perhaps the "pressure" President Kennedy felt about approving the assassination plots came from his own brother, the attorney general.

Helms's testimony before the Church Committee was filled with evasions and lapses of memory. He "did not recall," or "doubted," or had "no knowledge," or "could not remember." He sounded "like an amnesia victim," Thomas Powers concludes. "When investigators nailed him with a piece of paper, he answered as he could. All the rest he had forgotten. It is said men begin life with a *tabula rasa*; Helms ended it that way."

If we assume that Robert Kennedy directed the assassination plans, he certainly discussed them with the president. The brothers were intimate and the matter too important. President Kennedy must have authorized the plots. Because he felt at least slightly guilty about attempting to murder Castro, he talked about it with Szulc and Smathers.

*

Unaware of Operation Mongoose, news stories continually harped on the Kennedy administration's "weakness" in handling Castro. Communists were "getting away with murder" in Cuba while Washington did nothing. By late summer 1962, growing Soviet arms shipments to Cuba led several Republicans to attack the administration. Kennedy's critics accused the Soviets of violating the Monroe Doctrine, invoked by the United States for more than a hundred years to bar European nations from interfering in the Western Hemisphere.

Few U.S. officials thought that Khrushchev would deliver offensive nuclear weapons to Cuba. Such a daring move would be too risky; besides, the Soviets had never placed offensive missiles outside their country. But in fact the Soviets planned to deploy in Cuba 36 SS-4 medium-range ballistic missiles (MRBMs) and 24 SS-5 intermediate-range ballistic missiles (IRBMs). Cuba also bristled with 42,000 Soviet troops—far more than U.S. intelligence estimated—40 MiG-21 planes, surface-to-air missiles, 6 IL-28 bombers, 12 Luna missiles, and 80 cruise missiles for short-range nuclear strikes.

Why did Khrushchev act so rashly? Protecting Cuba was one reason. Soviet assistance allowed Cuba to survive "right in front of the open jaws of predatory American imperialism," he proudly claimed afterward. Inserting offensive missiles into Cuba was also a short cut to gaining nuclear parity with the United States. Khrushchev confidently believed that the installation of the missiles could be kept secret until they became fully operational following the November 1962 elections. Once deployed, the burden of changing the status quo would fall on Kennedy.

At 8:30 p.m. on Monday, October 15, 1962, McGeorge Bundy was notified that a U-2 reconnaissance aircraft had discovered medium-range ballistic missiles in Cuba. They were offensive missiles, the kind the Soviets had promised never to install there.

Instead of assembling the National Security Council or the Cabinet, Kennedy gathered around him those advisers and experts whose judgment he trusted. The group, soon labeled the Executive Committee of the National Security Council, or Ex-Comm, included Dean Rusk, Ted Sorensen, Robert Kennedy, McGeorge Bundy, Robert McNamara, Douglas Dillon, Maxwell Taylor, John McCone, Undersecretary of State George Ball, Ambassador Llewellyn Thompson, and a few others. "We had to force the issue before any missiles were fully installed or we risked their being fired," George Ball pointed out.

The Soviet action infuriated ExComm partly because it was surreptitious and deceitful. The United States had openly installed its own missiles in Turkey. "The intensity of the American reaction in October was very largely a function of the deception," Bundy later said. No U.S. president could politically survive if he allowed the Soviet Union brazenly to enter the Western Hemisphere and establish missile bases ninety miles off Florida. It would have undermined NATO's confidence in the will and determination of the United States and disturbed all the nations in North and South America.

The crisis lasted for thirteen days as ExComm secretly debated options. One factor in the debate was the U.S. missiles in Turkey. In late 1957 the Eisenhower administration had publicly offered to deploy intermediate-range Jupiter missiles in Turkey, a U.S. ally. In the fall of 1962, with the installation completed, the United States turned the missiles over to the Turks. Inaccurate, vulnerable, and outdated, the liquid-fueled Jupiters were useful only for a first nuclear strike and were therefore provocative. President Kennedy judged that the only negotiating ploy he could offer would be to withdraw the Jupiters from Turkey in return for the Soviets' withdrawal of their missiles from Cuba.

By October 18 ExComm focused on two major options: an air strike against the missile installations, coupled with a possible invasion; or a blockade. The hard-liners thought it was crucial to destroy the missiles without delay. If Washington warned Cuba of an attack, Castro would disperse or hide them. But the air-strike option raised several serious difficulties. A "surgical" strike was an illusion. With so many targets, massive bombardment would be needed to destroy them all. Even then there was no assurance that all the missiles could be destroyed or that some of the missiles would not fire first, landing devastatingly on American soil. Finally, the air strike would undoubtedly kill Russians as well as Cubans, and therefore risked Soviet military retaliation. Most of ExComm's air-strike advocates agreed that their route would ultimately end in an invasion. But an invasion, with all its consequences, the president would not approve.

The blockade alternative gained adherents because, unlike the air strike, it was a limited, low-key military operation. Khrushchev could avoid a direct military clash simply by keeping his ships away. "It could at least be initiated without a shot being fired or a single Soviet or Cuban citizen being killed," Sorensen pointed out. If a naval engagement became necessary, having the confrontation just off U.S. shores was a major advantage.

The blockade signaled Khrushchev that the United States was resolute; yet it wasn't sudden or humiliating and would probably avoid casualties. Beginning at the lowest level of action was also least likely to alienate U.S. allies. What's more, the blockade applied only to offensive weapons, not defensive arms or food and supplies that would affect innocent Cubans.

ExComm decided on a blockade, now renamed a quarantine to overcome legal objections. On Monday evening, October 22, Kennedy explained the crisis and his decision when he addressed the American people on national television.

The president insisted on keeping track of every detail during the crisis. Each morning he reviewed the location of every ship approaching the quarantine line and the instructions given U.S. commanders. His worst nightmare was that the Soviets might decide that since total war was inevitable, they should launch a preemptive nuclear strike against the United States.

The quarantine went into effect at 10 a.m. on October 24. American ICBMs, nuclear submarines, and almost every available bomber—about fourteen hundred—were on alert. As Kennedy had hoped, on October 25 Khrushchev ordered Soviet missile-carrying ships to turn back. So far the quarantine had sparked no shooting. But the major problem remained: how to get the Soviet nuclear missiles out of Cuba? Kennedy resumed contingency plans for an air strike and an invasion.

On Friday evening, October 26, the White House received a long, confidential letter from the Soviet premier, appearing to have been written by Khrushchev himself. He suggested a compromise: a pledge by the United States not to invade Cuba in exchange for the Soviet withdrawal of their missiles.

The letter delighted ExComm and seemed to be the basis for a deal. But hope evaporated the following morning. Shortly after ExComm met at 10 a.m., a second letter arrived from Khrushchev—different in tone and substance, and it seemed to have been written by a committee. Instead of just the no-invasion pledge, the new letter proposed a missile swap: the United States would remove its Jupiters from Turkey, then the Soviets would withdraw their missiles from Cuba. ExComm members were angered by the new condition.

"It was unmistakably Black Saturday," recalled George Ball. "One might reasonably infer from the evidence that the Soviets really intended war and were simply stalling until they were better prepared."

Dealing with Saturday's nightmare may well have been Kennedy's greatest day as president. He remained calm and analytical. "He seems more alive to the possibilities and consequences of each new development than anyone else," said historians Ernest R. May and Philip Zelikow. "He is the only one in the room who is determined not to go to war over obsolete missiles in Turkey." ExComm devised an ingenious solution to the problem of the two letters: it responded to the first and ignored the second.

On Saturday evening, October 27, acting as the president's personal emissary, Robert Kennedy met privately in his office at the Justice Department with Soviet ambassador Anatoly Dobrynin. The situation was urgent, Kennedy emphasized; time was running out. If the Soviets retaliated, "before this was over, while there might be dead Americans, there would also be dead Russians." If the Soviets agreed to remove the missiles, the United States would agree not to invade Cuba. And although the United States could not agree publicly to remove the Jupiter missiles from Turkey, he offered assurance that they would be removed in four or five months. The Soviets agreed, and the crisis ended.

Kennedy emerged from the Cuban Missile Crisis a national hero, an almost "Lincolnesque" figure. Walter Lippmann praised him for having shown "not only the courage of a warrior, which is to take the risks that are necessary, but also the wisdom of the statesman, which is to use power with restraint."

But some historians allege that Kennedy's conduct during the crisis was irresponsible and reckless. Driven by his machismo character, his hatred of Castro, his rage over the Soviet deception, and his selfish concern for political advantage, Kennedy exaggerated the missile danger, rejected a possible diplomatic solution, and insisted on a dangerous public showdown. He should have negotiated a settlement, giving Khrushchev the chance to save face. While pursuing his foolish policy, the argument goes, Kennedy risked nuclear war "to satisfy his own psychic and political needs."

Actually Kennedy showed remarkable restraint. At each stage of the crisis he chose the moderate and prudent course. As Tony Judt has observed, "Instead of an invasion he favored an air strike on missile bases; instead of a blanket air strike he favored selective strikes only; he insisted that no strikes, however selective, should happen until warning had been given. He opted for a naval blockade over immediate military action, and a partial naval quarantine over a blanket blockade on all shipping."

At every stage of the crisis Kennedy gave Khrushchev time to reflect and reappraise. "It seems especially odd," notes historian Alonzo Hamby, "that he has been criticized for impulsiveness when he sought the advice of an 'executive committee' composed of most of the major foreign policy authorities of the United States, or that he has been accused of playing out irrational machismo impulses when he accepted the most pacific alternatives seriously offered to him."

The ExComm meetings were far superior to the deliberations during the Bay of Pigs. Kennedy himself was far better informed and far more perceptive. ExComm's "intellectual interchange," George Ball recalled, "was the most objective I ever witnessed in government—or, for that matter, in the private sector."

Arthur Schlesinger was mostly correct when he concluded, several decades ago, that Kennedy's combination of "toughness and restraint, of will, nerve and wisdom, so brilliantly controlled, so matchlessly calibrated, . . . dazzled the world."

11

Vietnam

THE FIRST major foreign crisis President Kennedy faced was in Laos. It was a precarious situation. A small, impoverished, landlocked county with a population of about two million, Laos together with Vietnam and Cambodia emerged out of French Indochina after the Geneva Conference of 1954. It was of little strategic importance except that its border with North Vietnam furnished a route for communist insurgents to travel to South Vietnam.

Soon after the Geneva Conference, a violent civil war broke out in Laos between the Communist Pathet Lao and the American-supported royal government. In an attempt to bring peace, Laotian prince Souvanna Phouma established a neutral government in 1957 with the aid of his half-brother, Prince Souphanouvong, leader of the Pathet Lao. But the Eisenhower administration, viewing neutrality as an "accommodation with evil," rejected the coalition arrangement. With U.S. backing, Gen. Phoumi Nosavan, the right-wing leader of the royal army, staged a coup, forcing the Pathet Lao and Souvanna to flee to the hills, where they conducted successful guerrilla warfare against Phoumi. Sustained by North Vietnam and a large Soviet airlift of supplies, the Pathet Lao won several military victories in 1961, bringing them precariously close to swallowing all of Laos.

On May 1, 1961, President Kennedy discussed the Laotian problem with the Joint Chiefs of Staff, who had urged sending ten thousand U.S. troops. Kennedy remained skeptical of the Chiefs' recommendations, and at one meeting asked probing questions of them and received what he considered poor answers.

Kennedy instructed Averell Harriman, the U.S. representative at Geneva, to attempt to negotiate a reliable neutral government in Laos, an exceptionally delicate and complex task. "Operating against heavy odds, Harriman worked a series of near-miracles at Geneva," notes Edmund Wehrle. "These included maintaining a cease-fire, eliciting Soviet support for Laotian neutrality, and persuading the American-supported, anticommunist royal government of Laos to cooperate." The Geneva negotiations finally succeeded in June 1962. Kennedy had displayed restraint, skill in negotiations, and a willingness to compromise.

In nearby Vietnam the facts about U.S. involvement startle. In 1969, at the height of U.S. engagement in the Vietnam War, the United States had 540,000 troops stationed in that tragic Southeast Asian nation. Fifty-eight thousand Americans died in the war; 313,000 were wounded. About 2.1 million Vietnamese soldiers and civilians perished. The United States spent roughly $200 billion in its search for victory. In the end the United States and its ally South Vietnam lost the war.

From 1950 through 1975 both Democratic and Republican presidents supported the U.S. intervention in Vietnam, and so did most leaders of both parties in Congress. U.S. involvement began slowly with military "advisers" sent to South Vietnam, the number rising from 685 in 1960 to 16,900 at the time of Kennedy's death. Kennedy had also escalated the rhetoric and the rationale for a strong U.S. presence. Off the record he had serious questions about fighting there and hoped to find a way to hold South Vietnam with a minimal number of American troops. Kennedy's successor inherited not his inner doubts but his deeper commitment and his forceful public statements justifying the importance of saving South Vietnam.

Kennedy justified U.S. assistance to President Diem on idealistic grounds: South Vietnam was one battleground in the broader conflict between freedom and communism. He warned of "the Communist conspiracy," "the Communist tide," "Communist efforts," and "the Communist advance." The United States must "bear the burden . . . of helping freedom defend itself" in South Vietnam. Kennedy's key advisers agreed.

Nuclear weapons could not deter Communist aggression in places like South Vietnam, Kennedy thought, because those conflicts were too limited to justify nuclear warfare. Washington needed military flexibility: "flexible response" would counter a variety of threats without resorting to nuclear devastation. The United States needed a strategy that could counter infiltration, assassination, sabotage, bribery—the weapons of guerrilla warfare.

Kennedy ordered the Special Warfare School at Fort Bragg, North Carolina, to prepare troops for the unique skills necessary for guerrilla warfare in underdeveloped countries. A new weapon was added to the cold war arsenal: counterinsurgency. "If the communists were going to lead guerrilla uprisings, then the West would have to learn how to fight back," notes Evan Thomas. The United States must win the "hearts and minds" of the people in places like South Vietnam. The new approach to combat insurgency was "bold, determined, and energetic," counterinsurgency expert Douglas Blaufarb concluded, "but it was also superficial and, responding to the perceived urgencies of the threat, too hasty." Counterinsurgency required responsive, honest government and professional behavior by the host country's armed forces. Unfortunately, in South Vietnam the very government the United States wanted to help was the biggest roadblock because it lacked the support of its own people.

Kennedy had little choice but to work with Diem, but this proved prickly because of Diem's personality and his controversial inner circle. Ngo Dinh Nhu, Diem's chief adviser and younger brother, brutally directed the police services. Cynical and devious, he systematically used corruption and terror to maintain Diem in power. U.S. officials repeatedly urged Diem to remove or exile Nhu, but he refused.

Kennedy hoped South Vietnam's leader would initiate reform, but the president was reluctant to push too hard. Diem worried that in a crunch Washington might abandon him. Instead Kennedy made it his main priority to convince Diem that the United States supported him.

In late October 1961, in preparation for a major presidential review, Kennedy sent a top-level mission to Vietnam, headed by Maxwell Taylor and Walt Rostow. Before Rostow left for Vietnam, the president spoke to him alone. Rostow recalled:

> He kept coming back to the fact that the French put in more than 250,000 good troops, and were run out. . . . He wanted my judgment on whether the Viet Cong had nationalism on their side. Did the people of South Viet Nam really want Ho Chi Minh? We can't commit as many troops as the French; the South Vietnamese must fight this themselves—can they? Do they want to see it through?

The ensuing Taylor Report sparked two weeks of intense high-level debate within the administration. It portrayed the Vietcong insurgency as one facet of the global Communist threat. It recommended "a quick U.S. response . . . to help save Vietnam." The commitment "must include the sending to Vietnam of some U.S. military forces." The United States needed to change its relationship with South Vietnam from simply giving advice to a "limited partnership." Soon Washington must declare its intention "to attack the source of guerrilla aggression in North Vietnam and impose on the Hanoi Government a price for participating in the current war." The most controversial section of the report recommended dispatching eight thousand U.S. combat troops to South Vietnam. More might be needed later. Nothing would be so reassuring to the South Vietnamese as the introduction of U.S. troops.

Kennedy's closest advisers endorsed the report. Anything less than 8,000 troops would fail to restore Diem's confidence, McNamara wrote. In fact, 8,000 troops would probably not be enough. In the future, he stated, "I believe we can safely assume the maximum U.S. forces required on the ground in Southeast Asia will not exceed six divisions, or about 205,000 men."

A few critics disagreed, but the dissenters were not among Kennedy's inner council. Senator Mike Mansfield wanted the president to proceed cautiously. The United States would be engaged without the support of significant allies; South Vietnam could become quicksand. "Where does an involvement of this kind end?" U.S. intervention could also be viewed by Southeast Asians "as a revival of colonial force." The responsibility of defending the country rested "on the shoulders of the South Vietnamese, whose country it is and whose future is their chief responsibility."

At a dramatic meeting of the National Security Council on November 15, 1961, the president expressed grave concern about introducing American combat troops, far greater concern than his primary advisers expressed during his entire presidency. He worried about becoming involved simultaneously on two military fronts—Berlin and South Vietnam—on opposite sides of the world. The wisdom of becoming more involved in Vietnam was not clear to him. By comparison, the Korean War had involved a case of clear aggression, opposed by the United States and other members of the United Nations; in South Vietnam the aggression was more obscure and less flagrant. Kennedy said he "could even make a rather strong case against intervening in an area 10,000 miles away against 16,000 guerrillas with a native army of 200,000, where millions have been spent for years with no success."

Kennedy compared the obscurity of the issues in South Vietnam to the clarity of the U.S. position in Berlin. Rusk remarked that the Berlin problem showed that firmness and resolve might also work in Vietnam without causing full-scale war. Kennedy disagreed, saying that "the issue was clearly defined in Berlin and opposing forces identified whereas in Vietnam the issue is vague and action is by guerrillas, sometimes in a phantom-like fashion."

In the end Kennedy decided to go ahead with most of the Taylor Report's recommendations, but not the call for eight thousand troops. He was most comfortable with a middle way. There would be no U.S. combat troops, no dramatic action that would rile the American people, but enough expertise from additional U.S. advisers and enough firepower to get the job done and avoid political crucifixion at the hands of Republicans.

Yet the middle way nonetheless meant escalation. Kennedy's decisions in November were a major turning point in American involvement in South Vietnam. "Rejecting the extremes of negotiations on the one hand and the dispatch of combat troops on the other, Kennedy settled on a limited commitment of aid and advisers," observes historian George Herring. Within two years the small American contingent in South Vietnam escalated to 16,900 advisers, making a future decision to withdraw much harder.

On February 12, 1962, Kennedy established the Military Assistance Command, Vietnam (MACV) to direct the expanded military effort. Maxwell Taylor personally selected his protégé Gen. Paul Harkins as commander.

Kennedy tried to conceal the combat role of U.S. advisers so as not to rattle the American public. In mid-February, though, after eight American advisers were killed in a plane crash, a *New York Times* editorial criticized the administration for concealing the facts about America's increased involvement. On the same day the *Times* carried a column by James Reston, who flatly declared that "the United States is now involved in an undeclared war in South Vietnam. This is well known to the Russians, the Chinese Communists, and everyone else concerned except the American people."

Criticism of administration policy was the exception, though, not the rule. During 1962 the "strategic hamlet" program became the centerpiece of Kennedy's counterinsurgency plan. The scheme was to gather Vietnamese peasants into compact enclaves, protect them with barbed wire and mines, and provide them with radios to contact military forces. Inside the hamlets there would be homes, schools, a community center, and other services. Diem put his brother Nhu in charge of construction, and by the end of the summer of 1962 Nhu bragged that he had built 3,225 hamlets and relocated more than 4 million peasants into them.

During 1962 the conflict seemed to take a turn for the better. U.S. advisers went along with South Vietnamese Army units; American helicopters shuttled soldiers to attack guerrillas; American pilots flew missions against Vietcong concentrations; and from Washington's perspective the strategic hamlets were thriving. Ambassador Frederick Nolting and General Harkins issued glowing reports on the war. "There is no doubt we are on the winning side," Harkins claimed. Nolting reported "substantial progress in pacification and stability."

In Washington, Kennedy, who had many issues on his mind, cheerfully accepted the optimistic reports from men in whom he had confidence. For eighteen months after the debate on the Taylor Report, he set aside the Vietnam problem. He assumed that the strategic hamlet program was succeeding and that U.S. assistance would help quell the insurgency.

But policymakers badly underestimated the nationalism of Ho Chi Minh's movement, the determination and perseverance of the enemy, their organizational skills and their superior strategy. Not just terrorists, the insurgents were close to their nation's pulse, deep believers in their cause, and willing to endure monumental sacrifices to gain victory.

Conversely, U.S. officials overestimated the strength and cohesiveness of South Vietnam. To most Washington officials Saigon's army, the ARVN, seemed viable. It was well equipped with radios, airplanes, artillery, and fighter planes while the enemy had only light infantry. The ARVN needed only a little prodding, it was thought, "an adviser or two."

Nhu's decision to establish hamlets in remote areas to "show the flag" disregarded U.S. advice. Only 20 percent of the settlements met U.S. standards. "Most would be overrun within a year, enabling the Vietcong to capture thousands of American weapons," observes James Giglio. Nor did Nhu provide the crucial social, political, and economic reforms that might have made the strategic hamlet program effective. "Money the United States allocated for such purposes never reached the peasants," Giglio notes. Kennedy, his Washington advisers, Nolting, and Harkins remained oblivious to the failure.

Kennedy's advisers—McNamara, Bundy, Taylor, and Rostow—knew little about the region's history, language, culture, or values. McNamara later recognized that he and his associates had been "setting policy for a region that was terra incognita. We were flying blind," he added, because "we had no counterparts" to the State Department's Soviet experts. In the last six months of Kennedy's life the inattention, mistakes, misjudgments, and faulty assumptions relating to Vietnam returned to haunt his presidency.

1963

IN EARLY 1963, while Kennedy and his top advisers still shared the illusion of growing success in South Vietnam, a cadre of journalists began to criticize the war effort, describing a situation far different from the official version. Starting in 1962 and reaching a peak the following year, three American correspondents in Saigon—David Halberstam of the *New*

York Times, Neil Sheehan of United Press International, and Malcolm Browne of the Associated Press—disparaged Diem's regime and U.S. ineffectiveness.

These journalists reported from an anti-Diem perspective. "What we were reflecting was reality as seen by American and Vietnamese officers who were fighting the war," Halberstam later claimed. "Our conflict was with people who were in Saigon at the official level who reflected not what was happening in the field, but what they wanted to happen in the field." The correspondents accused the U.S. mission in Saigon of deliberately lying to them about the Diem regime and the progress of the war.

In May 1963, without warning, events in South Vietnam suddenly careened out of control. For years the Catholic-dominated Diem government had discriminated against Buddhists. One decree placed legal restrictions on Buddhist associations but not on Catholic organizations. Catholics could display the Vatican flag, but Buddhists could not fly their own flag.

Pent-up frustration among Buddhists exploded on May 8, 1963. When Diem forbade Buddhists from flying their religious flag on the anniversary of Buddha's birth, more than a thousand Buddhist protesters gathered at the radio station in Hue to demand that the order be revoked. When they refused to disperse, government troops opened fire, killing eight people. The following day ten thousand Buddhists showed up to renew the protest. Diem's government refused to accept responsibility for the deaths, blaming Vietcong agents for stirring up the crowd.

The Buddhist crisis irritated and bewildered Kennedy. "How could this have happened?" he demanded of aides. "Who are these people? Why didn't we know about them before?"

International outrage against Diem's regime reached new intensity on June 11. To protest the government's discrimination, a seventy-three-year-old Buddhist monk knelt on a major intersection in Saigon. After a colleague doused him with gasoline, the monk lit a match and immolated himself in front of a large crowd which included newsmen and photographers. The poignant picture of the monk, engulfed in flames, appeared on front pages and on television throughout the world. Thereafter the Buddhists deftly used immolations, demonstrations, and public statements to generate sympathetic media coverage.

In August Kennedy appointed his old foe, Henry Cabot Lodge, to replace Frederick Nolting as ambassador to South Vietnam. When he asked Lodge to be ambassador, the president held up Malcolm Browne's photo of the monk's fiery suicide and sadly remarked, "I suppose these are the worst press relations to be found in the world today."

On August 21 Nhu's Special Forces ransacked pagodas and arrested more than fourteen hundred Buddhists in Saigon, Hue, and other cities. Americans were outraged. After the attack Lodge, who had just arrived at his Saigon post, requested guidance from Washington. Despite sharp disagreement among Kennedy's advisers, Lodge was given permission to cautiously encourage a coup. On the morning of November 1 a group of South Vietnamese generals and their forces attacked the presidential palace in Saigon. The following day the White House learned that Diem and Nhu had been captured and murdered.

The coup turned out badly for the United States. A series of ineffective military strongmen assumed control in Saigon, but it might have been just as bad or worse if Diem had remained in power and continued to alienate groups in his country.

*

Beginning in 1956 and lasting to the day he died, John Kennedy's public remarks expressed nothing but determination to support the South Vietnamese government and defeat the Communist insurgents. In public he never hinted that the

United States should withdraw. Some argue that these public statements were merely a smokescreen to conceal Kennedy's real intentions. Roger Hilsman later claimed that Kennedy told him, "over and over again," that Hilsman's job was to keep American involvement minimal so that the United States could withdraw at the first opportunity.

Charles Bartlett claimed that Kennedy frankly told him, "We don't have a prayer of prevailing there. Those people hate us. They are going to throw our tails out of there at almost any point. But I can't give up a piece of territory like that to the Communists and then get the American people to reelect me."

No one can know for sure what policy Kennedy would have followed in Vietnam had he lived, but that hasn't stopped people from speculating. Clark Clifford, who knew both President Kennedy and President Johnson, noticed profound differences in their personality and style. He believed that Kennedy never would have allowed U.S. involvement to escalate as Johnson did.

> I often saw President Johnson personalize the actions of the Vietcong, interpreting them as somehow aimed personally at him. He reacted by thinking, *They can't do this to Lyndon Johnson! They can't push me around this way!* On the other hand, I believe President Kennedy would have treated the attacks strictly as an international problem—not something aimed at him personally. In reacting to the same events, I believe he would have thought, *I don't like the looks of this. I don't like the smell of it. Sending more troops may just increase the costs—let's hold off for awhile and see what happens. I'm not going to get us more deeply involved.*

Arthur Schlesinger, Ken O'Donnell, and Ted Sorensen have all claimed that Kennedy would have avoided further involvement in Vietnam. After-the-fact reminiscences, though, may only be wishful thinking to protect Kennedy's reputation.

The most intriguing recollection involves Kennedy's conversation with Senator Mike Mansfield, whose integrity and probity are impeccable. In the spring of 1963 Mansfield criticized the U.S. involvement in the Vietnam War at a congressional leadership breakfast at the White House. Afterward, according to O'Donnell, the president invited Mansfield to his office for a private talk. (O'Donnell listened to the conversation.) The president told the majority leader that he had come to agree with Mansfield on the need for the United States to withdraw. "But I can't do it until 1965—after I'm reelected," Kennedy said. If he announced a withdrawal before the 1964 election, conservatives would castigate him during his reelection campaign.

Mansfield later confirmed O'Donnell's recollection of the conversation, but he denied there was any discussion of the 1964 election. "The only thing discussed at that meeting . . . was the President's desire to bring about a withdrawal but recognizing that it could not be done precipitantly but only over a period of months."

Complicating the picture are several leading advisers who dispute the notion that Kennedy would have withdrawn from Vietnam. Dean Rusk, for example, has insisted that Kennedy never mentioned disengaging from the war. "I talked with John Kennedy on hundreds of occasions about Southeast Asia," Rusk later wrote, "and not once did he suggest or even hint at withdrawal."

What seems peculiar, historian Gregory Olson has perceptively observed, "is that the President never discussed withdrawal plans for Vietnam with his brother, Robert. If Kennedy had actually committed to withdrawal after his reelection, Robert would have known." Asked in 1964 whether his brother considered pulling out of Vietnam, Robert Kennedy answered, "No." The Kennedy administration, he said, thought "we should win the war in Vietnam."

Still, in John Kennedy's uncertainty about sending troops to Vietnam, like his rejection of hard-line advice during the

Cuban Missile Crisis, he acted more judiciously than his major advisers. Perhaps he would have recognized that the costs of fighting in South Vietnam outweighed the possible benefits. In any case, he had made the commitment to Diem without much enthusiasm and with grave misgivings.

12

Mind, Personality, and Image

AMONG KENNEDY'S prominent qualities of mind were flexibility, breadth of interest, curiosity, wit, and detachment. He was an analytical and skeptical person. He preferred ideas he could use, practical ideas. A superb listener, he tried to find the area of another person's expertise and to keep the dialogue on that subject. After meeting Kennedy, the British philosopher and author Isaiah Berlin remarked, "He exhausts you by listening."

"He was able to resist the temptation, to which so many other great men have yielded, to sound off himself and be admired," noted George Kennan. "He asked questions modestly, sensibly, and listened very patiently to what you had to say."

Kennedy gathered information effectively from listening, but he retained more when he read. He preferred written briefings. If his aide Fred Dutton sent the president a forty-page memo, Kennedy returned it within thirty-six hours with editorial notes all over the margins. "It was incredible—his ability to consume paper, to read it, [and] make intelligent comments," Dutton said.

History, biography, and current events dominated Kennedy's leisure reading. Many of his insights about leadership came from his study of great men. He read almost every book by the prolific Winston Churchill. He admired Churchill's

graceful style and often read passages to savor their craftsmanship.

Fiction rarely appeared on his reading list. Critics believe
that the president spent evenings immersed in the fantastic
tales of Ian Fleming's British secret agent James Bond, and
that Fleming's stories encouraged Kennedy to engage in espionage. Of the film version of Fleming's *From Russia with Love*,
Ben Bradlee observed that Kennedy "seemed to enjoy the cool
and the sex and the brutality." But suggestions that the Bond
book and the movie were favorites, that they stimulated his
support for covert action, that Bond typified his personal
style, or that he had an intimate friendship with Ian Fleming
are all exaggeration.

Kennedy often told friends about his two favorite books.
"*Pilgrim's Way* is a book of great beauty and strength," wrote
a reviewer of John Buchan's book, published in 1940. Kennedy read the book shortly after it appeared.

Of Scottish Puritan background, modest, with a genius for
friendship, John Buchan spent most of his life writing scores
of books—fiction, biography, and history. In *Pilgrim's Way* he
offers portrait sketches of the outstanding men he knew and
loved: Alfred Milner, Aldous Huxley, Rudyard Kipling, H. G.
Wells, Ramsay MacDonald, T. E. Lawrence, George V, and
Arthur Balfour.

Buchan's most memorable portrait, the one Kennedy
found most inspiring, described Raymond Asquith. Young
Asquith was the son of Herbert Asquith, the eminent British
politician and prime minister (1908–1916). "There are some
men whose brilliance in boyhood and early manhood dazzles
their contemporaries and becomes a legend," Buchan wrote.
"They march on into life with a boyish grace, and their high
noon keeps all the freshness of the morning." Raymond Asquith had "great beauty of person; the gift of winning speech;
a mind that mastered readily whatever it cared to master;
poetry and the love of all beautiful things; a magic to draw
friends to him; a heart as tender as it was brave. One gift only

was withheld from him—length of years." While leading his military unit, young Asquith was killed in 1915.

In Kennedy's post–World War II notebook he inscribed Buchan's final testimony to Asquith: "He will stand to those of us who are left as an incarnation of the spirit of the land he loved. He loved his youth and his youth has become eternal. Debonair, brilliant and brave, he is now part of that immortal England which knows not age or weariness or defeat."

With friends Kennedy often talked about Raymond Asquith. "I remember him saying over and over that there was nobody in our time who was more gifted," Jack's friend David Ormsby-Gore recalled. "Whether Jack realized it or not, I think he paralleled himself after Asquith."

Kennedy's other favorite book was a distinguished biography. In 1939 David Cecil published *The Young Melbourne*, a study of William Lamb who became Lord Melbourne and the prime minister of Great Britain from 1834 to 1841. The book scrutinized Melbourne's life up to the time he became prime minister. Cecil planned to cover Melbourne's entire life in one volume, but World War II interrupted his plan; he published what was finished, hoping he could later complete his study. Reviewers praised the book as an unusually fascinating portrait.

In 1954 Lord David Cecil, now professor of English literature at Oxford and renowned for his sensitive, stylized biographies, completed his study and published the two parts in one volume, *Melbourne*. Although fifteen years apart, Cecil gracefully fused the two sections. Kennedy read *Melbourne*, not Cecil's earlier book.

Reviewers heaped praise on *Melbourne*. "A classic," said the *Chicago Tribune*; "superb," wrote reviewer John Lukacs; "a work of art," concluded George Dangerfield in the *Saturday Review*. The book was listed briefly on the *New York Times* best-seller list.

Melbourne was not a great person, not one to be emulated by John Kennedy. Indecisive, he much preferred to put off decisions than make them. He was indolent and cynical. Reform movements were dangerous, he said, because they aroused expectations that government and society could actually be improved. He even opposed popular education.

David Ormsby-Gore insightfully observed that Kennedy "liked the way [the book] was written, he liked the style of the writing and he was interested in the period. I think these were all elements which gave him great pleasure. . . . He certainly never talked about Melbourne as being one of the great figures of the 19th century."

Exquisite prose style, captivating narrative, brilliant portraits—these were the primary attractions of *Pilgrim's Way* and *Melbourne*.

Kennedy once defined himself politically as "an idealist without illusions." He must strive for excellence in all his activities—in administering of his office, in his speeches, programs, and appointments, in the arts—but this goal had to be tempered by realism and must not unduly risk his political defeat.

The lives of great men—Winston Churchill, Raymond Asquith, Jefferson, Lincoln, Napoleon—captivated him. When he discussed them, Isaiah Berlin concluded after a discussion with Kennedy, "his eyes shone with a particular glitter, and it was quite clear that he thought in terms of great men and what they were able to do." He respected distinction in many fields and tried to foster it, dotting his conversation, as well as his formal speeches, with the sayings of great people.

"He was a hard man, casually cruel," concludes Richard Reeves in his study of Kennedy:

> I did not like the man who jabbed a needle into his buddy Red Fay's leg to show the pain of his own daily medical regimen. . . .
>
> I did not like the man who refused to talk to his friend Ben Bradlee for months to punish him for a small criticism. . . . And I did not like the man who ran meetings from the

bathtub, giving the orders of the day to assistants sitting on toilets and leaning on sinks.

Reeves's specific examples are accurate, and there were others, but the author exaggerates. For the most part Kennedy was not a vindictive man and did not harbor grievances. "There was no 'Kennedy treatment' comparable with the 'LBJ treatment,'" noted Dean Rusk.

Reeves also judges Kennedy as egocentric, a person who used his charm to manipulate people for his own selfish ends. Kennedy was "an artist who painted with other people's lives. He squeezed people like tubes of paint, gently or brutally, and the people around him—family, writers, drivers, ladies-in-waiting—were the indentured inhabitants serving his needs and desires." This was true in some cases, particularly with ladies-in-waiting, but he was seldom brutal with anyone. He brandished his charm and squeezed people primarily because that was what politicians did. He turned on his charm to convince Congress and the American people to support his programs; he turned on his charm so he could be reelected in 1964 and continue to push his program.

Others had a different impression of Kennedy's ego. "He did not fall victim to the pervading virus of vanity which so frequently seems to attack the holders of great positions of power in any government," said Robert Lovett. "All three presidents I served—Truman, Kennedy, and Johnson—had lively senses of humor, but Kennedy's was the best," said Dean Rusk. Kennedy used humor, sardonic wit, and teasing with everyone, including himself. His laugh was usually restrained and seldom boisterous; his face crinkled and his eyes twinkled as he broke into a broad grin.

His best-remembered witticisms were original, as when he hosted a large group of Nobel Prize–winners at the White House: "This is the most extraordinary collection of talent, of human knowledge, that has ever been gathered together at the White House, with the possible exception of when Thomas Jefferson dined here alone."

From the time he recovered his health in the late 1950s, Kennedy no longer had a morbid fascination with death. Still, there were moments when his own possible assassination entered his mind. His physician, Dr. Janet Travell, reported that once, when the president was reading the newspaper in his limousine, he glanced up and saw a boy in the back seat of a sedan ahead of him holding a large motion-picture camera against the back window with its lens pointed at the president. Instantly Kennedy's muscles tensed.

"It's only a child with a movie camera," Travell assured him.

The president took a deep breath and said, "I will not live in fear. What will be, must be."

*

Kennedy cultivated and protected his public image. He avoided being photographed eating food or wearing his glasses. His attractive personal style offset his mistakes, masked his ineptness, and enhanced his popularity. Much of Kennedy's image involved his family life with his two adorable children and glamorous wife. A photographer observed: "You couldn't miss with him. It was just like French cooking. No matter what you did, you always came up with something fine."

Kennedy used television the way Franklin Roosevelt used radio: to give him direct, instantaneous, and unmediated access to the public. On January 25, 1961, only five days after his inauguration, Kennedy stood before cameras for the first-ever live televised presidential news conference. The luxurious new State Department auditorium hosted the unprecedented event. More than four hundred reporters gathered for the president's debut.

The 6 p.m. broadcast was an enormous popular success, with an estimated television audience of 65 million. "His performance was almost flawless," said reporter Charles Roberts. "I sensed from the moment the President walked on stage that the presidential press conference would never be the same again." Indeed, Kennedy had opened a new era in political communications.

The week before a scheduled press conference, Pierre Salinger gathered materials on current issues. The State Department prepared a large briefing book, listing possible questions and answers on issues of foreign policy; the Council of Economic Advisers did the same for major economic developments. All the various reports were gathered for the president to study. On the morning of the press conference Kennedy had breakfast with key advisers who grilled him with questions.

The president was quicker and far more articulate in his responses to news conference questions than his predecessor. Ike's syntax had been obscure and convoluted; Kennedy's was clear and direct. The news conferences kept the president's mind razor-sharp, like preparing for a final exam. James Reston noted wonderingly, "How Kennedy knew the precise drop in milk consumption in 1960, the percentage rise in textile imports from 1957 to 1960, and the number of speeches cleared by the Defense Department is not quite clear, but anyway, he did. He either overwhelmed you with decimal points or disarmed you with a smile and a wisecrack."

Besides sixty-four news conferences in three years, Kennedy went on television nine other times to issue important statements about a single subject, like the Berlin crisis. He also held informal television interviews, the most memorable in late 1962 when the three television networks teamed up to make available an hour of prime time for a review of Kennedy's first two years as president.

The Kennedy administration opened itself to the press. Each day scores of printed handouts flowed from Salinger's office. The White House released everything that could be safely released—task-force reports, toasts at state dinners and official lunches, speeches the president made in the Rose Garden. Kennedy was receptive to Salinger's suggestion to remove many of the traditional barriers standing between the president and the media. The rule against live television at his press conferences was the first barrier to go. Under President Eisenhower, reporters could rarely interview any White House staff member. Under Kennedy, correspondents could visit the administration's top advisers in their offices or at lunch.

Kennedy began the practice of inviting the country's leading publishers to lunch at the White House; he held twenty-five such lunches, state by state. By and large the publishers found the sessions informative and stimulating. One publisher observed: "I was amazed. He did not dodge a single question."

But Kennedy could overreact to what he considered careless or biased reporting, leading critics to accuse him of whining about picayune matters. Merriman Smith of United Press International, the dean of White House correspondents at the time, was amazed at the president's close attention to everything written about him. "How they can spot an obscure paragraph in a paper of 3,000 circulation 2,000 miles away is beyond me. They must have a thousand little gnomes reading the papers for them." Fletcher Knebel of *Look* magazine wrote: "Never before have so few bawled out so many so often for so little."

Every president, from Washington to Eisenhower, has been accused of censorship, managing news, manufacturing news, or blacking out news. The media insist on their duty to report everything happening in government; the president insists on his right to conceal or withhold information whose publication might damage national security. Normally the media defer to the government only in wartime. But in the cold war, was an actual declaration of war necessary before the president could invoke extraordinary controls on the flow of information?

Kennedy thought the media had responsibilities as well as rights—the responsibility to get the facts correct, to consider the national interest, and to place their opinions on the editorial page. Because the cold war could turn into a hot war, the administration needed to conceal some operations and sometimes maneuver secretly. If prevented from concealing critical maneuvers, the government would lose a key weapon in the cold war—the right of the enemy not to know.

Critics then and later charged that the Kennedy administration engaged in suppression, distortion, and outright lies. A few reporters were cut off from all news sources at the White House because an item they wrote did not win approval at the White House. Correspondents whose papers criticized the president sometimes received the silent treatment. "If you want to be an insider, the best thing to do is to let Ted Sorensen write your stories for you," said one detractor. Ben Bradlee felt the president's sting for a brief and mildly critical comment he made for a feature story in *Look* magazine. "It's almost impossible," Bradlee said, "to write a story they like. Even if a story is quite favorable to their side, they'll find one paragraph to quibble with." For this remark Kennedy socially banished Bradlee for almost three months.

Edward P. Morgan enjoyed social contact with the president but didn't feel it warped his professional approach to his job. "I could produce commentaries that were highly critical of something that the Administration did." Still, Morgan found something insidious about his social relations with the president. "It's very difficult to go to a man's house for dinner and have a hell of a good time in the process—let alone to the White House for dinner and enjoy an intimate relationship with the President and the First Lady of the land—and then go off . . . and be enormously critical."

In sum, Kennedy did attempt to manage the news in a few instances, and by his social flattery of journalists and close friendship with several he certainly hoped to influence news coverage. But detractors exaggerate when they claim that his actions seriously compromised the independence and freedom of the media. His attempts at management and social flattery applied to only a tiny segment of the news industry, and they often had little impact. "Kennedy has committed no serious offenses against press freedom," said *Time*.

"Beyond any reasonable doubt, the Kennedy Administration has deliberately sought to magnify each of its accomplishments and minimize its shortcomings," concluded *Newsweek*. "But here's the rub. Virtually every government in history has done the same thing."

13

White House Life: Work and Family

THE AUTHOR Garry Wills, a severe critic of John Kennedy, sarcastically observed that the "official Kennedy literature is drearily joyful in repeating how much fun Kennedy had being President." But it was true—he did enjoy it. "John F. Kennedy was a happy president," said Sorensen. "He liked the job, he thrived on its pressures."

White House staff meetings and weekly Cabinet meetings were a thing of the past under Kennedy. Nor would he have an assistant president's job, the post held by Sherman Adams in the Eisenhower White House. He abolished the National Security Council (NSC) Planning Board and the Operations Coordinating Board because he thought they engaged in needless paperwork and blocked the president's contact with his responsible officers. Eisenhower wanted his advisers to present him with a consensus, an agreement on a course of action by all relevant parties with the arguments neatly summarized. Then he would say "Yes" or "No." Kennedy's Cabinet and NSC meetings were largely symbolic, conducted to satisfy the public's desire for order and regularity.

Unlike Ike, Kennedy wanted a part in the process of decision-making. Documents presented to him should be vivid and forceful, offering different points of view. "He was not interested in unanimous committee recommendations which stifled alternatives to find the lowest common denominator of compromise," Sorensen commented.

The president collected information from many sources: magazines, books, television, radio, elder statesmen, friends, politicians, experts, polls, and especially newspapers. He often phoned aides and Cabinet members, seeking more facts, documents, or evidence.

He took very seriously his responsibility to uphold high standards of government service even on problems some might judge as minor. In early November 1963 he was shocked to learn of the spread of polio in the Trust territories in the Pacific. "It seems to me that this is inexcusable," he wrote Stewart Udall, his interior secretary. "I would like to have an investigation made into why there were inadequate funds in 1958 for administering preventive medicine and why no action was undertaken between 1958 and 1963 when the spread of the disease again became acute. How much would it have cost to have taken precautionary steps?. . . . I would like a complete investigation into the reason why the United States government did not meet its responsibility in this area. Would you expedite this matter?"

Instead of regular Cabinet meetings and National Security Council meetings, Kennedy established small, interagency task forces to gather facts, isolate issues, and make recommendations. There were task forces on Laos, Cuba, Vietnam, NATO, minimum-wage policy, and integration in federal employment. In addition, Kennedy usually held three or four small daily meetings, more often on foreign policy than on domestic matters.

The president gave Cabinet officers free rein to run their own departments and seldom meddled. "He knew what you were doing, and he followed it closely, and he was very alert," observed Secretary of Agriculture Orville Freeman.

The NSC staff became a "little State Department," with its own area specialists. Each member had his own portfolios, not just ad hoc assignments. Bundy and his staff kept in touch with every aspect of foreign affairs—from disarmament negotiations to NATO troop levels, from the aid program in India to conditions in Yemen. Unlike the State Department, Bundy gave the president quick, clear, intelligent responses. A facilitator, he managed the flow of business, knowing and coordinating everything to do with foreign policy. Bundy's staff often duplicated the State Department's responsibilities, but Kennedy didn't care. Since he had little faith in the State Department and didn't know most of its personnel, he felt more confident in receiving information and opinions from Bundy's staff because he knew the issue would be carefully studied.

The president relied extensively on his brother. Robert Kennedy hated incompetence, laziness, stupidity, and pretense. Earning a bad reputation in the bureaucracy for his explosive temper, he once stormed into a State Department meeting, expressed his displeasure, and slammed a chair on the floor. He chastised bureaucrats in front of their peers, not seeming to care whom he offended.

But though he was prickly, Robert attacked his responsibilities as attorney general with energy and dedication. He recruited an excellent staff of talented and idealistic lawyers from leading law firms and universities, and his team remained exceptionally loyal to him. Under his direction the Justice Department's Organized Crime Section and the Tax Division convicted 570 racketeers. He turned a huge, slumbering, bureaucratic department into a vibrant and effective organization.

Bobby was the only person in the administration who could be absolutely candid with the president. "That is a terrible idea," he would declare. He realized that one of his most important roles was to speak frankly, to contradict his brother at times, and to nudge him onto the right course.

In a crisis, with his older brother relying on his advice and support, Bobby was usually wise, calm, restrained, and realistic in getting to the facts at the heart of a problem. The president trusted his judgment and depended on him to handle problems. But it was John Kennedy who weighed alternatives and made decisions. "*Nobody* told President Kennedy what to do," said Ken O'Donnell. "The President was much the toughest of the Kennedy brothers."

*

During Kennedy's presidency the White House sponsored a successful series of outdoor concerts, giving talented young amateurs—students of music and dance—a chance to perform. In a brief welcoming address Kennedy tried to inspire each group. One chilly spring day in 1962 the Greater Boston Youth Symphony Orchestra played on the south lawn for an audience of children. The president apologized for not being able to stay for the entire concert, but he promised to leave his office door open so he could listen.

While a tour guide once took a group of spastic children on a special private tour of the mansion, the president, who was late for an appointment, spotted them. An observer recalled:

> He crossed the lawn to us, insisted on being introduced to each child, and either picked up each limp, paralyzed hand to shake it, or touched the child on the cheek. He had a different conversation with each child. . . . He knelt down by the side of a young boy and held a long conversation with him. Then he dashed back into his office, returned with an old PT boat skipper's hat he had used in the war, and plopped it down on the boy's head.
>
> The child's face radiated a joy totally impossible to describe. . . .
>
> "His father was in PT boats, too," the President said to me by way of explanation. "His father is dead."

In the summer the president still preferred going to Hyannis Port. Anticipating his arrival, a mob of Kennedy grandchildren gathered in the driveway. Rose Kennedy recalled, "Jack then would come up onto the front porch where his father was sitting so proudly in his wheel chair." (Joe Kennedy suffered a stroke in 1961.)

Before the inauguration, William Walton assisted Jackie in renting Glen Ora, forty miles west of Washington, located in the horse-and-hunt country near Middleburg, Virginia. Glen Ora was the president's concession to Jacqueline's desire to ride horses. The four-hundred-acre estate included stables, pastures, a guest house, and an Olympic-size swimming pool.

A few weeks before Christmas 1962 the Kennedys began to build a new home also in the hunt country near Middleburg. To please her husband, Jackie christened it Wexford, a bow to the Kennedys' roots in County Wexford, Ireland. Jack never liked Wexford, never felt comfortable there. "Wexford epitomized the differences in their taste," observed Ralph Martin. "He liked the open sea and she loved the sweeping forest and mountains." Jackie could ride her horses, but the house had no swimming pool, no beach to walk or ship to sail.

In the spring of 1963, with Wexford under construction, the first couple spent weekends at Camp David, the presidential retreat in the Catoctin Mountains of Maryland. A mountaintop complex, surrounded by woods, Camp David is miles from civilization. With beautiful scenery, comfortable living quarters, guest houses, stables with horses, bowling alleys, a movie theater, a heated swimming pool, a three-hole golf course, and complete and secure privacy, it resembles a splendid resort. "If only I'd realized how nice Camp David really is, I'd never have rented Glen Ora, or built Wexford," Jackie said wistfully.

In the summer of 1963 the Kennedys rented a weathered-shingled home on Squaw Island, still close to Hyannis Port but far enough away to escape the family tumult at the Kennedy compound.

Boating relaxed Kennedy the most, even on overcast and chilly days. Once, while Jackie served hot dogs to guests on board, the president teased, "This is history in the making: 'The First Lady with the elegance and dignity of the White House hostess she is, serving the humble hot-dog to her distinguished guests at sea.'"

When he sailed, Kennedy sat at the bow, clinging to the forestay. "He loved the view from there and seemed to listen to the sound of the water being parted by the bow into a rush of surging white that swept aft along both sides," reported Julius Fanta. A naval aide recalled seeing him "gazing over the sea, lost in thought, and idly chewing on the frame of his sunglasses."

Private screenings of films were a frequent pastime at the White House, but unless the movie was very dramatic the president walked out after the first twenty-five minutes, usually to read or work. His favorites were *The Guns of Navarone* and *Spartacus*.

*

"Americans in 1960 elected a president with arguably the most extensive medical problems ever; surely, no president required more prescription medication," observes James Giglio, an expert on Kennedy's health.

After his inauguration, Kennedy appointed Dr. Janet Travell as his White House physician, the first woman ever to hold the post. He also inherited Adm. George C. Burkley, who had worked in the Eisenhower administration. By having on staff two primary doctors, Kennedy invited friction.

Medical attention was a part of Kennedy's daily routine. As Robert Dallek has noted, "He was under the care of an allergist, an endocrinologist, a gastroenterologist, an orthopedist, and a urologist," along with Travell and Burkley.

In the first six months of his presidency, "Kennedy suffered stomach, colon, and prostate problems, high fevers, occasional dehydration, abscesses, sleeplessness, and high cholesterol, in addition to his ongoing back and adrenal ailments," Dallek records. His physicians administered large doses of so many drugs that Travell kept elaborate records. Yet he missed only one day of work.

Kennedy's unstable and painful back remained a major cause of concern. In the summer of 1961 Dr. Edwin Cave, an outside orthopedic consultant, was asked to analyze the x-rays of Kennedy's back. In his report, Cave attributed the president's pain to "the scar in the region of his previous operation[s]." He never mentioned compression fractures or osteoporosis, Dallek's major contentions. X-rays of 1962 showed evidence of osteoarthritis.

Of the many orthopedic surgeons Kennedy had seen for his back pain, he received the most sensible advice from Dr. Hans Kraus of New York. In the fall of 1961 Dr. Burkley brought in Dr. Kraus to implement exercise therapy. Kraus recommended gradually increased strengthening exercises for weak muscles, and limbering and stretching exercises for stiff muscles. (Kraus disdained Travell's procaine injections.)

Three times week Kennedy followed Kraus's regimen, exercising in the small gymnasium next to the White House swimming pool. Kraus reported steady progress in the strength and flexibility of the president's back, and Kennedy's pain diminished.

As president, Kennedy became overly preoccupied with his health, concerned that his stomach would act up, that his voice would be weak, or that he was about to catch a cold. Over many years, scores of doctors, nurses, and school officials had attended to his ailments. His many visits to doctors and hospitals led him to an exceptional concentration on *imagined* as well as real health problems.

"The President received no other treatments that were not authorized or indicated by me," Burkley later stated, seemingly oblivious to the famous intervention of another doctor who was injecting Kennedy with a dangerous compound. In the fall of 1960, during the presidential campaign, Kennedy told his friend Charles Spalding that he felt fatigued, his muscles "weak." Spalding arranged a confidential consultation with Dr. Max Jacobson, who injected the candidate with what was apparently the physician's standard concoction: amphetamines, steroids, calcium, placenta, and vitamins. "After his treatment," Jacobson later claimed, "he told me his muscle weakness had disappeared. He felt cool, calm and very alert."

"Dr. Feelgood," as he was known, continued to treat Kennedy for the next three years. Born in Germany, Jacobson had emigrated to the United States in 1936 and established a medical practice in New York. Denied hospital privileges in 1946, thereafter he practiced out of his office.

Amphetamine (also known as speed) is a powerful stimulant, once widely and rashly prescribed. In the early 1960s doctors used it to treat depression and prevent fatigue. Amphetamines were not illegal at the time, and the drug's dangers and addictive properties were not widely known: amphetamines can cause nervousness, impaired judgment and overconfidence. Jacobson claimed that the dose levels of amphetamines he prescribed were too small to lead to dependence. Besides, he said during an interview, "Amphetamine is not an addictive drug. Heroin is. Morphine is." Now most experts would strongly disagree with his opinion.

Prominent patients of the doctor included writer Truman Capote, filmmakers Cecil B. DeMille and Otto Preminger, singer Eddie Fisher, and playwright Tennessee Williams. Many of Jacobson's patients swore by his compound and claimed that his shots gave them boundless energy, allowing them to lead more productive and pleasurable lives. In his ramshackle office, which doubled as an unauthorized drug laboratory, the unkempt Jacobson didn't maintain quality control or sterility standards. He treated patients while wearing bloodstained surgical garb. In 1975 the New York State Board of Regents revoked his license to practice medicine.

In late May 1961 Jacobson was invited to the White House to treat the president's back pain. Shortly after receiving his shot, Kennedy stood up and walked back and forth several times. "I feel very much better." The president convinced Jacobson to accompany him to Europe for the Vienna summit, where he injected Kennedy several times. According to gate logs, Jacobson came to the White House more than thirty times. He insisted that his treatments helped Kennedy manage the Vienna summit, the Cuban Missile Crisis, a threatened steel strike, and the James Meredith affair in Mississippi. There is no evidence that Jacobson treated Kennedy after May 1962.

In her oral history and in her published autobiography, Dr. Travell never mentioned Jacobson; nor did Dr. Burkley in any of his public comments. Both were privately suspicious of him. Burkley apparently spied on Jacobson but was helpless to stop his White House visits. There is no evidence that Jacobson's treatment affected Kennedy's behavior at Vienna or during the Cuban Missile Crisis or at any other time. He never appeared to have symptoms of excessive amphetamine usage.

That Jacobson intervened in managing Kennedy's health care replicated a long-term problem. For most of his life Kennedy received fragmented medical care from too many physicians, with no one doctor in charge of his overall management and having all the available information. No single physician coordinated all the drugs he received.

Although Kennedy's handling of major crises after Jacobson had treated him remained adroit and cautious, even the possibility that his thinking and judgment might have been impaired at crucial moments is chilling. His ailments and treatments notwithstanding, Kennedy appeared to the public to be in robust health—young, trim, and vigorous. He overcame his medical problems partly through his remarkable will and fortitude. "Therein, perhaps, lies his real profile in courage," observes James Giglio.

*

Jackie contributed to her husband's presidency by vastly improving the beauty of the White House, encouraging the performing arts, and serving as a charming ambassador on her husband's trips. On the other hand, she hated many of the customary duties of the first lady and was often uncooperative.

In her triumphant trips abroad with her husband, Jackie captivated foreigners with her youth, beauty, poise, clothes, and brief speeches in French or Spanish. In June 1961 she was the star in Paris. Her knowledge of France, her fluency in the subtleties of French, and her entertaining conversation captivated Charles de Gaulle. At his Paris press conference, the president said, "I do not think it altogether inappropriate to introduce myself to this audience. I am the man who accompanied Jacqueline Kennedy to Paris, and I have enjoyed it."

Often moody, easily fatigued, and naturally shy, Jackie found excuses for avoiding the traditional responsibilities of the first lady. She detested many of the rituals: attending luncheons, meeting ambassadors' wives, or greeting foreign leaders she thought were unimportant. She refused to meet with such major charitable organizations as the Muscular Dystrophy Association and the American Red Cross.

Raising children became one of Jack's favorite topics of conversation. In 1963 Caroline was six years old, and John was three. "He was very affectionate and attentive to his children," said Secret Service agent Larry Newman. "No matter how pressing his duties were," said nanny Maud Shaw, "he always found time to listen to the children."

While he relaxed in his rocking chair, Caroline and John would climb all over him. "I'll race you over to the pool," he would say, and the two children were off like a shot. Caroline and John walked with him to his office almost every morning. Five or ten minutes later Maud Shaw would take John back to the mansion and Caroline to her school.

Loose in the west lobby of the White House, Caroline chatted with reporters. One asked her what her father was doing. "Oh, he's upstairs with his shoes and socks off, not doing anything." Salinger said it was the girl's last press conference.

"In the first year or so in the White House, Jackie and Jack related to each other like professionals," Angier Biddle Duke observed. "They were co-workers. But then, after the Cuban missile crisis, they became more personal with each other. . . . Jackie started to talk about him in a more personal way. Like, 'Angie, the President is tired; lay off him, okay?' She seemed more concerned about him as a person." By 1963, holding his hand, Jacqueline would walk with the president to Air Force One, not caring about the spectators watching them.

In early August 1963, while the Kennedys vacationed on Squaw Island, Jackie was pregnant and due in mid-September. But on August 7, five and a half weeks early, she felt birth pangs. A helicopter landed on Squaw Island and flew her to Otis Air Force Base hospital on Cape Cod.

The baby boy, four pounds, ten and a half ounces, was christened Patrick Bouvier Kennedy after Jack's grandfather. Doctors diagnosed Patrick as having hyaline membrane disease and rushed the child to Boston Children's Hospital later in the afternoon. With the disease, most common in premature infants, a membrane coats the air sacs in the lungs, hindering the baby's ability to pass oxygen into the bloodstream.

At 4:04 a.m. on Friday, August 9, fewer than forty hours after his birth, the baby died. Jack and Jackie were devastated. Only thirteen people were invited to attend the Mass of the Angels presided over by Cardinal Cushing in Boston the next day. (Jackie was unable to attend.) After the other mourners left for the cemetery, Kennedy remained behind. Cushing watched him circle "the tiny coffin with his arm, as if he wanted to take it with him." He placed a St. Christopher medal inside the casket next to the baby's body. The president was weeping and so was Cushing. "My dear Jack, let's go, let's go. Nothing more can be done."

Two months after Patrick's death, O'Donnell and Powers accompanied the president to the Harvard-Columbia football game at Harvard Stadium. Near the end of the first half, Kennedy turned to O'Donnell and said, "I want to go to Patrick's grave, and I want to go there alone, with nobody from the newspapers following me." O'Donnell organized the maneuver. At Patrick's grave the president prayed quietly for a few moments, then laid a yellow chrysanthemum bouquet by the tombstone.

*

Past presidents and their wives had never refurbished the entire White House. Instead they had merely altered a wall or two to suit their own taste, never blending the modifications with the rest of the decor. As a result the White House was a poorly decorated mansion.

Jackie did a more thorough renovation. On February 23, 1961, she launched the historic project by appointing a twelve-member Fine Arts Committee. This formidable group of experts were mostly wealthy, influential Republicans, and their work turned out to be impressive. The collective effort yielded more than five hundred new acquisitions for the White House, including chairs, tables, lighting fixtures, and mantels. Eventually Jackie's project stimulated her husband's imagination. He had never expressed an interest in furniture, wall paintings, curtains, or rugs, but now he gave tours to guests, pointing out the aesthetic atrocities the Kennedys had inherited. "Look," he said, crawling on his hands and knees to examine a table. "It's not even a good *reproduction.*"

The White House social secretary was Letitia Baldrige. Exceptionally capable, statuesque, a congressman's daughter and a veteran of American embassies in Europe, Baldrige helped organize receptions and dinners for heads of state. Kennedy instructed that a diversified group be invited to receptions—political figures, businessmen, Negroes, labor leaders, artists, writers. "Make sure that Hubert Humphrey and his wife are invited to one of our State dinners," he advised. "We ought to . . . make sure that everybody in the Senate gets invited rather than just the same old names."

For after-dinner entertainment Jackie welcomed esteemed performing artists: cellist Pablo Casals, violinist Isaac Stern, and pianist Eugene Istomin, among others. On the evening of November 13, 1961, the White House invited 153 guests to a musicale in the East Room to hear Casals, eighty-four, one of the world's greatest performing musicians. The evening's music, declared *Time*, "sent shards of rapture through the world of serious music."

Casals had exiled himself from his native Spain in 1939 to protest the rule of fascist Francisco Franco. Since then he had refused to play his cello in any country that recognized the Franco government. But when President Kennedy learned that Casals approved of his administration, he asked him to play at the White House, and Casals accepted.

At the end of the concert the audience, led by the president, gave Casals a standing ovation. Leonard Bernstein, his head buried in his hands during most of Casals's performance, said afterward, "I was deeply moved by the entire occasion, not merely by the music of Casals but by the company in which it was played."

"The Casals evening has had an extraordinary effect in the artistic world," Schlesinger wrote the president shortly after the performance. "You probably saw John Crosby's column this morning ('President Kennedy is the best friend culture . . . has had in the White House since Jefferson')." Schlesinger recommended that the president go a step further and appoint a special assistant for culture who could survey areas of actual or possible government support. Schlesinger suggested August Heckscher as the best person for the job. Heckscher directed the Twentieth Century Fund, a nonprofit research institution that subsidized studies of economic, political, and social issues. The president acted immediately, asking Heckscher to join the White House team to work on cultural matters.

Over the next year and a half, serving as the administration's cultural liaison, Heckscher accumulated volumes of information. His report disapproved of governmental design standards—for coins, stamps, federal buildings—and urged the government to use independent panels of experts for aesthetic advice. Furthermore the report "called attention to the inadequate condition of America's cultural facilities, suggested educational reforms, decried the run-down appearance of the national capital, and even offered tax reforms." In consultation with Heckscher the president issued an executive order establishing the President's Advisory Council on the Arts.

Although unfamiliar with an artistic concept, Kennedy nonetheless appreciated its merit. "He simply understood the *quality* of greatness," said Baldrige. In terms of government policy toward the arts, the Kennedy administration made only incremental progress. The White House dinners were mostly symbolic, Heckscher's report merely a beginning. Still, as John Wetenhall contends, Kennedy's effort displayed "sensitivity to the rising concerns for culture in America." The New Frontier formed practical recommendations and endowed the cultural agenda with a "vocabulary of idealism that left a legacy of national values to the legislation that would follow."

14

Women and Sex

KENNEDY TOLD his friend Charles Bartlett that in the White House he intended to curb his womanizing. He would keep the White House "white." In fact the presidency never stopped Kennedy from pursuing attractive women. Although the White House and the media's glare confined and restricted him, the aura of his office, his constant travel, Jackie's frequent absences, solicitous procurers, plus the discreet attitude of the Secret Service enabled him to continue his philandering.

One of his adulterous affairs burst into the national headlines on December 17, 1975. A month earlier the Church Committee, in its report on CIA assassination attempts, had discreetly stated that a "close friend" of President Kennedy had also been a close friend of mobsters John Roselli and Sam Giancana. Shortly after, the *Washington Post* leaked the person's identity—it was a woman, Judith Campbell Exner. On December 17, sitting next to her second husband, Dan Exner, and hiding behind large sunglasses, Exner, then forty-one, held forth at a press conference and denied any knowledge of underworld activities. Two years later, in her sensational autobiography *My Story* (1977), Exner recounted her sexual tryst with Kennedy and her simultaneous relationship with Giancana, plus her friendship with Roselli.

Of all the Kennedy sex scandals, the Exner story may be the one that troubles his admirers most. It is also a tale that remains clouded with uncertainty. Exner changed it several times, amplifying her original confession of an affair into bizarre claims about her role in a conspiracy involving Kennedy and the Mafia. The first accusations were bad enough; the later ones would seriously injure Kennedy's reputation as president, if true.

Exner's friend Sam Giancana, a short, dour, homely Sicilian, held forth at the Armory Lounge in Forest Park, Illinois, ordering murders and managing his crime empire. An extraordinary criminal, Giancana was a leading member of La Cosa Nostra, the national crime syndicate, successor to Al Capone in Chicago. Giancana's friend and associate, John Roselli, represented the Chicago mob on the West Coast.

On the evening of February 7, 1960, the singer Frank Sinatra introduced Judith Campbell to Senator Kennedy at Sinatra's table at the Sands lounge in Las Vegas. After their encounter, Kennedy phoned her frequently, telling her how much he missed her and wondering when they could meet again. They finally rendezvoused on March 7 at the New York Plaza Hotel, where they had their first sexual encounter.

In Florida in late March 1960, Sinatra also introduced Campbell to a man named "Sam Flood." It took a while for Campbell to learn that the man who befriended her in Florida was actually Sam Giancana. Was it just a coincidence, critics wondered, that within a two-month period Sinatra's introductions had sparked Exner's romances with a future president and a notorious criminal? Was Giancana using Exner because she was Kennedy's girlfriend? In her autobiography Exner dampened such speculation: It "never occurred to me that Sam's interest in me was simply because of my association with Jack Kennedy."

Throughout the fall of 1961 and the winter and spring of 1962, she continued seeing Kennedy. At the White House their routine seldom varied. Evelyn Lincoln made reservations for her at the Mayflower Hotel. In the evening the White House car drove her to the East Gate, the one used by tourists in the daytime. After her arrival about 7:30 p.m., she and the president usually had frozen daiquiris and then dinner. By late spring 1962 their romance had cooled. He phoned her infrequently, and she returned his calls less often.

Was Exner's story true? By the time she wrote her autobiography in 1977, Kennedy, Giancana, and Roselli were all dead.

Exner had told the Church Committee that her relationship with Kennedy was only personal, and that she had no knowledge of any relationship between Giancana and Kennedy. She made the same denials in her press conference in December 1975 and in her autobiography, which reviewers found to be credible. The evidence she offered—addresses, telephone numbers, descriptions of White House decor— "makes the defensive protestations of the keepers of the Kennedy flame somewhat dubious," said a review in the *New York Times*.

But eleven years after her book was published, Exner began telling another, very different story. In 1988 *People* magazine published an article by Kitty Kelley, based on the author's interviews with Exner. "I lied when I said I was not a conduit between President Kennedy and the Mafia," Exner stunningly told Kelley. "I lied when I said that President Kennedy was unaware of my friendships with mobsters. He knew everything about my dealings with Sam Giancana and Johnny Roselli because I was seeing them for him." She claimed to have acted as a courier between Kennedy and Giancana and Roselli.

For example, she claimed that a few days after the bungled Bay of Pigs invasion in April 1961, Kennedy called her in California and asked her to fly to Las Vegas, pick up an envelope from Roselli, and deliver it to Giancana in Chicago. Then she was to arrange a meeting between the president and the Mafia boss, one that took place in her suite at the Ambassador East on April 28, 1961.

For eighteen months in 1960 and 1961, Exner claimed, she served as the president's link with the Mob. At Kennedy's

request she crisscrossed the nation carrying envelopes between the president and Giancana, and arranged about ten
meetings between the two, one of which, she thought, took
place inside the White House.

"They were sealed but not taped," Exner said of the plain
nine-by-twelve manila envelopes. "I never looked inside. . . .
I didn't know what they contained." Not until 1975, when
the Church Committee made its report, did Exner become
convinced that "I was probably helping Jack orchestrate the
attempted assassination of Fidel Castro with the help of the
Mafia."

In 1997, eighteen years after the publication of *My Story*,
Exner again amplified her account. In separate interviews
with journalists Liz Smith (for her article in *Vanity Fair*) and
Seymour Hersh (for his book *The Dark Side of Camelot*),
Exner unveiled sensational new allegations. She now claimed
that Kennedy had revealed to her the contents of envelopes
she subsequently delivered to Giancana and Roselli. "I knew
they dealt with the 'elimination' of Castro and that Sam and
Johnny had been hired by the CIA. That's what Jack explained
to me in the very beginning."

For the first time Exner implicated Robert Kennedy in the
CIA-Mafia-Castro story. "I used to be at the White House
having lunch or dinner with Jack, and Bobby [Kennedy]
would often come by," she told Liz Smith. "He'd squeeze my
shoulder solicitously and ask, 'Judy, are you O.K. carrying
these messages for us to Chicago? Do you still feel comfortable doing it?'"

Exner's autobiography had been convincing because her
key contentions could be documented with FBI reports, Secret
Service logs, White House telephone records, witnesses, and
evidence in her own possession. The same is not true for her
revelations after 1977. Her sensational charges—that money
and documents were directly exchanged between the president and Giancana, and that Robert Kennedy colluded with
Giancana as well—all rely primarily on Exner's testimony.

Several serious weaknesses cast doubt on Exner's post-1977 allegations. Secret Service agents who candidly testified about the president's womanizing do not confirm any of Exner's contentions about his relations with Giancana. "Ms. Exner has, like all of us, read about the CIA's attempt to use Giancana to assassinate Castro," noted Garry Wills of Exner's revelations to Hersh, "so—sure enough—Kennedy relied on her to send messages and documents to Giancana dealing with this explosive matter. What documents? Hersh might have asked himself at this moment."

Exner's post-1977 observations defy logic. Why would Kennedy select her as his courier to the Mafia? He had plenty of aides who could have performed the role of courier far more safely and capably than Exner. Would Kennedy really have used a "none-too-bright girlfriend to handle something so incredibly sensitive as passing bribes to the Mafia?" asks Evan Thomas.

Even conservative critics, who might have been expected to treat Exner's later revelations more favorably, were unimpressed. After reading Exner's 1977 autobiography, columnist William Safire severely chastised Kennedy. But Exner's subsequent revelations left him cold. "She's changed her story too often over the decades," Safire concluded.

Exner had a long history of instability, making her an exceptionally unreliable witness. She admitted to lying repeatedly and changed her story several times. She became addicted to alcohol and amphetamines, suffered from depression and paranoia, seriously contemplated suicide, endured two divorces, and feared death at the hands of the Mafia. Her background and problems do not inspire confidence in her veracity.

Historians may never prove or disprove Exner's assertions. Scholarship on the Mafia and on the presidents' private lives, observes historian Michael Beschloss, "is not subject to the same precision as the study of diplomatic history, for which there are official documents drafted and preserved according to professional standards in public archives." Perhaps evidence will emerge in the future to bolster Exner's recent contentions. Until then we should assume that the first story regarding the affair was true, because it was supported by evidence; but that her later claims about her role in an alleged Giancana-Roselli-Kennedy triangle, because they are not supported by other sources, are fantasy.

*

Several White House employees performed sexual favors for the president. Two young women, Fiddle and Faddle, regularly serviced him. Fiddle was Priscilla Wear; Faddle was her close friend Jill Cowen. Both were in their early twenties and had attended Goucher College. Fiddle had nicknamed herself as a child; Kennedy's staff naturally tabbed her sidekick Faddle.

They volunteered for the 1960 campaign, and after the election Wear went to work as Evelyn Lincoln's assistant while Cowen was the Girl Friday to Pierre Salinger in the press office. Kennedy partied with the two women in the White House swimming pool, a focal point for his sexual activity. Waiters, household staff, and Secret Service were told to stay away from the pool. Then Fiddle and Faddle skinny-dipped with the president and other male guests. Later the president had sex with them in a small adjoining room. "It was common knowledge in the White House," said Secret Service agent Larry Newman, "that when the President took lunch in the pool with Fiddle and Faddle, nobody goes in there."

When Jackie Kennedy left for Glen Ora, the president gulped his bowl of soup and hit the pool with Fiddle and Faddle. "When [Jackie] was there, it was no fun," said Newman. "He just had headaches. You really saw him droop because he wasn't getting laid. He was like a rooster getting hit with a water hose."

For about a year Kennedy had a White House affair with Mary Meyer, a descendant of a prominent American family, the Pinchots of Pennsylvania. In the mid-1950s Mary moved to Washington, D.C., and became an artist. Her sister, Tony Bradlee, was the wife of Kennedy's journalist friend Ben Bradlee of *Newsweek*. (The Bradlees later divorced.)

Together with the Bradlees, Mary was invited to many of the big White House dances and smaller dinners arranged by Jackie Kennedy. Mary refused Kennedy's first advance, but on January 22, 1962, with Jackie away at Glen Ora, the president's offer to send a White House limousine to Mary's townhouse proved irresistible. They continued their affair into early 1963.

President Kennedy viewed Hollywood star Marilyn Monroe as an exceptionally desirable notch to add to his belt. On one occasion, in March 1962, he managed to add the notch, but many accounts of their relationship are exaggerated. Some allege that secret FBI records, wiretaps, tape recordings, photographs, sworn depositions, and police reports all prove that Kennedy and Monroe had a long-standing intimate—often salacious—relationship, including liaisons in the White House. But the authors of these sensational tales never produce documentation for independent experts to study.

The president's clandestine womanizing created frightful problems for the Secret Service. The agents' stories added a new dimension to Kennedy's reckless behavior. Agent Larry Newman was assigned to the presidential detail in the fall of 1961, and his first assignment—to protect the president in Seattle in November—proved traumatic, his "baptism by fire." Agents had sealed the president's floor at the Olympic Hotel, and Secret Service protocol dictated that access be limited to those with special clearance.

Suddenly a local Democratic sheriff came out of the elevator with two prostitutes, on his way to the president's suite. "I stopped the man," said Newman, but he loudly proclaimed that the "two girls were for the President's suite." Several policemen were there. Before long, Dave Powers came out of the suite, thanked the sheriff for bringing the women, and ushered them into the president's suite.

Newman was embarrassed. Before leaving the floor, the sheriff had warned the two women that "if any word of this night gets out, I'll see that you both go to Stillicoom [a state mental hospital] and never get out."

What Newman and other agents experienced in Seattle became commonplace. Tony Sherman served two years on the Kennedy detail. "It was just not once every six months, not every New Year's Eve, but was a regular thing," Sherman said of the president's womanizing.

"Dave Powers was the interface on these occasions," said Newman. The women would remain in the president's suite for three or four hours. "This became a matter of great concern," Newman said, "because we didn't know who these people were and we didn't know what they had on their person. You would just look up and see Dave Powers mincing down the hall and saying 'Hi pal.'" The agents had no way to stop it, and were told by their superiors not to interfere.

Powers angered the Secret Service agents because he prevented them from conducting even a cursory security check of the women. Newman complained, "We didn't know if these women were carrying listening devices, if they had syringes that carried some type of poison, or if they had Pentax cameras that would photograph the President for blackmail." Security was only as good as its weakest link, and Powers was the weak link. Agent William McIntyre speculated that a public scandal was inevitable. "It would have had to come out in the next year or so. In the [1964 presidential] campaign, maybe."

In the fall of 1963 the president came within an eyelash of causing his own dramatic "Profumo Scandal" because of his links to the roguish Bobby Baker and the prostitute Ellen Rometsch. Only luck and adroit political maneuvering saved him from public disgrace.

The dashing John Profumo, minister of war in Harold Macmillan's government in England, had an affair with prostitute Christine Keeler, who had also had a sexual relationship with Evgeny Ivanov, the Soviet naval attaché in London. Profumo resigned in disgrace in June 1963 after admitting he had lied about the affair. A subsequent investigation found that Profumo had not divulged national secrets, but the scandal embarrassed and damaged Harold Macmillan's government.

Bobby Baker, a native of Pickens, South Carolina, started out as a Senate page boy and rose to become secretary for the Democratic majority in the Senate and a protégé of Lyndon Johnson. In his autobiography, *Wheeling and Dealing*, Baker called himself "a Capitol Hill operator." Accused of influence peddling in 1963 for taking payoffs in return for steering federal contracts to his friends, Baker resigned from his Senate position on October 7, 1963, and eventually served eighteen months in a federal prison for fraud and tax evasion.

Baker not only brilliantly guided the Senate's legislative process, he did personal favors for senators, congressmen, lobbyists, and friends. The favors included providing them with women. He helped found the Quorum Club, a private suite in the Carroll Arms Hotel in Washington patronized by legislators and lobbyists on Capitol Hill. There beautiful Ellen Rometsch served as a hostess and a high-priced call girl. Kennedy's disreputable friend Bill Thompson, always on the lookout for beautiful women to take to the president, spotted Rometsch and arranged through Baker to bring her to the White House.

But the FBI, worried that Rometsch was a security risk, had been keeping tabs on her. As a youth in East Germany she had belonged to two Communist party organizations. After defecting to the West, she married a sergeant in the West German air force and accompanied him on his assignment in Washington. Rometsch, twenty-seven, met Kennedy in the spring of 1963. Baker estimated that she visited the president at least ten times in the spring and summer that year.

On July 3, 1963, FBI chief J. Edgar Hoover informed Robert Kennedy that the FBI believed Rometsch was having illicit relations with highly placed governmental officials. Fearing that Rometsch worked for the Communists and was gathering incriminating information, the FBI, with Robert Kennedy's approval, arranged to have her and her husband quietly sent back to West Germany in August 1963. President Kennedy didn't know about Rometsch's background and didn't realize that she might be a Communist spy.

The Rometsch story remained quiet until October 26, 1963, when investigative reporter Clark Mollenhoff published a dispatch in the *Des Moines Register* revealing that the Senate Rules Committee studying the Bobby Baker scandal was also planning to hear testimony about Ellen Rometsch and her abrupt expulsion from the United States. "The evidence also is likely to include identification of several high executive branch officials as friends and associates of [Rometsch], the part-time model and party girl," Mollenhoff wrote.

Mollenhoff's story horrified President Kennedy. In an exceptionally unusual entry in her diary, Evelyn Lincoln wrote on October 28: "The President came in all excited about the news reports concerning the German woman and other prostitutes getting mixed up with government officials, Congressmen, etc. He called Mike Mansfield to come to the office to discuss the playing down of this news report."

To ward off a security scandal—like the Profumo affair—that might destroy the Kennedy presidency, Robert Kennedy maneuvered behind the scenes to prevent the Senate investigation of Baker's influence peddling from disclosing Baker's use of call girls such as Rometsch. After Mollenhoff's exposé appeared, the White House phone lines between the attorney general, O'Donnell, and the president burned up.

On Monday morning, October 28, Robert Kennedy met with Hoover and told him that the president "urgently wished the FBI director to brief the Senate leadership on the dangers of the Rometsch case. If word got out that senators and executive branch officials were carrying on with a woman suspected by the FBI of spying, the integrity of the country would be damaged."

The same day Hoover met secretly with Senator Mike Mansfield and the Republican minority leader, Everett Dirksen, at Mansfield's home. He told them that Rometsch was not a spy, had not been involved with anyone at the White House, but that the FBI had the names, dates, and places where Bobby Baker's girls had entertained U.S. senators.

The strategy worked. Fortunately for the Kennedy presidency, most senators, particularly the Democrats, wanted to handle the Baker matter discreetly. The Senate had a long-time reluctance to police its own members, therefore the investigation was not very searching. It ignored Baker's and the senators' link to Rometsch and other women—and President Kennedy's sexual relationship with Rometsch.

Why did John Kennedy engage in such behavior? As a model for his womanizing, he had an example of someone he admired, respected, and loved all his life: his own father.

Lem Billings recalled Jack saying that "getting it off with beautiful people was sort of reaffirming the life-force and escaping life's pressures all at the same time." Escape from boredom was also a factor, Billings thought. Kennedy believed in living "for the moment, treating each day as if it were his last, demanding of life constant intensity, adventure, and pleasure." His chronic ill health may also have contributed to his obsession with women. As Garry Wills has suggested, his sexual performance was "a way of cackling at the gods of bodily debility who plagued him, as if to say, 'I'm not dead yet.'"

Whatever the causes of his behavior, Kennedy pursued women with an urgency and single-mindedness that made ordinary courtship seem casual and desultory, and with a recklessness that jeopardized his marriage, his career, his health, and the health of his partners. After all, he may have reasoned, his father's public career seemed undamaged by womanizing. Joseph P. Kennedy was one of America's wealthiest businessmen and had served in the New Deal and as ambassador to Great Britain—yet he simultaneously held his family together and avoided public scandal.

Unburdened by conscience or guilt, Jack rationalized that because Jackie didn't satisfy all his emotional and sexual needs, he would enjoy companionship and sex with other women. Besides, if he didn't act on his urges, he remained horny, suffered headaches, and grew restless.

His sexual gamesmanship required concentration, self-control, persistence, and persuasiveness. Through repetition and practice, he mastered the game's rules and techniques. It shored up his ego and reinforced an inner sense of potency, attractiveness, and power. As a connoisseur of the sexual game and a habitual deceiver in his courtship, he assumed a seductive mask, keeping his genuine feelings deeply hidden from his partners. His exceptional charm and sensitivity appeared natural, spontaneous, and sincere but was usually deliberate and manipulative. By adroit questioning and probing, he induced a woman to talk about herself and flattered her in the process.

Kennedy's personal life did indeed affect his performance as president. His retention of Hoover as director of the FBI, for example, can partly be explained by his womanizing. Hoover's bulging file on the president's sexual encounters went back to Kennedy's affair with Inga Arvad during World War II. Kennedy may have kept Hoover in his post because the president feared that Hoover would make incriminating information public.

The link between Kennedy's private life and his presidential performance, though, should not be exaggerated. He disconnected his personal life from his work. "He was as consistently cautious in his policy-making as he was reckless in private," historian Mark White has accurately observed. Kennedy didn't send American soldiers into Cuba during the Bay of Pigs debacle, or deploy combat troops in Vietnam, and preferred the blockade option rather than the dangerous air-strike alternative during the Cuban Missile Crisis. "If

Kennedy had displayed the machismo and recklessness in his political life that he exhibited privately, he would have fought in Vietnam and over Cuba," White says.

Nonetheless Kennedy's sexual liaisons were damaging, or potentially damaging, in several ways. They exposed him to blackmail from scorned women, the Mafia, the FBI, the Teamsters, the Soviets, or some hostile foreign intelligence service. Fortunately for him, none of his lovers objected to being used and discarded. None complained and found the ear of a brave reporter or editor.

There was always the chilling possibility that Sam Giancana would threaten to publicize evidence of Kennedy's sexual relationship with Judith Campbell Exner. Then, suggests Michael Beschloss, the president "could have been faced with a choice between giving in to whatever demands Giancana made or allowing himself to be driven out of office."

"We were told that the Soviets had women who were very good agents," said Larry Newman. Distressed and annoyed, the Secret Service felt powerless to intervene. Agent Tony Sherman agreed. "I never knew the names of the outsiders, where they came from, where they were, or anything," said Sherman. "I opened the door and said good evening and they said good evening. And in they went and the door shut. And when I reported for my next shift the next day, the President was still alive."

Given Kennedy's acute sensitivity in most aspects of his political career, his reckless philandering is almost incomprehensible. He must have convinced himself that the media and the Republican opposition would continue to be discreet. "He seemed to have an aristocratic view of public leaders and their private sexual adventures," historian James Giglio correctly observes. "Kennedy felt sorry for [John] Profumo, without thinking that the same thing could happen to him." He might not have survived a second term without a devastating exposé.

15

Searching for Peace

ON THE FIRST LEG of his European trip in June 1963, President Kennedy's reception in West Germany, in the words of *Time*, was "almost beyond the bounds of reality." Huge crowds chanted "Ken-ah-*dee*! Ken-ah-*dee*! Ken-ah-*dee*!" Hundreds of thousands of hand-held American flags fluttered in the air.

With his back to the Berlin Wall, to a crowd of 150,000 Kennedy gave his version of the difference between the Communist and the free world:

> There are many people in the world who really don't understand, or say they don't, what is the great issue between the Free World and the Communist world. *Let them come to Berlin*. There are some who say that communism is the wave of the future. *Let them come to Berlin*. . . . And there are some who say in Europe and elsewhere, we can work with the Communists. *Let them come to Berlin*. And there are even a few who say that it is true that communism is an evil system, but it permits us to make economic progress. "Lass' sie nach Berlin kommen." *Let them come to Berlin*!
>
> Freedom has many difficulties and democracy is not perfect, but we have never had to put a wall up to keep our people in, to prevent them from leaving us. . . .
>
> All free men, wherever they may live, are citizens of Berlin, and, therefore, as a free man, I take pride in the words "Ich bin ein Berliner."

Before the trip to Berlin, while Ken O'Donnell talked with the president about the travel plans, Kennedy told him, "I've decided that I want to go to Ireland, too." The trip would be personal and have nothing to do with foreign policy except to foster goodwill. Before the visit he studied the history of his forefathers and the history of Ireland, and was filled with a mixture of nostalgia, pride, and Irish patriotism. He had always been inspired by Irish poetry and literature and its stories of tragedy and desperate courage.

On the first morning he visited Dunganstown and the old Kennedy homestead. Mary Ryan, her family, and cousins from miles around welcomed him. "Cousin Jack came here like an ordinary member of the family," Mary Ryan later said. "He crouched at the fire and blew the bellows. He asked everything about the family and the farm."

He asked questions about the people he met, the landmarks he viewed, and the remarks he heard. "He wanted an explanation of everything," said Sean Lemass, Ireland's prime minister. "He was asking questions from an intense and lively interest."

Relaxed, playful, and witty, Kennedy announced that in 1968 he would support whichever Democratic candidate promised to appoint him ambassador to Ireland. He introduced people in his entourage who had Irish ancestors, among them Monsignor Michael O'Mahoney, "the pastor of a poor, humble flock in Palm Beach, Florida." Everyone roared.

The Bunratty singers, in fifteenth-century costumes, sang Irish songs. While the president listened, he whispered to Dave Powers, "Ask them to sing 'Danny Boy.'" As the Irish girls sang the song, Kennedy joined in the singing. Another group enchanted the president with one of his favorite Irish tunes: "We are the boys of Wexford, who fought with heart and hand to burst in twain the galling chain and free our native land." As he listened to still another singing group, he "had the sweetest and saddest kind of look on his face," said Kennedy's friend James Reed. "He was standing by himself, leaning against the doorway, and just seemed transported into a world of imagination."

In Ireland he dotted his speeches with wit, graceful literary quotations, and acclaim for the country's courageous past, its literary and artistic genius, and its contributions to America. On Friday morning, June 28, he flew to Cork where he addressed the combined houses of parliament. Ireland was "the first country to lead what was the most powerful tide in the twentieth century, the desire for national independence, the desire to be free."

"This is an extraordinary country," he continued. "George Bernard Shaw, speaking as an Irishman, summed up its approach to life: Other people, he said, 'see things and say: "Why?". . . But I dream things that never were and I say: "Why not?"'"

At the airport, instead of saying he was flying to England, Kennedy told the crowd he was "going to another country." Everyone laughed. He would return "in the Springtime," he said, to see "old Shannon's face once again." As he left he told a friend that his visit had been the "happiest days I've ever spent in my life."

*

"We arm to parley," Kennedy often said, quoting Churchill. A well-armed country had more bargaining power for disarmament talks. "Our arms," he said, should be "sufficient beyond doubt." At a cost of about $17 billion in additional appropriations, Kennedy vastly strengthened U.S. military power and made it far more versatile.

It is not true, as some have argued, that in conducting foreign policy he purposely created an atmosphere of crisis. He much preferred seemingly endless talks with the Soviets rather than direct confrontation. "You can't have too many of those [confrontations], because we are not sure on every occasion that the Soviet Union will withdraw." Peace was a long process—"the sum of many acts." He wanted to redirect world affairs, Dean Rusk thought, so that it moved "toward a period of consultation, negotiation, and agreement rather than a period of competition, hostility, and ideological opposition."

Kennedy needed to assure allies of his willingness to use nuclear weapons in a crisis, but he had deep forebodings about a nuclear confrontation. He worried that he might be required to decide to launch a retaliatory strike without any warning at all. He prudently ordered that electronic locks be placed on strategic nuclear weapons to prevent unauthorized use, and then intentionally leaked the technology to the Soviets so their weapons would also be more secure.

Kennedy sought strong conventional forces as well as nuclear forces in Europe, and a higher nuclear threshold. He did not wish to be confronted with the awful choice of having to use nuclear weapons or concede territory to the Soviets. He needed a broader range of choices. Non-nuclear forces needed to be built up, including those of NATO allies, in order to avoid a rash move to nuclear weapons.

While Britain sought to sustain its role as America's favorite ally, the French kept their distance. In the French view, Britain's special relationship with the United States was merely a junior partnership, neither available to the French nor desired. Charles de Gaulle wanted supremacy in Western Europe, and to create for France a nuclear capability exclusively under French control. Why should France run the risk of becoming a battlefield but not have possession of nuclear weapons that would probably decide the outcome of the war? De Gaulle feared that military integration with the powerful United States would make the French subordinate. Although he supported the concept of European unity and wanted the United States to come to the assistance of European nations in the event of attack, he opposed NATO. The United States should help defend Europe but should not interfere in Europe's affairs.

It irritated Kennedy that while the United States supplied most of the military forces in Europe to protect West Berlin, de Gaulle received credit for taking the toughest line toward the Soviets. "We find it difficult to understand the apparent determination of General de Gaulle to cut across our policies in Europe. If it is desired that we should cease to carry the load in Europe, nothing could be better from our point of view," Kennedy said.

There was little the president could do that didn't play into de Gaulle's hands. Charles Bohlen, U.S. ambassador to France beginning in 1962, recommended that Kennedy "avoid any open confrontation or row with de Gaulle." Washington should continue "to treat him with great courtesy; to recognize that there are many areas in which cooperation with France continues and should be maintained."

According to Bohlen, Kennedy "finally came to the conclusion that de Gaulle needed some form of friction with the United States for his own personal policies, domestic and otherwise, but Kennedy was equally determined that he was not going to oblige him."

*

In the summer of 1963 Kennedy concentrated much of his attention on negotiations for a nuclear test-ban treaty. A major impetus for the ban was his concern about the Chinese Communists. The president had no mandate to change U.S. relations with Communist China. To abandon Taiwan and normalize relations with China was far too sensitive for him to consider only a dozen years after Republicans had accused Democrats of losing China to the Communists.

The ideological and political differences between China and the Soviets had widened considerably since the late 1950s. The Communist Chinese constantly criticized the Soviet Union, challenging its dominance of the international Communist movement and accusing the Soviets of "revisionism" and submission to U.S. imperialism. Kennedy tried to exploit the tension between the Soviet Union and China, hoping the Soviets might join the United States in taking military action against Chinese nuclear facilities. Ideally Kennedy would have liked an unidentified airplane to fly over China and destroy its nuclear facilities. "They've only got a couple," he told aides, "and maybe we could do it. Or maybe the Soviet Union could do it."

Several administration officials later testified that such drastic action was only speculative contingency planning. It was only "talk, not serious planning or real intent," recalled McGeorge Bundy. Still, fear of Communist China's nuclear program remained at the forefront of Kennedy's thinking as he sought to curb nuclear testing.

The danger of testing nuclear weapons first became a major concern to the world on March 1, 1954, when the United States detonated a hydrogen bomb at Bikini Atoll in the Pacific. The huge explosion showered radioactive debris on the crew of the Japanese tuna trawler *Lucky Dragon*, causing severe radiation sickness and one death. Radiation sickness spread to the Marshall Islands as well. World leaders called for a ban on nuclear tests.

After November 1958 the Soviet Union, the United States, and Great Britain joined in a voluntary moratorium on future atmospheric tests. Both the Americans and the Soviets developed the ability to test underground, a more expensive method but much safer. Underground tests, though, posed unique verification problems. American scientists could easily detect atmospheric nuclear explosions in the Soviet Union but had difficulty distinguishing underground tests from natural events like earthquakes.

On September 1, 1961, the Soviets ended the voluntary moratorium by exploding the first in a series of powerful tests in the atmosphere, climaxing with the explosion of a fifty-eight-megaton device, three thousand times more powerful than the bomb dropped on Hiroshima.

Kennedy was deeply disappointed. He had to calibrate carefully the test-ban policy he could sell to the American people, for the Soviet test series revived intense pressure from the military, Congress, and the Atomic Energy Commission to resume U.S. testing. The president refused to resume U.S. aboveground testing until early March 1962, and even then did so with great reluctance.

Kennedy hoped a test-ban treaty would reduce the danger to health from radioactive fallout, put a brake on the arms race between the superpowers, stimulate additional arms-control agreements, and, most important from his perspective, control the proliferation of nuclear weapons. He moved negotiations ahead despite Soviet obstructionism. Studying the issue in depth, he kept himself as well informed as any nonscientific person could be.

On June 10, 1963, one day before his eloquent speech on civil rights, Kennedy delivered another major address at American University in Washington. He sought to ease cold war tensions, limit nuclear weapons, and make an unprecedented appeal to Americans to understand the Soviet Union.

His speech addressed the "most important" topic on earth: "world peace."

> I am talking about genuine peace, the kind of peace that makes life on earth worth living, the kind that enables men and nations to grow and to hope and to build a better life for their children—not merely peace for Americans but peace for all men and women—not merely peace in our time but peace for all time.

Americans needed to rethink their attitude toward the Soviet Union:

> No government or social system is so evil that its people must be considered as lacking in virtue. As Americans, we find communism profoundly repugnant as a negation of personal freedom and dignity. But we can still hail the Russian people for their many achievements—in science and space, in economic and industrial growth, in culture and in acts of courage.

Kennedy graciously asked Americans to appreciate the horrific price the Soviet people had paid during World War II:

> No nation in the history of battle ever suffered more than the Soviet Union suffered in the course of the Second World War. At least twenty million lost their lives. Countless millions of homes and farms were burned or sacked. A third of the nation's territory, including nearly two thirds of its industrial base, was turned into a wasteland.

"Let us not be blind to our differences," he warned, but we should also stress common interests.

> For, in the final analysis, our most basic common link is that we all inhabit this small planet. We all breathe the same air. We all cherish our children's future. And we are all mortal.

Near the end of his address Kennedy made two important announcements. Great Britain, the United States, and the Soviet Union had agreed to high-level negotiations in Moscow toward agreement on a comprehensive test-ban treaty. Meanwhile the United States would conduct no nuclear tests in the atmosphere as long as other nations did not test.

In Moscow, Khrushchev was deeply impressed with the address, saying it was "the best speech of any American president since Roosevelt." He even allowed his countrymen to hear it by not jamming Voice of America broadcasts. Humphrey Trevelyan, the British ambassador in Moscow, thought that "for the first time" Soviet leaders judged Kennedy as "someone who was genuinely working for a détente and with whom they could do business."

Confident, magnanimous, lacking in cant, the lyrical address was one of Kennedy's finest speeches. It differed sharply from the traditionally shrill anti-Communist rhetoric of almost every American political leader since the end of World War II.

The president appointed Averell Harriman as U.S. representative to the negotiations in Moscow. Kennedy hoped to use the talks to explore the possibility of joint action with the

Soviets to stop China's nuclear weapons program. In Moscow Harriman never directly proposed a joint preemptive strike to the Soviets, and the Soviets flatly rejected the indirect proposals Harriman did suggest.

Nonetheless on August 5 Britain, the United States, and the Soviet Union signed the Test Ban Treaty in Moscow. (Technically it was called the Treaty Banning Nuclear Weapons Tests in the Atmosphere, in Outer Space, and Under Water.) Because it applied only to aboveground testing, it lacked the complications of inspections and other control machinery. Public opinion in the United States decisively favored the treaty. The dramatic public support made Republicans reluctant to criticize Kennedy's effort.

Kennedy carefully orchestrated the strategy to gain support for the treaty in the Senate. He discussed it with senators and persuaded the wary Joint Chiefs of Staff to endorse it when they testified before Senate committees. In a shrewd political move, the president convinced the Senate's minority leader, Everett Dirksen, to announce his support in the Senate. With every able-bodied legislator voting, on September 24, 1963, the Senate approved the treaty 80 to 19.

Along with the treaty, Kennedy found other areas of common interest with the Soviets. In the summer of 1963 the two superpowers signed the "hot line" agreement, establishing a twenty-four-hour communications link to avoid a situation like the one they encountered during the Cuban Missile Crisis when critical messages took a long time to transmit. In October they agreed on the sale of U.S. wheat to the Soviets.

Kennedy displayed intense interest and skill in negotiating the test-ban accord and in securing Senate ratification. The treaty "opened the door to future agreements, a broadening of trade and exchanges, increases in American and Russian tourism, and a general lessening of Cold War tensions," concluded Dean Rusk. This was the legacy of what Kennedy believed was his greatest achievement.

16

Death in the Fall

IN THE FALL OF 1963 Kennedy, now forty-five years old, had strands of grey on the fringes of his hair and furrows in the corners of his eyes. In November he phoned a friend to say that he was sending a recent photo of himself, adding that it "shows my battle scars and wrinkles, although I don't see any warts. I'm not the skinny kid you once knew. In the picture I'm looking upward, watching eternity."

After the 1962 midterm elections a small group of Kennedy loyalists plotted the president's reelection in 1964. Politics was an ever-present reality in the Kennedy White House, Sorensen noted, used as a "criterion for trips, visitors, appointees and speeches, as an unspoken force counterbalancing the unrealistic, checking the unreasonable, occasionally deterring the desirable and always testing the acceptable."

The South seemed lost for Kennedy in 1964. "There is no hope for Kennedy in this state," said a Kennedy supporter in Jackson, Mississippi. On the other hand, Kennedy's increased popularity among Negroes, young males, and voters in the West—especially in California—more than offset Southern losses.

Kennedy much preferred having conservative Republican Senator Barry Goldwater as his opponent in 1964. He feared, though, that Republicans might nominate a more dangerous candidate, either Nelson Rockefeller or George Romney.

Rockefeller, a liberal Republican, had been elected governor of New York in 1958. Glamorous and urbane, he won reelection easily in 1962. But when Rockefeller divorced his wife in March 1962 and remarried two months later, he badly damaged his political career.

"The one fellow I don't want to run against is Romney," the president privately said in the spring of 1963. The former president of American Motors Corporation, George Romney, fifty-five, had captured the governor's office in Michigan in 1962. Because Romney was popular, dynamic, and capable, the president worried that he might win the Republican nomination. Kennedy seldom mentioned Romney's name lest the suggestion "build him up."

Kennedy did ask his aides to mention Goldwater as having presidential stature. "We had worked with Goldwater and we just knew he was not a very smart man and [he was] just going to destroy himself," said Robert Kennedy. The president worried "that he would destroy himself too early and not get the nomination."

"Give me good old Barry," the president said. "I'd never have to leave this Oval Office."

On September 24, 1963, the same morning the Senate ratified the test-ban treaty, Kennedy left Washington for a five-day, ten-thousand-mile trip through eleven mostly Western states. Ostensibly it was a conservation tour, but its real purpose was political. Of the eleven states on the tour, Kennedy had lost eight in the 1960 election.

By the time the president left Billings, Montana, and flew to Jackson Hole, Wyoming, he knew that people in the West wanted no more dry speeches about conservation. What interested them was war and peace.

To the thirty thousand people who heard him in Hanford, Washington, Kennedy stressed that "No one can say . . . with certainty . . . whether we shall be able to control this deadly [nuclear] weapon, whether we shall be able to maintain our life and our peaceful relations with other countries." He promised to try. "It is for this reason that I so strongly supported the test ban treaty, recognizing as I did its limitations, as a step on the long road to peace."

On Thursday, November 21, the president and Jackie flew to Texas. On Friday Kennedy began his day in Fort Worth. After a breakfast appearance sponsored by the Fort Worth Chamber of Commerce, the president and his entourage flew on to Dallas.

What happened in Dallas that day has been described and debated in thousands of books and countless other venues. While in his motorcade, Kennedy was shot twice and killed, and the nation wept.

On Saturday morning his body lay in the flag-draped closed casket in the East Room of the White House, the same spot the murdered Abraham Lincoln had lain a century earlier. Shortly after noon the president's coffin was moved from the White House to lie in state in the rotunda of the Capitol. On Sunday a huge crowd, at one point stretching forty blocks, stood in line to view the coffin. The same day, as Dallas police walked him through the basement of the Dallas police station, the alleged assassin, Lee Harvey Oswald, was shot and killed by Jack Ruby in full view of a national television audience.

President Johnson declared Monday, November 25, a day of national mourning. Across the nation and the world, millions watched the mournful events on television. The Kennedy family, with marching troops and bands, escorted the caisson from Capitol Hill to funeral services at St. Matthew's Church, and from there to Arlington National Cemetery in Virginia. In the long processional came foreign dignitaries, including crowned heads of state and the magisterial Charles de Gaulle of France. The cadence of muffled drums throbbed throughout the march. Black Jack, a riderless horse, symbolizing a lost leader, was led behind the casket.

With the funeral service at St. Matthew's Church completed, the casket team carried the coffin slowly down the church steps. Jackie, Caroline, and John Jr. waited at the bottom of the steps. As the band struck up "Hail to the Chief," soldiers snapped from parade rest to present arms. Mrs. Kennedy leaned down and whispered to her son, "John, you can salute Daddy now and say good-bye to him."

"Of all Monday's images, nothing approached the force of John's salute," wrote William Manchester. "His elbow was cocked at precisely the right angle, his hand was touching his shock of hair, his left arm was rigidly at his side, his shoulders were squared and his chin in." It was heart-wrenching.

After the church service the mourners journeyed down Constitution Avenue, around the Lincoln Memorial, over Memorial Bridge, to Arlington Cemetery. A million people gathered to watch the procession.

During the playing of the national anthem at Arlington, fifty jet planes, one for each state, screamed over the cemetery in salute, followed by Air Force One. After the lighting of a perpetual flame, at 3:34 p.m. John Kennedy's body was lowered into the ground.

Columnist Mary McGrory wrote, "It was a day of such endless fitness, with so much pathos and panoply, so much grief nobly borne."

Kennedy had served as president for only two years and ten months. He had little time. "It was as if Jackson had died before the nullification controversy and the Bank War, as if Lincoln had been killed six months after Gettysburg or Franklin Roosevelt at the end of 1935 or Truman before the Marshall Plan," Arthur Schlesinger reminded us. James Reston wrote: "What was killed in Dallas was not only the President but the promise."

A Note on Sources

Essential early studies of Kennedy include James MacGregor Burns, *John Kennedy: A Political Profile* (New York, 1959); Arthur M. Schlesinger, Jr., *A Thousand Days: John F. Kennedy in the White House* (New York, 1965); and Theodore Sorensen, *Kennedy* (New York, 1965). The books by Schlesinger and Sorensen praise Kennedy, causing pundits to label the authors as Camelot historians.

Nigel Hamilton's *J.F.K.: Reckless Youth* (New York, 1992) exhaustively covers Kennedy's early life. It is based on extensive research, but its judgments are flawed. Still essential is Doris Kearns Goodwin, *The Fitzgeralds and the Kennedys* (New York, 1987).

Three modern biographies, based on new materials made available at the John F. Kennedy Library in Boston, are Robert Dallek, *An Unfinished Life: John F. Kennedy, 1917–1963* (Boston, 2003); James Giglio, *The Presidency of John F. Kennedy,* 2nd ed. (Lawrence, Kans., 2006); and Michael O'Brien, *John F. Kennedy: A Biography* (New York, 2005).

Two highly critical accounts of Kennedy are Joan Blair and Clay Blair, Jr., *The Search for JFK* (New York, 1976), and Thomas C. Reeves, *A Question of Character: A Life of John F. Kennedy* (New York, 1991).

Other noteworthy general studies are Thomas Brown, *JFK: History of an Image* (Bloomington, Ind., 1988); Ralph

G. Martin, *A Hero for Our Time: An Intimate Story of the Kennedy Years* (New York, 1983); Herbert S. Parmet, *Jack: The Struggles of John F. Kennedy* (New York, 1980); Hugh Sidey, *John F. Kennedy, President* (New York, 1963); Richard Reeves, *President Kennedy: Profile of Power* (New York, 1993); and Harris Wofford, *Of Kennedys and Kings: Making Sense of the Sixties* (New York, 1980).

Several books on the Kennedy family merit attention. Joseph P. Kennedy is criticized in David E. Koskoff, *Joseph P. Kennedy: A Life and Times* (Englewood Cliffs, N.J., 1974), and in Richard J. Whalen, *The Founding Father: The Story of Joseph P. Kennedy* (New York, 1964). More favorable are Edward M. Kennedy, ed., *The Fruitful Bough: A Tribute to Joseph P. Kennedy* (Halliday Lithograph, 1965), and Amanda Smith, ed., *Hostage to Fortune: The Letters of Joseph P. Kennedy* (New York, 2001). Rose Kennedy is described in Charles Higham, *Rose: The Life and Times of Rose Fitzgerald Kennedy* (New York, 1995). Rose tells her own story in Rose Fitzgerald Kennedy, *Times to Remember* (Garden City, N.Y., 1974).

Robert Kennedy is the subject of many studies. The best are James W. Hilty, *Robert Kennedy: Brother Protector* (Philadelphia, 1997); Arthur M. Schlesinger, Jr., *Robert Kennedy and His Times* (Boston, 1978); and Evan Thomas, *Robert Kennedy: His Life* (New York, 2000). John Kennedy's older brother is described in John F. Kennedy, ed., *As We Remember Joe* (Cambridge, Mass., 1945), and Hank Searls, *The Lost Prince: Young Joe, the Forgotten Kennedy* (New York, 1969). His sister's life is told in Lynn McTaggart, *Kathleen Kennedy, Her Life and Times* (Garden City, N.Y., 1983).

Memoirs of aides and cabinet members have Kennedy as their primary focus. The most essential is Lawrence F. O'Brien, *No Final Victories* (Garden City, N.Y., 1974). Other memoirs are George W. Ball, *The Past Has Another Pattern: Memoirs* (New York, 1982); McGeorge Bundy, *Danger and Survival* (New York, 1988); Evelyn Lincoln, *My Twelve Years with*

John F. Kennedy (New York, 1965); Robert S. McNamara, *In Retrospect: The Tragedy and Lessons of Vietnam* (New York, 1995); Kenneth P. O'Donnell and David F. Powers, *"Johnny, We Hardly Knew Ye": Memories of John Fitzgerald Kennedy* (Boston, 1970); Dean Rusk, *As I Saw It* (New York, 1990); Pierre Salinger, *With Kennedy* (Garden City, N.Y., 1966); and Maxwell D. Taylor, *Swords and Plowshares* (New York, 1972).

Friends of Kennedy also present useful reminiscences. They include Benjamin Bradlee, *Conversations with Kennedy* (New York, 1975); Igor Cassini, *I'd Do It All Over Again* (New York, 1977); Clark Clifford, *Counsel to the President: A Memoir* (New York, 1991); Paul B. Fay, Jr., *The Pleasure of His Company* (New York, 1966); and John Kenneth Galbraith, *Ambassador's Journal: A Personal Account of the Kennedy Years* (New York, 1988).

Especially rewarding for the life of Jackie Kennedy are Sarah Bradford, *America's Queen: The Life of Jacqueline Kennedy Onassis* (New York, 2000), and Mary Barelli Gallagher, *My Life with Jacqueline Kennedy* (New York, 1969). Kennedy's sexual philandering is detailed in Nina Burleigh, *A Very Private Woman: The Life and Unsolved Murder of Presidential Mistress Mary Meyer* (New York, 1998), and in Judith Exner, *My Story, as Told to Ovid Demaris* (New York, 1977).

Kennedy's domestic policy is analyzed in David Burner and Thomas R. West, *The Torch Is Passed: The Kennedy Brothers and American Liberalism* (St. James, N.Y., 1984). Nick Bryant, *The Bystander: John F. Kennedy and the Struggle for Black Equality* (New York, 2006), describes his civil rights record. The Peace Corps is covered well in Gerald T. Rice, *The Bold Experiment: JFK's Peace Corps* (Notre Dame, Ind., 1985). Three books that survey Kennedy's economic policies are Jim F. Heath, *John F. Kennedy and the Business Community* (Chicago, 1969); Walter W. Heller, *New Dimensions of Political Economy* (Cambridge, Mass., 1967); and

Kim McQuaid, *Big Business and Presidential Power: From FDR to Reagan* (New York, 1982).

Four outstanding books focus on Kennedy's foreign policy: Michael R. Beschloss, *The Crisis Years: Kennedy and Khrushchev, 1960–1963* (New York, 1991); Lawrence Freedman, *Kennedy's Wars: Berlin, Cuba, Laos, and Vietnam* (New York, 2000); Ernest R. May and Philip D. Zelikow, eds., *The Kennedy Tapes: Inside the White House During the Cuban Missile Crisis* (Cambridge, Mass., 1997); and Robert Weisbrot, *Maximum Danger: Kennedy, the Missiles, and the Crisis of American Confidence* (Chicago, 2001).

Life in the White House is described in Letitia Baldrige, *Of Diamonds and Diplomats* (Boston, 1968). The role that Catholicism played in Kennedy's life and career is presented in Thomas Carty, *A Catholic in the White House?* (New York, 2004); and Lawrence H. Fuchs, *John F. Kennedy and American Catholicism* (New York, 1967). His death and funeral is detailed in William Manchester, *The Death of the President* (New York, 1967).

Index

A NOTE ON THE AUTHOR

Michael O'Brien was born in Green Bay, Wisconsin, and studied at the University of Notre Dame and the University of Wisconsin at Madison, where he received a Ph.D. in history. He is the author of a full-scale biography of John F. Kennedy as well as biographies of Senator Philip Hart, Vince Lombardi, Father Theodore Hesburgh, and Joe Paterno, and *McCarthy and McCarthyism in Wisconsin.* He is now emeritus professor of history at the University of Wisconsin, Fox Valley, and lives in Menasha, Wisconsin.